RETURN ON INVESTMENT MANUAL

RETURN ON INVESTMENT MANUAL

Tools and Applications for Managing Financial Results

ROBERT RACHLIN

SHARPE PROFESSIONAL
An imprint of M.E. Sharpe, INC.

658.15
R11r

Library of Congress Cataloging-in-Publication Data

Rachlin, Robert, 1937–
Return on investment manual : tools and applications for managing
financial results / Robert Rachlin.
p.   cm.
Includes bibliographical references and index.
ISBN 0-7656-0014-5 (hardcover : alk. paper)
1. Investments—Handbooks, manuals, etc.
2. Rate of return—Handbooks, manuals, etc.
I. Title
HG4521.R24   1997
658.15′2—dc21
97-12691
CIP

Printed in the United States of America

To

Brian, Matthew, and Jeremy

ABOUT THE AUTHOR

Robert Rachlin is Assistant Dean for Business Studies, UCCE, Hofstra University, and is an internationally known educator, author, lecturer, and consultant in the areas of strategic planning, budgeting, and financial management. He has previously held key financial positions with SCM Corporation, Texaco, General Foods, Gulf & Western, and several banks.

Professor Rachlin received his bachelor's degree in accounting from Pace University and his master's degree in management and economics from St. John's University. He served as an Adjunct Associate Professor of Management at New York University and the New York Institute of Technology. Currently he is full Adjunct Professor of Management at Hofstra University. He is a frequent lecturer to professional groups, companies, and practicing professionals and is the recipient of the "Fellow" Award for outstanding service to the planning profession by the Planning Executives Institute, an organization he served as New York Chapter President.

He is a prolific author and coauthor in the areas of finance and management. His writings include *Handbook of Strategic Planning; Handbook of Budgeting; Successful Techniques for Higher Profits; Handbook of International Financial Management; Total Business Budgeting: A Step-by-Step Guide with Forms; Managing Cash Flow and Capital during Inflation;* and *Accounting and Financial Fundamentals for Non-Financial Executives.*

WHAT THIS MANUAL WILL DO FOR YOU

Return on Investment Manual: Tools and Applications for Managing Financial Results is a comprehensive, concise, easy-to-use manual that provides virtually everything you need for making better decisions that will ensure a profitable return on investment. The manual is complete with ratios, calculations, examples, and sample policies. It provides guidelines for isolating problem situations for immediate corrective action and precautionary indicators in establishing future goals.

Return on investment (ROI) continues to be regarded as a key technique for increasing profitability and establishing corporate objectives, as well as measuring results in quantitative terms. Therefore, a company must develop decision-making strategies in order to direct its activities toward achieving maximum results from those objectives.

The manual should be kept within arm's reach to help accomplish those objectives by providing the latest techniques and practical applications in key areas of your company's activities, such as pricing, capital investments, working capital, human resources, shareholder value, marketing, cash management, cost control, break-even, cost of capital, inventory control, receivables management, leasing, and establishing ROI rates for segments of the business and the total company. Management activities reflect in financial results; therefore, it is vitally important to establish key return on investment strategies in areas that have major impact on return on investment performance.

Here are just some of the many ways this manual will help you:

- How to maximize profits with minimum risk and how to use funds to ensure maximization of long-term growth given various levels of risk
- How external factors impact return on investment decisions

- How to analyze capital investment proposals
- How to analyze product-line performance using return on investment techniques
- How to establish correct pricing structures to meet return on investment objectives
- How to measure the impact of mergers, acquisitions, and divestments on return on investment
- How activity-based costing and activity-based budgeting are used in decision making, how standards are derived, and who is responsible for unfavorable variances
- How to use capital investment evaluation techniques to increase return on investment
- How to evaluate energy conservation using return on investment techniques
- How human resource management impacts return on investment performance
- For those situations when setting up a spreadsheet is impractical, the book concludes with a complete set of present value tables and compound tables are provided

The manual is designed for business professionals, whether they possess a strong financial knowledge or little or no knowledge. The more experienced professionals who want to sharpen their skills in formulating strategic directions will find this manual extremely valuable. Inexperienced professionals will find it useful in upgrading their skills so that they can apply the practical knowledge contained herein to everyday situations. In addition, this manual provides the basic knowledge and skills necessary for starting a new business or maintaining a successful business. The manual will also be useful to those readers who need to solve specific problems relating to return on investment and to those wanting information on the subject for general interest. In general, it is a manual for everyone who has an interest in the technique of return on investment and how it applies to everyday decision making and, ultimately, success.

You should keep in mind that not every tool and application will apply directly to every specific business situation. Specific tools and applications should be customized to fit specific needs, using those developed in the manual. Management techniques vary among different industries and companies, so this customized approach would be the most beneficial.

Return on Investment Manual provides all the tools, new thinking, latest rules, and recent approaches dealing with the concepts, strategies, and applications of return on investment.

The author wishes to thank his editor, Olivia Lane, for her support on the project; my family, for their tolerance during the writing of this book; and all those business professionals from whom I have gained expertise and cooperation.

Robert Rachlin
Plainview, New York

CONTENTS

ILLUSTRATIONS

EXHIBITS

FIGURES

Return on Investment Manual

1

KEY RETURN ON INVESTMENT CONSIDERATIONS FOR DEVELOPING EFFECTIVE DECISION-MAKING STRATEGIES

As competition becomes tougher, small versus medium-sized companies, large versus large companies, products versus products, and markets versus markets, it becomes evident that success is largely based on financial performance. One universally accepted performance guide is return on investment. Why?

Return on investment (ROI) is the culmination of all activities of a company. For example, when expenses are incurred with no corresponding revenue benefits, profits decrease, as well as return on investment rates. When human resources are unproductive, profits decline, and return on investment rates decline. When capital investments do not live up to their expectations, declining return on investment rates can be expected. When too much money is expended for working assets (i.e., accounts receivable and inventories) without gains in revenues, both profits and return on investment rates will show downward trends. When marketing segments of a company fail to produce expected revenues and reasonable control of accounts receivable and inventories, overall company performance is affected.

These and many other factors tend to present challenges to operating managers of all sizes of companies. Whether a company is small, medium, or large, the common thread prevails—a manager must manage the company's resources. The ability to do so will result in higher return rates. One can safely say that all activities of any organization ultimately have some impact on return on investment rates. The challenge to business executives is to manage in such a way that positive decisions outweigh negative decisions. Since return on investment results are looked upon as how well a company is managed and its potential expectations for the future, both private and public owners of companies look closely at these results.

Not only will the ROI concept measure the impact of decisions, but it will also reflect the many internal and external factors used to accomplish growth and financial objectives. For example, interest rates, labor and material costs, tax rates and changes, capital spending, capacity utilization, money supply, technological changes, market share, and industry growth are just a few of the contributing factors and decisions that ultimately end up in one or more parts of the return on investment equation, or

The Basic
ROI Equation

$$\frac{Profit}{Investment}$$

In addition, many of these factors involve determining certain risk objectives and the ability to carry out these objectives with internal management skills.

The success or failure of an organization lies within the ability of internal management to make sound and profitable decisions and is usually within a business executive's control. It is not always external factors that cause companies to earn less than expected on monies invested in the business. A key role is also played by such major internal decisions as allocating resources between major segments of the business to maximize earnings and growth, providing adequate funds at the lowest possible cost, providing adequate flows of funds in future years through long-term investments, developing human resource skills to coincide with the needs of the organization, and establishing controls, reviews, and reporting processes needed to monitor the business. It is obvious that the concept of return on investment is impacted by a series of external and internal factors, as well as the strategies employed in managing a business.

WHY A BUSINESS NEEDS TO MAINTAIN AN ADEQUATE RETURN ON INVESTMENT RATE

A survival test of any business is how well it can cover its risks and provide an adequate return to its owners. Three major ways of accomplishing this objective follow:

- Utilizing the funds of the company to ensure maximization of long-term profits given anticipated levels of risk.

- Maximizing other resources of the company to ensure that it obtains the highest possible return without assuming any excessive undue risks.
- Allocating resources between segments of the organization to produce the highest possible return on investment.

To increase owners' wealth, an operating manager must simultaneously accomplish the following two activities:

- Maximize profits, which is accomplished by increasing revenues, increasing margins, and decreasing operational expenses.
- Minimize investment, which is accomplished by increasing inventory turnover, speeding up the collection of receivables, and minimizing unprofitable investments in property, plant, and equipment.

Although these activities seem fundamental, accomplishing them is not always possible. The internal and external environments are not always favorable. Most well-managed companies are continuously aiming to accomplish these two activities, but sometimes circumstances do not create the perfect environment. When both activities are accomplished, companies prosper and growth occurs. Nevertheless, one must keep in mind that other factors, such as cash flow, human resources, economic environment, market share, product quality, and the product life cycle also play a major role in the success or failure. From an ROI point of view, however, maximizing profits and minimizing investment are paramount.

It is important to recognize that ROI concepts will never replace sound business judgments but, instead will aid in supporting or raising questions as to the validity of these business judgment factors. Return on investment is what it is intended to be: a financial management tool that defines the problem, evaluates and weighs possible alternative investments, and brings into focus those qualitative factors affecting the decision that may not be expressed in quantitative terms.

THE VITAL ROLE OF ROI

The concept of ROI assists management in maintaining the necessary growth for survival. It assists in highlighting historical performance and enables managers to use such data in projecting future performance. This use is easily seen in the evaluation of capital investments where future cash flows are projected and used to evaluate expected ROI. In addition, future overall company financial objectives are established using historical data as a base. Because ROI is recognized as an acceptable measurement technique, its value is unquestioned. It is used by investors, the business community, the financial community, economists, and students of business techniques and applications.

ROI is also important because it provides management with an easy and understandable mathematical calculation. This calculation is used to enhance the decision-making process through better planning, by assisting in the evaluation of investment opportunities, by evaluating management performance, and by evaluating the overall position of the company in relation to the marketplace.

What Is ROI?

Return on investment is a management tool that systematically measures both past performance and future investment decisions. In other words, it is a financial tool that measures historical and anticipated results. ROI rests on the assumption that the best alternative investment is one that maximizes profits.

The definition of ROI depends upon the investment base used. If equity is used as the denominator base, the definition is "return on equity." If assets are used as the base, the definition is "return on assets." The numerator is the profit expected from that investment, such as before taxes or after taxes. Like the investment base, it can vary. The ratio for return on investment is earnings divided by investment.

Table 1-1 illustrates some of the variations that can exist and the differing titles used to describe the ROI concept. Note the various data used for the numerator and denominator. These are just a few of the examples of how return on investment is calculated. Therefore, ROI can be considered a generic term and must be specifically defined before calculations can be made. The key to remember is that the calculations must be consistent with historical data and with other comparative data. For example, you must be consistent with the same calculations when comparing return on assets of last year with those of this year. In addition, when trying to compare your own company's results with industry standards, the same numerator and denominator must be used. Consistency of calculations is necessary to develop trends and to formulate company ROI objectives.

Five Key Reasons Why ROI Is Recommended

In today's complex business environment, technological, economic, and competitive pressures tend to complicate managerial decision making. Return on investment provides management with an easy method of more effectively evaluating and communicating both past and anticipated future

TABLE 1-1   Varying ROI Calculations

Numerator	÷	Denominator	=	ROI definition
Net income		Total assets		Return on total assets
Net income		Shareholder equity		Return on shareholder equity
Net income		Capital employed		Return on capital employed
Operating profit		Total assets		Return on total assets
Operating profit		Capital employed		Return on capital employed
Net income + interest expense		Total Assets		Return on total assets
Income before interest and taxes		Total assets		Return on total assets
Net income		Net assets		Return on net assets

performance in an effort to increase growth and productivity. The ROI concept is unique in that it creates an atmosphere that is healthy for any organization. It defines a specific problem within the company, such as production efficiency, growing obsolescence of plant and machinery, lack of new product introductions, or decreasing share of market. Identifying problems is the first step toward solving them.

Once the problem is identified, alternatives are presented and weighed against each other. An action plan is developed to carry out the selected alternative, and the investment begins to materialize. Thus the ROI concept accomplishes many management tasks. The following list highlights why ROI is recommended and what the concept may do toward enhancing the decision-making process.

1. To force planning. Corporate management must have a plan, whether it be short term or long term, in order to measure efficiency and set goals.
2. To provide a basis for decision making. It takes certain decisions out of the realm of intuition into that of supportive and quantitative basis.
3. To evaluate investment opportunities. This can include not only initial capital investments but also the cost of additional working capital, the economic life of the investment, and the effect on company profitabil-

ity. These investment opportunities will also include alternative investments or new product opportunities.

4. To aid in evaluating management performance. This includes performance of responsibility or profit-center heads, as well as total company performance against a common denominator or against planned measures of performance or predetermined objectives. It aids in eliminating inequities that might arise between managers or operating units resulting from differences in size and makeup of operations, that is, highly intensified capital operations versus distributive operations that may have very little capital investment. In addition, performance measurement can be used to evaluate management's use of assets, cash flow, capital, equipment or other facilities, and internal control.

5. To measure responses to the marketplace. ROI measures management's response to changes in the marketplace on pricing and need, as well as profitability and cost-reduction measures.

Managers must be involved at all levels of the organization, since ROI results occur from participation of all disciplines at all levels. It must be kept in mind that ROI is the concern of everyone involved in the business.

MAJOR USES AND APPLICATIONS OF ROI

That ROI is everyone's concern is evidenced by the various uses and applications of ROI within an organization. While these uses and applications create total involvement throughout the company, some employees are affected more than others. The following list identifies and briefly explains the major uses and applications of ROI.

External measurement compares external performance with internal performance or the company's performance with industry standards.

Internal measurement determines how well the segments of the organization are performing in relation to planned objectives.

Improving asset utilization shows how best to utilize the company's assets in order to maximize profits.

Capital expenditure evaluation uses concepts such as payback, accounting methods, and discounted cash flow techniques to measure expected returns on a proposed investment.

Establishing profit goals is a tool used to set financial goals based on past performance and future potential.

Management incentives are a means of rewarding management for meeting stated ROI objectives.

Product-line analysis is used to evaluate the impact of adding or eliminating product lines.

Make or buy decisions are tools to evaluate whether to make or buy a product.

Lease or purchase decisions evaluate lease decisions versus purchase decisions.

Pricing measures the impact of certain pricing decisions and is used to establish pricing where certain ROI objectives are required.

Mergers, acquisitions, and divestments measure the impact of the activity of mergers, acquisitions, and divestments.

Evaluating marketing segment is used to maintain overall objectives through marketing, such as generating revenue, and maintaining reasonable levels of accounts receivable and expected levels of inventory for sale.

Evaluating human resources is a concept still in the early stages of development; however, determining the return on investment in people employed by the company may have a useful application.

Inventory control measures the incremental changes of inventory and earnings generated from that additional investment.

These major uses and applications of ROI highlight its far-reaching effects on the company. Most decisions have an impact in some way on ROI performance.

METHODS FOR MEASURING HISTORICAL VERSUS ANTICIPATED FUTURE EARNINGS

As previously stated, ROI is concerned with both evaluating the past and estimating or projecting the future. Different methods and techniques can be applied to measure historical results or project future results. Table 1-2 highlights some of those methods and stresses the need to integrate all functions of a business and develop an overall company objective.

THREE CAUTIONS ABOUT USING THE ROI CONCEPT

Using the ROI concept in evaluating external and internal performance requires three cautions. Like all methods of evaluation, improper interpretation can result from measuring different sets of comparative data with a single measurement device. The tool of return on investment is a vital management tool, but recognition must be given to three important factors.

First, you cannot rely totally on absolute numerical results. Too often,

TABLE 1-2   Historical versus Anticipated Future Earnings

Historical	Future
Performance Measurement through	Capital Evaluation through
Return on capital employed	Payback methods
Return on total assets	Accounting methods
Return on controllable assets	Discounted cash flow methods
Return on equity	
for	for
Internal measurement	Improving asset utilization
External measurement	Capital expenditure evaluations
Distributive channels	Mergers, divestments, and acquisitions
Incentives	Setting of profit goals
Pricing	Lease versus purchase decisions
Product reviews	Make or buy decisions
	Human resources

managers make decisions by comparing absolute relationships between sets of data without an understanding of how the calculations were made and how they relate to other sets of numerical data. This misconception can lead to wrong decisions, unless further interpretations are given to the meaning of the results, whether the data compare products, departments, divisions, companies, or industries. The nature of comparative products, quality of products, nature of selling, production costs, and corporate structure are but some of the operations areas to be considered before any sound conclusions can be reached.

A second consideration is the rule of consistency, which is among the most important cautions that can be mentioned. This rule, which states that incremental changes from period to period are more important than absolute values, will continuously be referred to, since it is the basis from which the concept of ROI was conceived. The rule of consistency is important if you understand how ROI functions. Since ROI measures comparative data over a period of time, it is important to be consistent in measuring like data with like time periods. Once a method of comparison is chosen, the ground rules must remain consistent.

For example, Table 1-3 illustrates how guideline changes affect the return on investment rate. If the ROI calculation in 19X1 used net income as a percentage of total assets, the calculation resulted in a 17.3% rate. When comparing the same set of data for 19X2, a rate of 19.2% resulted, or an

TABLE 1-3	Changing Guidelines and the Impact on ROI Results	
	19X1	*19X2*
Net income	$ 45,000	$ 50,000
Net income before interest and taxes	93,000	100,000
Total assets	260,000	260,000
Net income over Total assets	$\dfrac{\$45,000}{\$260,000} = 17.3\%$	$\dfrac{\$50,000}{\$260,000} = 19.2\%$
NIBI&T over Total assets	$\dfrac{\$93,000}{\$260,000} = 35.8\%$	$\dfrac{\$100,000}{\$260,000} = 38.5\%$

increase of 1.9 percentage points. If in 19X2 the numerator was changed to net income before interest and taxes (NIBI&T), however, the calculations would be 38.5% or an increase of 21.2 percentage points (38.5% − 17.3%). In a very simple way, this illustrates the need to use the same set of data when comparing return on investment results. If any changes occur between comparative periods, they must be changed to reflect a true trend accurately. Remember, consistency between comparative periods must be adhered to if accurate decisions are to be reached.

A third and final caution is not to ignore other methods of appraising performance. Although return on investment is an important barometer of financial success, it is not the ultimate evaluation technique. Supporting measures of performance, such as share of market, percentage of sales changes, management philosophies, meeting budgeting objectives, and other evaluation techniques, must also be considered in order to evaluate accurately the performance of an individual and/or segment of a company.

GUIDELINES FOR ALLOCATING CONTROLLABLE VERSUS NONCONTROLLABLE DATA

As we have seen, it is important to assign and maintain consistency in net sales, net income, and investment properly. In addition, segments for evaluating performance should be allocated, such as divisions, product lines, departments, accountability centers, marketing segments, and the like.

Should all data be allocated, or only data for which a manager has responsibility and authority? If you accept the rule of consistency, it does not matter how you allocate as long as you are consistent in measuring like data from period to period. The ultimate return on investment rate can be adjusted upward if lower investments are allocated and adjusted downward if higher investments are assigned to the segment. A similar result happens when earnings are defined differently, for example, net income versus net income before interest and taxes. Therefore, it appears that the more likely approach should be to measure performance in accordance with what a manager is responsible for and what authority a manager is given.

I recommend that only data that can be identified as controllable by a manager be used. Data that may be allocated apart from a manager's authority could lead to erroneous decisions and force an operating segment to make decisions detrimental to the operation, for example, increasing prices to meet ROI objectives. The other unassigned data can be used to complete the entire company's operation in the establishment of overall goals. For example, the format can be used in determining controllable return on investment by segment and the relationship to the entire company. You can see in Table 1-4 that each operation can be measured on those components that are controllable by a manager. Each operation is given an ROI objective and should coincide with the overall objective after other noncontrollable data are included.

I suggest that income before taxes be used on the controllable components, and net income on the overall company. Since taxes are difficult to compute on an individual segment, only net income should be used for overall evaluation. In addition, I recommend that for short evaluation periods, that is, less than one year, period-end balances be used for the investment base. For periods of one year or longer, year-end balances should be used for the investment base or a variation of the average of the beginning and closing yearly balances, moving averages, or any other variation. The conclusion will not alter as long as consistency is followed. Remember, the absolute rates are not as important as are the incremental changes that occur from period to period. This indicates the performance trend and will act as an indicator of performance in the past, as well as the future.

DECISION-MAKING STRATEGIES

- Develop return on investment policies and procedures.
- Identify both internal and external factors that affect return on investment performance.

TABLE 1-4   Allocating Controllable versus Noncontrollable Data

Controllable Data	Net Sales	Net Income	Investment	Return on Investment
Operation A	xxx	xxx	xxx	x
Operation B	xxx	xxx	xxx	x
Operation C	xxx	xxx	xxx	x
Operation D	xxx	xxx	xxx	x
Total controllable	xxx	xxx	xxx	x
Noncontrollable data				
Other sales	xxx	xxx		
Other expenses		xxx		
Corporate overhead		xxx		
Taxes		xxx		
Other investments			xxx	
Total company	xxx	xxx	xxx	x

- Assess both internal and external factors as to their importance to the organization's performance and level of risk.
- Communicate with employees and educate them concerning the significance of return on investment concepts.
- Define how return on investment is to be calculated at various levels of the organization as well as in various applications.
- Be sure not to place so much emphasis on return on investment as to create manipulative techniques for increasing ROI performance, thereby sacrificing short-term in favor of long-term growth.
- ROI performance, however, should be partially directed toward long-term objectives and not totally toward the short-term.
- Maintain consistency in evaluating ROI performance to ensure comparative analysis.
- Clearly define how overhead is allocated to operating units.

2

HOW TO ANALYZE, MANAGE, AND ESTABLISH YOUR COMPANY'S RETURN ON INVESTMENT RATE

Chapter 1 introduced return on investment as a decision-making tool. Since return on investment results from all activities of an organization, the functional activities can be reflected using a typical organization to define the components that make up the ROI equation, that is, the profitability rate and the turnover rate discussed later in this chapter.

THREE KEY COMPONENTS OF ROI

To understand ROI, it is important to grasp its three components: net sales, net income, and investment. They are derived from the two major financial statements: the consolidated statement of income and the consolidated balance sheet. To illustrate the calculations of the components and other data that will be used throughout the book, hypothetical statements of income and balance sheet are presented in Tables 2-1 and 2-2. These financial statements of a fictitious organization, The Great Company, Inc., will serve to illustrate many of the concepts and applications of ROI.

From the financial statements of The Great Company, Inc., the two major components of ROI are formulated, namely, the profitability rate and the turnover rate. The profitability rate is computed by dividing net income by net sales:

TABLE 2-1   The Great Company, Inc.

Statement of Income

19X2

Net sales	$700,000
Cost of sales	525,000
Gross profit	175,000
Other operating expenses	
Depreciation	5,000
Selling expenses	30,000
Administrative expenses	25,000
General expenses	15,000
Operating income	100,000
Other (income) expenses	2,000
Income before income taxes	98,000
Income taxes	48,000
Net income	$ 50,000

*ROI
Equation
Using
Profitability
Rate and
Turnover Rate*

$$\frac{\text{net income}}{\text{net sales}}$$

The turnover rate is computed by dividing net sales by investment:

$$\frac{\text{net sales}}{\text{investment}}$$

When both components are combined, they form the basis of return on investment, which results in

$$\frac{\text{net income}}{\text{net sales}} \times \frac{\text{net sales}}{\text{investment}}$$

which can be mathematically reduced to

$$\frac{\text{net income}}{\text{investment}}$$

TABLE 2-2   The Great Company, Inc.

Balance Sheet

19X2

Assets

Current assets

Cash in banks	$ 5,000
Marketable securities at cost which approximates market	7,000
Accounts receivable—net of allowance for doubtful accounts	80,000
Inventories	40,000
Prepaid expenses	5,500
Total current assets	137,500
Fixed assets—net of accumulated depreciation	118,000
Other assets	4,500
Total assets	$260,000

Liabilities

Current liabilities

Accounts payable	$ 38,000
Debt due within one year	4,500
Accrued expenses	10,000
Income taxes payable	12,500
Total current liabilities	65,000
Long-term debt	24,000
Total liabilities	$ 89,000

Shareholders' Equity

Common stock	$ 40,000
Capital in excess of par value	10,000
Earnings retained in business	121,000
Total shareholders' equity	$171,000
Total liabilities and shareholders' equity	$260,000

by eliminating the net sales in each of the profitability rate and the turnover rate. Before one can appreciate this ratio, however, it is important to understand each segment because each reacts differently, and different decisions will have to be made in order to increase either of the segments.

TABLE 2-3	Investment Dollars Needed to Support Sales Increases		
	Current Level	*Proposed Level*	*Increase*
Net sales	$700,000	$770,000	$70,000
Assets			
Cash	5,000	5,300	300
Accounts receivable	80,000	86,000	6,000
Inventories	40,000	43,000	3,000
Machinery and equipment	118,000	125,700	7,700
Total assets	$243,000	$260,000	$17,000

Step One: Determine Investment Dollars to Support Sales Revenues and Turnover Rate

The "turnover rate," or investment turnover, is an indicator of how capital-intensive a business is, or how many dollars in investment are needed to support dollars in revenues. At a given level of sales dollars, one will find a somewhat linear relationship to investment dollars. As net sales increase, additional investments will be needed to support these increases in sales, such as cash, accounts receivable, inventories, and sometimes additional machinery and equipment.

Referring to the statement of income for The Great Company, Inc. (Table 2-1), suppose the company is planning an increase of sales from $700,000 in the present year to $770,000 in the following year. Additional investment dollars will be needed, as illustrated in Table 2-3. Using the hypothetical set of data in the table, you can see that a sales dollar increase usually requires an additional investment in assets. For example, if we look at total assets as a base, the reasoning behind this statement is as follows: To support sales, assets are needed. Sales result in either cash or accounts receivable. Inventories are needed to support sales levels. Plant, property, and equipment are needed to produce the product that ends up in inventory, and either cash or receivables are created when the product is sold. Other assets usually are insignificant. Sales dollars will usually follow a linear pattern, since such a pattern is needed to support the sales volume. Most companies within an industry will find this turnover rate consistent over a period of time. Certain industries have a high turnover rate because of the nature of the business. Once a company's acceptable level of turnover is found, every effort should be made to improve this rate or, at the least, to maintain this level.

Although these data do not reflect the normal increase of assets with increases in sales, they do illustrate that sales increases do in fact affect assets. The extent to which assets will increase depends upon the nature of the company and the industry in which the company competes.

The impact of the turnover rate is:

	Current Level	Proposed Level
Net sales	$700,000	$770,000
Assets	$243,000	$260,000
Turnover rate	2.88	2.96

Figure 2-1 illustrates how the various accounts are combined to calculate the turnover rate. In order to utilize the chart as illustrated effectively, each account should reflect two or more comparisons, such as this year versus last year, actual versus budget, or one's company versus the competition. Figure 2-1 illustrates the data for the year 19X2, Table 2-2. Remember, when using other investment bases, such as capital employed or return on equity, the accounts would change. But the same formula would be used, that is, net sales divided by investment.

Step Two: Determine the Profitability Rate to Increase ROI

The profitability rate, or earnings divided by net sales, reveals how much of earnings is generated from each dollar of net sales. It is probably the most critical relationship in the ROI calculation. It provides the financial base on which companies will support their future growth. When excessive earnings result, they are put back into the business to support the future objectives of the company. Because the use of internal funds is generally cheaper than external borrowing, it is extremely important that every effort be made to maximize sales dollars into higher earnings. Lack of earnings, and ultimately of cash flow, is one of the primary reasons why companies fail.

Another reason why the profitability rate is important is that it is the most sensitive to business decisions. In the short run, the profitability rate can be changed easily by merely reducing expenses. This is a short-run remedy, however, and may jeopardize the company's existence if caution is not exercised. In addition, it is the one segment that can vary substantially in calculating ROI. For example, using the data from The Great Company, Inc., Statement of Income, Table 2-1, the profitability rate for 19X2 was

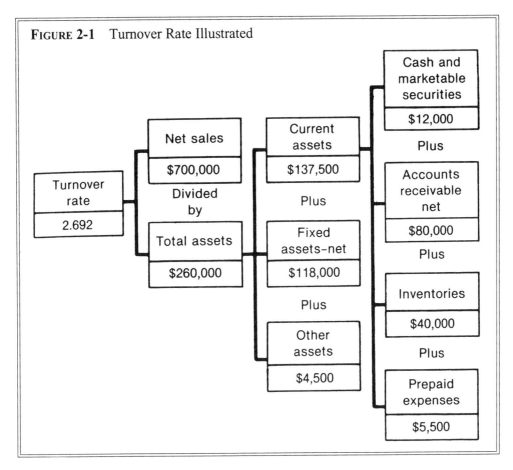

FIGURE 2-1 Turnover Rate Illustrated

7.1%, or net income of $50,000 divided by net sales of $700,000. Assume that the company reduced expenses as follows: selling expenses by $3,000, by limiting salesperson's expenses; administrative expenses by $8,000, by decreasing the administrative staff by one person; and general expenses by $2,000, by lowering general overhead. This results in increasing the profitability rate from 7.1% to 8.1% as shown in Table 2-4.

It is generally accepted that reducing expenses can be quicker than reducing investment dollars. As we discuss later in the chapter, other decisions can increase the profitability rate, such as pricing decisions, increasing volume, and reducing costs and expenses.

In order to control, evaluate, and monitor the profitability rate, the data composing the profitability rate can be structured by product line, geographic market, operating divisions, responsibility centers, profit centers, or any other business segment deemed necessary for the managing of the business. Each of these segments should have a profitability rate

TABLE 2-4   How Reducing Expenses Affects the Profitability Rate

	19X2 as Shown in Table 2–1	After Reduction of Expenses	Change
Net sales	$700,000	$700,000	—
Cost of sales	525,000	525,000	—
Gross profit	175,000	175,000	—
Other operating expenses			
Depreciation	5,000	5,000	
Selling expenses	30,000	27,000	($3,000)
Administrative expenses	25,000	17,000	(8,000)
General expenses	15,000	13,000	(2,000)
Operating income	100,000	113,000	13,000
Other (income) expenses	2,000	2,000	—
Income before income taxes	98,000	111,000	13,000
Income taxes	48,000	54,390*	6,390
Net income	$ 50,000	$ 56,610	$6,610
% of net sales	7.1%	8.1%	1.0%

* Assume same rate of 49% as calculated in Table 2–1.

objective, which must be measured against actual performance periodically. I suggest that this evaluation be made no less than once a month.

Figure 2-2 shows how the profitability rate is displayed and how it can be analyzed at each separate account level using data from Table 2-1. Remember that, like each account in the turnover rate, each account in the profitability rate can be compared as to actual versus budget, this year versus last year, one's company versus competitors, and so forth. Note that different accounts can be displayed, depending upon the business and the needs of the company.

THE ROI EQUATION USING RETURN ON TOTAL ASSETS

We have now discussed the two major components of the ROI equation, namely, the turnover rate and the profitability rate. The two components formulate the basis for calculating the return on investment rate. Looking

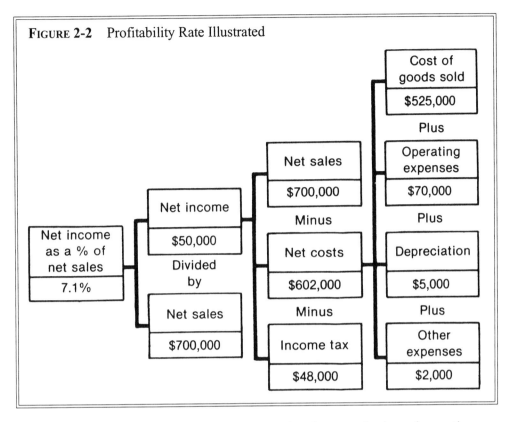

FIGURE 2-2   Profitability Rate Illustrated

at the two components, you can see that the net sales in each equation can
be canceled, resulting in the following:

*ROI
Equation
Using Return
on Total
Assets*

$$\frac{\text{Net income}}{\text{Investment}}$$

As pointed out previously, the reason the ROI ratio is broken down into
two components is to review the relationship of earnings to sales and the
rapidity with which committed capital is being used effectively. In addition,
you can see that to improve the ROI rate a manager can increase the
profitability rate by increasing sales, reducing expenses, or a combination
of both. Also, the ROI rate can increase by working existing investments
harder, thus increasing the turnover rate. These outcomes assume that all
these factors are under the control of the manager being measured. For
example, let's assume that two managers have the responsibility for individual operations. The following facts are presented to illustrate the point.

	Manager A	Manager B
Net sales	$700,000	$700,000
Net income	50,000	66,500
Total assets	260,000	348,432
Profitability rate	7.1%	9.5%
Turnover rate	2.692	2.009
Return on total assets	19.1%	19.1%

You can see that both managers have the same sales dollars and the same ROI rate. Which manager is more effective? Without a detailed analysis of each operation, Manager B could be considered the better manager because Manager B generates a higher profitability rate, which has a heavier weight when calculating ROI. Many questions can be raised regarding this conclusion:

- Manager B operates with $88,432 more total assets ($348,432–$260,000), thereby tying up more of the company's funds. Is this the nature of the business or is Manager A able to operate with fewer assets by managing more effectively?
- What has been the trend in the profitability rate over several years and what are the expectations for the future?
- What will the investment in fixed assets, for example, machinery and equipment, be in future years? How old are the fixed assets in each operation?
- What is the sales potential for each operation?
- What are the ROI potentials for each operation?
- How does the ROI rate compare with like operations, industries, competition, and so forth?

The list highlights the need to analyze financial results further and to be extremely cautious in drawing any conclusions based on pure numerical results.

Calculating Return on Total Assets

By combining the turnover rate in Figure 2-1 and the profitability rate in Figure 2-2, return on total assets can be calculated, as shown in Figure 2-3.

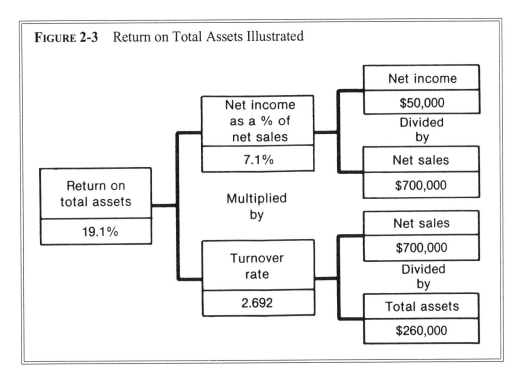

FIGURE 2-3   Return on Total Assets Illustrated

CALCULATING RETURN ON NET ASSETS (RONA)— AN EXAMPLE

Exhibit 2-1 is an example of using net assets as the denominator calculating return on investment. Motorola, Inc., a major electronics company, uses the calculation of return on net assets, commonly referred to as RONA, in measuring performance for the total company, all sector/groups, divisions, and units and subsidiaries of the corporation. Exhibit 2-1 illustrates how a company can develop an ROI policy and procedure that takes the user through a detailed analysis of how to calculate return on net assets (RONA).

HOW TO DETERMINE INDUSTRY ROI RATES

A major part of the decision-making process for both evaluating ROI results and providing a company with the ability to establish attainable ROI objectives for the overall business, as well as business segments, is the reviewing of industry results. It is through this process that strategies are established by analyzing competitive data.

For example, it is important to focus on both overall ROI ratios such as

---

EXHIBIT 2-1—Sample Policy

MOTOROLA, INC.
WORLDWIDE CORPORATE FINANCIAL
PRACTICES AND POLICIES

RETURN ON NET ASSETS (RONA)

Effective Date:
Revised Date:
Current Date:

Revised By:
Reviewed By:

Approved By: Accounting Policy Council

PURPOSE

To define the RONA Ratio, the components which make up the RONA Ratio and the time periods to be employed in the measurement and reporting of RONA.

SCOPE

This WWCFP is applicable to Total Motorola and all Sector/Groups, Divisions, units and subsidiaries of the Corporation.

CONTENTS

1.0   RONA Ratio
2.0   Net RONA Assets
3.0   RONA Receivables/Payables
4.0   RONA—Total Motorola
5.0   Responsibility

1.0   **RONA Ratio**

1.1   The RONA Ratio is a measurement relating profitability to asset management. The basic RONA Ratio can be stated as follows:

$$\frac{\text{Sum of 12 Months Net Profit \$}}{\text{Sum of 12 Months Net Sales \$}} \times \frac{\text{Sum of 12 Months Net Sales \$}}{\text{Average of 13 Months Net RONA Assets}}$$

OR

Net Profit % × Net RONA Asset Turnover = RONA

1.2   "Sum of 12 Months" is the current month just ended plus the prior 11 months.

1.3   "Average of 13 Months Net RONA Assets" is the sum of RONA assets for the month just ended plus the prior 12 months divided by 13.

1.4   Net Profit equals the profit after tax appearing on the Sector/Groups P&Ls for full profit visibility.

2.0   **Net RONA Asset Outline**

2.1   **Qualified RONA Assets**

2.1.1   Cash
2.1.2   Accounts Receivable Net
2.1.3   *Rona Receivables* (Section 3.0)
2.1.4   Cost Recoverable from Government Contracts
2.1.5   Inventories Net
2.1.6   Deferred Taxes Current
2.1.7   Other Current Assets
2.1.8   Net Plant and Equipment (Fixed and ELO)
2.1.9   Investment in Wholly Owned Subs
2.1.10 Investment in Nonconsolidated Subs
2.1.11 Sundry Assets

2.1.12 = (1) RONA Qualified Assets

     NOTE: By definition, Capitalized Leases are included in RONA Qualified Assets, since the related assets would be included in the balance sheet (i.e., Fixed Assets, etc.)

2.2 Qualified RONA Liabilities

2.2.1 Accounts Payable
2.2.2 Accrued Compensation
2.2.3 Federal Income Tax
2.2.4 Other Taxes
2.2.5 Profit Sharing
2.2.6 Accrued Warranties
2.2.7 Other Current Liabilities
2.2.8 *RONA Payables* (Section 3.0)
2.2.9 Deferred Taxes Non-Current
2.2.10 Other Non-Current Liabilities
2.2.11 Minority Interest

2.2.12 = (2) RONA Qualified Liabilities

     (1) minus (2) = Net RONA Assets

2.3 Items specifically excluded from Net RONA Assets are:

2.3.1 Cash Equivalents
2.3.2 Marketable Securities
2.3.3 Notes Payable
2.3.4 Current Portion of Long-Term Debt
2.3.5 All Related Party Accounts (Including Domestic Debt)
2.3.6 Long Term Debt
2.3.7 All Shareholders Equity (Including CTA Accounts)

The sum of items 3 through 7 above, less item 1 and 2, is the contra-balance to Net RONA Assets.

3.0 RONA Receivable/Payables

3.1 In order to reflect the effects of related party sales and purchases on the RONA base, RONA receivables/payables are stated on the Sector/Group balance sheet. The RONA receivables/payables should equal 1/12 of the original budgeted related party sales/purchases. This entry is made in January of each year and coordinated by Corporate Accounting to ensure that consolidated Motorola RONA receivables/payables equal zero.

4.0 RONA—Total Motorola

4.1 Net RONA Assets for Total Motorola do not equal the sum of the Sector/Groups Net RONA Assets. This difference is caused by the following:

4.1.1 Items appearing on Corporate books not allocated back to the Sector/Groups (i.e., economic translation gain/loss).

4.1.2 Corporate consolidation entries.

4.2 Net Sales and Net Profits % are used in the RONA Ratio by Corporate Accounting consistent with the Sector/Groups. (Net Profit % is Net Profit divided by Net Sales.)

     The total Net Sales and Net Profit % for Total Motorola will not equal the sum of the Sector/Groups because of:
        —Corporate Sales/Profits.
        —Corporate consolidation entries.

5.0 Responsibility

5.1 Sector/Group controllers are responsible for ensuring that RONA numbers reported are per these definitions.

Return on Assets (ROA), leverage, and Return on Stockholders' Equity (ROE); and components of ROI such as profit margin percentage and the turnover rate.

If we look at ROE (net income divided by stockholders' equity) as a measurement tool, we can see that this ratio reflects the amount of net income generated by each dollar of equity and provides an investor with the opportunity to evaluate how well management, and especially the chief executive officer, is performing.

Caution: As a result of changes in accounting practices, caution should be given to evaluating ROE rates between different industries, as each industry has different accounting conventions and can alter the ROE rate. Nevertheless, comparing these rates within industries has validity. Also, with better inventory management techniques (see chapter 9) companies have been able to increase sales with lower investments in inventory as a result of just-in-time inventory and economic order quantity (EOQ) techniques.

To illustrate this concept, Tables 2-5 through 2-9 represent a list of twelve companies from *Fortune*'s 500 industrial companies that are sales leaders, that is, companies having the most sales revenues for their respective industries for the year 1995. The companies are ranked in these tables according to their total sales revenues.

Profit Margin Percentages

Table 2-5 shows twelve companies by their revenue ranking for 1995. Profit margin percentages represent net income divided by revenues, or net sales. It is one of the equations needed to compute ROI, as shown in Figure 2-3.

You will notice that the highest net income producers do not necessarily reflect the highest profit margin percentage. For example, General Motors has the highest net income but the fifth-highest profit margin percentage, whereas Philip Morris has the fourth-highest net income but the highest profit margin percentage. This reflects differences in how businesses are operated, but it is meaningful in showing what leading companies within different industries return on a dollar of sales. This may provide a strategy in helping a company determine what industries warrant potential acquisitions in terms of profitability.

Turnover Rate

This is the other part of the equation for determining ROI rates. It represents the net sales (revenues) divided by an investment base. In Table 2-6, the

TABLE 2-5   Profit Margin Percentage
(Net Income ÷ Revenues)

Top Twelve Companies by Revenue Ranking—1995

Company Name	Net Income ($ in billions)	÷	Revenues (sales) ($ in billions)	=	Profit Margin %
General Motors	$6.9		$168.8		4.1%
Ford Motor	4.1		137.1		3.0
Exxon	6.5		110.0		5.9
Wal-Mart Stores	2.7		93.6		2.9
AT&T	.1		79.6		.1
IBM	4.2		71.9		5.8
General Electric	6.6		70.0		9.4
Mobil	2.4		66.7		3.6
Chrysler	2.0		53.2		3.8
Philip Morris	5.5		53.1		10.4
Prudential Insurance	.6		41.3		1.5
State Farm Group	1.3		40.8		3.2

Source: Data compiled from "The Fortune 500," *Fortune*, April 29, 1996, pp. F-1 through F-20, © 1996 Time Inc. All rights reserved.

TABLE 2-6   Turnover Rate
(Net Sales ÷ Total Assets)

Top Twelve Companies by Revenue Ranking—1995

Company Name	Net Sales ($ in billions)	÷	Total Assets ($ in billions)	=	Turnover (Times)
General Motors	$168.8		$217.1		.78
Ford Motor	137.1		243.3		.56
Exxon	110.0		91.3		1.20
Wal-Mart Stores	93.6		37.9		2.47
AT&T	79.6		88.9		.90
IBM	71.9		80.3		.90
General Electric	70.0		228.0		.31
Mobil	66.7		42.1		1.58
Chrysler	53.2		53.8		.99
Philip Morris	53.1		53.8		.99
Prudential Insurance	41.3		219.4		.19
State Farm Group	40.8		85.3		.48

Source: Data compiled from "The Fortune 500," *Fortune*, April 29, 1996, pp. F-1 through F-20, © 1996 Time Inc. All rights reserved.

TABLE 2-7	Return on Assets (ROA) (Profit Margin % × Turnover Rate) Top Twelve Companies by Revenue Ranking—1995			
Company Name	Profit Margin %	×	Turnover Rate =	Return on Assets %
General Motors	4.1%		.78	3.2%
Ford Motor	3.0		.56	1.7
Exxon	5.9		1.20	7.1
Wal-Mart Stores	2.9		2.47	7.2
AT&T	.1		.90	.1
IBM	5.8		.90	5.2
General Electric	9.4		.31	2.9
Mobil	3.6		1.58	5.7
Chrysler	3.8		.99	3.8
Philip Morris	10.4		.99	10.3
Prudential Insurance	1.5		.19	.3
State Farm Group	3.2		.48	1.5

Source: Data compiled from "The Fortune 500," *Fortune,* April 29, 1996, pp. F-1 through F-20, © 1996 Time Inc. All rights reserved.

investment base is total assets. Other investment bases can include shareholders' equity (see Table 2-9), capital employed, return on net assets, or some other variation thereof. Both total assets and shareholders' equity are the most commonly used, however.

Again, highest net sales (revenues) does not always result in the highest turnover rate, as shown in Table 2-6. Since total assets play a major role, as well as types of industry, both must be considered. Table 2-6 shows Wal-Mart Stores number one in turnover, but fourth in revenues.

Return on Assets (ROA)

This ROI rate is calculated by using the results from Tables 2-5 and 2-6, that is, the profit margin percentage times the turnover rate. This measures the dollar return per dollar of invested assets. It is an excellent method used for internal purposes to measure how well executives can manage the assets to which they have been entrusted. It is a measurement used to evaluate a manager's performance level. Table 2-7 shows that while some companies, such as Philip Morris and General Electric, have high profit margin

TABLE 2-8   Leverage
(Total Assets ÷ Stockholders' Equity)

Top Twelve Companies by Revenue Ranking—1996

Company Name	Total Assets ($ in billions)	÷	Stockholders' equity ($ in billions)	=	Leverage
General Motors	$217.1		$23.3		9.3
Ford Motor	243.3		24.5		9.9
Exxon	91.3		40.4		2.3
Wal-Mart Stores	37.9		14.8		2.6
AT&T	88.9		17.3		5.1
IBM	80.3		22.4		3.6
General Electric	228.0		29.6		7.7
Mobil	42.1		18.0		2.3
Chrysler	53.8		11.0		4.9
Philip Morris	53.8		14.0		3.8
Prudential Insurance	219.4		11.4		19.3
State Farm Group	85.3		25.1		3.4

Source: Data compiled from "The Fortune 500," *Fortune*, April 29, 1996, pp. F-1 through F-20, © 1996 Time Inc. All rights reserved.

percentages, Philip Morris has the highest return on assets percentage (10.3%), while General Electric has the eighth-highest return on assets percentage (2.9%). This is because Philip Morris needed $53.8 billion of assets to generate $5.5 billion of net income, whereas General Electric needed $228 billion of assets to generate $6.6 billion of net income. It is difficult to draw any conclusions, since they are two different industries and must operate differently according to the nature of the business. If they were in the same industry, some conclusions could be drawn as to why one company could operate with less assets.

Leverage

Leverage is calculated by dividing total assets by stockholders' equity. This ratio answers the fundamental question on how a company finances its assets. Table 2-8 shows that Prudential Insurance has the highest leverage (19.4), whereas Mobil and Exxon have the lowest (2.3).

TABLE 2-9	Return on Stockholders' Equity (ROE) Profit Margin % × Turnover Rate × Leverage)

Top Twelve Companies by Revenue Ranking—1995

Company Name	Profit Margin % (Table 2–5)	×	Turnover Rate (Table 2–6)	×	Leverage (Table 2–8) =	Return on Stockholders' Equity (ROE)
General Motors	4.1%		.78		9.3	29.7%
Ford Motor	3.0		.56		9.9	16.7
Exxon	5.9		1.20		2.3	16.3
Wal-Mart Stores	2.9		2.47		2.6	18.6
AT&T	.1		.90		5.1	.5
IBM	5.8		.90		3.6	18.8
General Electric	9.4		.31		7.7	22.4
Mobil	3.6		1.58		2.3	13.1
Chrysler	3.8		.99		4.9	18.4
Philip Morris	10.4		.99		3.8	39.1
Prudential Insurance	1.5		.19		19.3	5.5
State Farm Group	3.2		.48		3.4	5.2

Source: Data compiled from "The Fortune 500," *Fortune,* April 29, 1996, pp. F-1 through F-20, © 1996 Time Inc. All rights reserved.

Return on Stockholders' Equity (ROE)

This calculation measures the profit return that stockholders receive on their investment. It is one of the most important ratios observed by outsiders, primarily investors, in determining how well a company has performed for the stockholders. It is computed by multiplying the profit margin percentage (Table 2-5), by the turnover rate (Table 2-6), by the leverage multiple (Table 2-8). The end results in return on stockholders' equity (ROE), as shown in Table 2-9. This table shows that Philip Morris leads the list at 39.1%, resulting from a higher profit margin percentage, lower turnover rate, and lower leverage multiple. Conversely, AT&T results last with the principle ratio being the profit margin percentage (.1%).

Again, as mentioned previously, caution should be given to measure like companies within like industries.

ESTABLISHING ROI RESPONSIBILITY USING THE ORGANIZATION CHART

Since ROI results represent decisions from all parts of the organization, it is possible to assign individual objectives to each part of the organization that makes up the total ROI equation. Figure 2-4 is an organization chart reflecting responsibility levels throughout the organization. Both the turn-over rate and the profitability rate are assigned as individual responsibilities. You can see how other functions of the organization, such as the turnover rate, contribute to the ROI equation. For example, cash and marketable securities and receivables are usually the responsibility of the treasurer of the company. Other major functions also are assigned to individual managers as their responsibility. Guidelines for effectively establishing these two assets can be developed as part of the decision-making process for monitoring and increasing ROI performance.

DETERMINE THE PROFITABILITY RATE AND TURNOVER RATE AT VARIOUS LEVELS OF ROI

In establishing desired ROI rates, it is important to develop objectives for both the profitability rate and the turnover rate. To illustrate this concept, a sampling of the various combinations of both the profitability rate and turnover rate are presented in Table 2-11. You can see that at different desired return on investment levels, different profitability and turnover rates are required. For example, to achieve a 10% return on investment rate, the profitability rate should be 5% and the turnover rate 2.0, as shown in Table 2-10.

Keep in mind that at any given level of ROI, many other combinations can be established. For example, using the 10% desired ROI rate, other combinations can be projected, as shown in Table 2-11. While this simple illustration shows the various rate combinations, it also serves to point out the specific objectives that can be established, as previously discussed. Both profitability and turnover rates require different objectives and are affected by different parts of the organization and ultimately by different financial statements.

HOW TO INCREASE RETURN ON TOTAL ASSETS

Operating decisions have a major impact on ROI results. Since most decisions are reflected in the financial statements and since ROI reflects

FIGURE 2-4   Establishing ROI Responsibility Using the Organization Chart

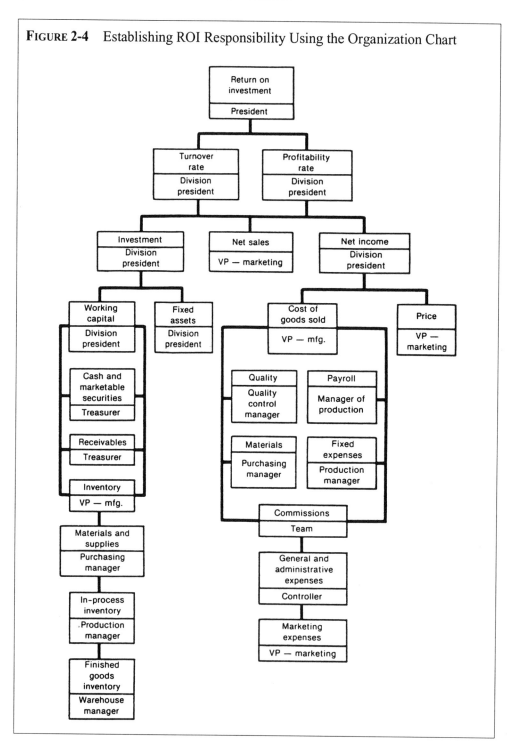

TABLE 2-10	Sampling of Determining the Profitability Rate and Turnover Rate at Various Levels of ROI	
Desired ROI Rate	Profitability Rate Should Be	Turnover Rate Should Be
6%	1.0%	6.00
7	2.0	3.50
8	3.0	2.67
9	4.0	2.25
10	5.0	2.00
11	6.0	1.83
12	7.0	1.71
13	8.0	1.63
14	9.0	1.56
15	10.0	1.50

TABLE 2-11	Various Profitability and Turnover Rate Combinations at a Desired ROI Rate of 10%
Profitability Rate	Turnover Rate
1.0%	10.0
2.0	5.0
3.0	3.3
4.0	2.5
5.0	2.0
6.0	1.7
7.0	1.4
8.0	1.3
9.0	1.1

financial results, to a large degree ROI results can be controlled by the company. The type and magnitude of the decisions will depend upon the achievable results that are desired. Some decisions may be easier than others. Remember, as pointed out earlier, decisions relating to the profitability rate may be easier to accomplish. This does not mean that areas relating to the turnover rate cannot be accomplished. It does mean that greater earnings may be easier to accomplish because of greater control on expenses, particularly human resource costs.

Briefly, the operating decisions that increase ROI or, in this example, return on total assets, are as follows:

Increase sales volume. Higher net sales will result, assuming that there are no price reductions.

Increase sales price. Higher net sales will result, assuming that there is no loss in sales volume.

Reduce production costs. Higher earnings will result, assuming that costs are not the result of lower production.

Reduce operating costs. Higher earnings will result by keeping costs at a level to produce low break-even points.

Reduce cash balances. Keep cash balances to minimal operating levels and use excess cash to generate additional income. This results in lowered investment balances, increased earnings, and ultimately higher ROI.

Reduce receivables. Keep receivables to workable levels in relation to sales. Outstanding receivables should not exceed normal credit terms. Lower receivables will reduce investment, make available additional funds for operating the business, and increase ROI.

Reduce inventories. Keep inventory turnover at acceptable levels. Enough inventory should be on hand to service customers, yet caution should be taken in watching for excessive inventory resulting from declining sales volume or product obsolescence.

Dispose of unprofitable facilities. Constantly watch for facilities that are uneconomical. They should be disposed of or used for other purposes.

Although the above operating decisions seem basic and are part of managing a successful and financially profitable company, they are frequently overlooked. Table 2-12 is a summary of decisions that result in an increase of return on total assets.

HOW TO ANALYZE ROI VARIANCES

It is often necessary to determine which part of the ROI equation (investment or earnings) is responsible for ROI variances; therefore, the two segments must be analyzed. By comparing actual performance versus budgeted performance, or two actual periods, the variance can be explained. By knowing what caused the variances a manager can redirect the resources and establish changes in operating procedures to turn unfavorable variances into favorable ones. Using the following data as an illustration you will see

TABLE 2-12   Summary of Decisions to Increase Return on Total Assets

	Increase	Decrease	Comments
Profitability Rate	X		Net earnings divided by net sales
Net sales	X		Objective is to increase revenues
Pricing	X	X	Maintain balance between market share, consumer acceptance, and competition
Volume	X		Must relate to above pricing strategies
Total costs and expenses		X	Maintain acceptable level of cost of sales as well as cost-effective distribution, marketing, and overhead expenses
Taxes		X	Minimize tax liabilities through effective tax planning
Net earnings	X		Generate more after-tax earnings per dollar of sales by concentrating on higher margins and by controlling operating expenses
Turnover Rate	X		Net sales divided by total assets
Cash and marketable securities		X	Maintain effective cash management program
Accounts receivable		X	Maintain tight control over credit and collection policies
Inventories		X	Maintain acceptable inventory turnover levels
Fixed assets		X	Maintain fixed assets that are cost-effective through technology and production efficiencies

how to analyze a variance. What part of the 5% variance was due to total assets, and what part to net income?

	Actual	Budget	Variance
Total assets	$260,000	$240,000	($20,000)
Net income	$ 50,000	$ 58,100	$ 8,100
ROTA	19.2%	24.2%	5.0%

To calculate the total asset variance, budgeted net income is divided first by budgeted total assets:

$$\frac{\$58,100}{\$240,000} = 24.2\%$$

and then by actual total assets:

$$\frac{\$58,100}{\$260,000} = 22.3\%$$

The unfavorable total asset variance was 1.9%.

To calculate the net income variance, budgeted net income is divided by actual total assets:

$$\frac{\$58,100}{\$260,000} = 22.3\%$$

and actual net income is divided by actual total assets:

$$\frac{\$50,000}{\$260,000} = 19.2\%$$

The unfavorable net income variance was 3.1%.

The total asset variance of 1.9% and the net income variance of 3.1% comprised the total ROI variance of 5%. These comparisons can also be made by periods, by competitors, by this year versus last year, and so forth. This analysis answers the question of where the shortfall or increase took place and highlights potential necessary actions.

DECISION-MAKING STRATEGIES

- Develop an organizational structure to meet the requirements for analyzing components of return on investment.
- Determine criteria for measuring return on investment, that is, profits and investment base.
- Analyze revenue mix and expenses for determining ways of increasing the profitability rate.
- Establish objectives for return on total asset measurements for both internal segments and the total company using such criteria as historical patterns, industry standards, and future expectations.
- Assign ROI objectives to functional areas of the company.
- Establish standards for both the profitability rate and the turnover rate.
- Reevaluate balance sheets periodically to determine the true investment value for calculating ROI results.
- Develop a strategy for earnings growth that depends less on the expansion of sales and more on the earning power of assets.
- Establish a strategy that determines whether to divest or invest in segments of the company that are below ROI standards.

3

How to Use Ratios to Monitor ROI Performance

Ratios can provide important information in establishing standards, controlling performance, and providing operational information necessary to meet changing conditions. For example, in chapter 2 we saw how ratio standards can be applied to the organizational chart and to the return on investment concept. Because ROI is in itself a ratio and the ROI ratio is a summation of many ratios created throughout the organization, the need to develop an understanding and interpretation of key ratios is paramount.

THREE APPROACHES TO ANALYZING RATIOS

The different approaches to analyzing ratios will serve several objectives in establishing and maintaining ROI performance. They will serve:

- To compare internal ROI results.
- To compare the total company or segments of the company with regard to competition.
- To measure trends in the business from period to period.
- As a basis for the allocation of resources within a company, that is, more resources to high-potential areas, and fewer resources to declining segments of the company.

Using this as a basis, ratios can be approached in the following ways:

1. Using the same time period to measure your company in comparison with competitors.

2. Using the same ratios over the same time period to measure trends for your company.
3. Combining the above two concepts to develop trends over time for your company and the industry in which it operates.

The first approach, using the same time period to measure and compare your competitors' performance, requires obtaining competitive financial data as published periodically by *Fortune* magazine, Dun & Bradstreet, governmental agencies, and trade associations. For example, industry data presented in chapter 2 were obtained from the *Fortune* 500 industrial companies. This kind of analysis can be used to compare ROI components by competitors over several periods of time. While only one company for each of twelve industries was presented, complete data for all companies within any industry are available from this source as well as other sources.

The second approach, using the same ratios over the same time period for a specific company, is used to evaluate internal performance. These ratios are used to establish objectives and monitor performance for such key areas as liquidity, debt, profitability, and accounts that make up working capital. These ratios assist in providing certain information for managing many segments of the organization that are reflected in the ROI equation.

The third approach, which combines the first two approaches by relating both competitive ratios with those of your own company, provides a basis for measuring how well your competitors compare with your own company in profitability and turnover of assets. Within these two components, other evaluations and objectives must be made, such as the speed of collections, number of days in inventory, working capital, and liquidity. These and many other factors ultimately result in a higher or lower return on investment.

THE RELATIONSHIP OF ROI TO FINANCIAL STATEMENTS

Since ROI is a financial tool, it measures outcome in financial terms. As previously discussed, ROI is derived from the two major financial statements, namely, the statement of income and the balance sheet. Therefore, it is possible to group ratios into three major categories. These categories highlight trends at different levels of the organization, much like an organization chart. Each category focuses on a different responsibility level within the organization and relates to different parts of the business and different financial statements.

Performance ratios. These follow the trend of the overall performance of the company. Because these ratios are viewed by the outside community as a way of measuring both current and potential performance, they are important to the overall success of the company.

Managing ratios. These assist in evaluating the various components of the balance sheet and are used in managing such major areas of the company as cash, receivables, inventories, and debt relationships.

Profitability ratios. These evaluate components of the earnings statement and effectively show how well a manager is performing, given his or her level of responsibility.

The following examples of the three categories of ratios utilize the financial data presented in Tables 2-1 and 2-2, in chapter 2.

Performance Ratios

Net income to shareholders' equity measures the return generated from the owners' equity in the business when considering all risks. This ratio is important because it serves as a barometer with which shareholders can measure future growth and, ultimately, provide additional capital in the form of buying a piece of the equity, such as shares. The greater the ratio, the more attractive the stock to outside investors.

$$\frac{\text{Net income}}{\text{Shareholders' equity}} = \frac{\$50,000}{\$171,000} = 29.2\%$$

Net sales to shareholders' equity measures the amount of sales volume supported by the equity of the company. A proper balance must exist, and this balance will be reflected over a period of time. A high ratio could mean heavier than usual debt to support high levels of sales, whereas a low ratio could mean an underutilization of the company's resources or insufficient sales to cover the business activity.

$$\frac{\text{Net sales}}{\text{Shareholders' equity}} = \frac{\$700,000}{\$171,000} = 4.09 \text{ times}$$

Net income to total assets represents the return on funds invested in the company by both the owners and the creditors.

$$\frac{\text{Net income}}{\text{Total assets}} = \frac{\$50,000}{\$260,000} = 19.2\%$$

Price/earnings ratio measures how much investors are willing to pay for the current earnings of the company. Companies that are anticipated to have high growth in the future usually have high P/E ratios. Conversely, low P/E ratios are reflected for those companies expected to have low growth in the future.

$$\frac{\text{Market price per share}}{\text{Earnings per share}} = \frac{\$80}{\$5} = 16 \text{ times}$$

Dividend yield measures the expected return to investors.

$$\frac{\text{Dividends per share}}{\text{Market price per share}} = \frac{\$2}{\$80} = 2.5\%$$

Dividend payout indicates how a company divides its earnings between common shareholders and reinvesting them within the company.

$$\frac{\text{Dividends per share}}{\text{Earnings per share}} = \frac{\$2}{\$5} = 40\%$$

Investment turnover measures how many dollars of net sales is generated from a dollar of total assets. Higher ratios reflect greater efficiency.

$$\frac{\text{Net sales}}{\text{Total assets}} = \frac{\$700,000}{\$260,000} = 2.7 \text{ times}$$

Managing Ratios

Current ratio measures the ability of the company to meet its current obligations. The margin of safety provided out of current assets to pay current debts and the adequacy of working capital are two major features of this ratio. The receivables and inventories must be carefully monitored, however, to ensure that they are in keeping with acceptable levels of performance. Other ratios, such as the collection period and inventory turnover ratios, will aid in this analysis.

$$\frac{\text{Current assets}}{\text{Current liabilities}} = \frac{\$137{,}500}{\$65{,}000} = 2.12 \text{ times}$$

Acid test ratio supplements the current ratio by measuring liquidity and the ability of the company to meet its current obligations. This ratio emphasizes those liquid assets that can be quickly converted into cash. Such assets include cash in banks, marketable securities, and those accounts receivable (net) that represent quick assets.

$$\frac{\text{Quick assets}}{\text{Current liabilities}} = \frac{\$92{,}000}{\$65{,}000} = 1.42 \text{ times}$$

Current liabilities to shareholders' equity measures the share that creditors have against the company as compared with the shareholders.

$$\frac{\text{Current liabilities}}{\text{Shareholders' equity}} = \frac{\$65{,}000}{\$171{,}000} = 38\%$$

Debt to equity measures the amount by which a company is financed by long-term debt or borrowed capital and the extent to which a company is financed by permanent contributed capital (shareholders' equity).

$$\frac{\text{Long--term debt}}{\text{Shareholders' equity}} = \frac{\$24{,}000}{\$171{,}000} = 14\%$$

This ratio is sometimes referred to as 7.13 to 1, which is the reciprocal of the given ratio; that is, for every $1 of long-term debt there is almost $7 of shareholders' equity.

Net sales to fixed assets—net reveals how efficiently a business is able to use its own investments in fixed assets. The higher the ratio, the more effective the long-term assets are being utilized. The lower the ratio, attention should be given to the marketing area of the business.

$$\frac{\text{Net sales}}{\text{Fixed assets—net}} = \frac{\$700{,}000}{\$118{,}000} = 5.9 \text{ times}$$

Net sales to working capital measures the ability of working capital to support levels of sales volume. Working capital is explored in chapter 6, which will reveal that an increase in sales volume requires an increase in working capital.

$$\frac{\text{Net sales}}{\text{Working capital}} = \frac{\$700,000}{\$72,500} = 9.66 \text{ times}$$

Fixed assets—net to shareholders' equity measures the amount of capital invested in nonliquid assets. High investments reduce monies for other investments, such as working capital. Favorable investments in fixed assets will provide favorable future earnings, however, and will result in greater funds being available to the company.

$$\frac{\text{Fixed assets—net}}{\text{Shareholders' equity}} = \frac{\$118,000}{\$171,000} = 69\%$$

Day's sales outstanding, referred to as the collection period ratio, indicates the average age of net customers' accounts receivable. It measures the efficiency of internal credit policies and potential bad-debt write-offs. The greater the number of days sales outstanding, the greater the possibility of past due accounts. The calculation is made in two steps. Step 1 measures the average daily credit sales.

$$\frac{\text{Net sales}}{\text{Number of days in a year}} = \frac{\$700,000}{365} = \$1,917.81 \text{ average daily credit sales in a year}$$

Step 2 computes the day's sales outstanding by dividing the average daily credit sales into accounts receivable (net).

$$\frac{\text{Accounts receivable—net}}{\text{Average daily credit sales}} = \frac{\$80,000}{\$1,917.81} = 41.7 \text{ day's sales outstanding}$$

Net sales to accounts receivable—net measures the turnover of accounts receivable during a year. Higher ratios indicate more rapid collections.

$$\frac{\text{Net sales}}{\text{Accounts receivable—net}} = \frac{\$700,000}{\$80,000} = 8.75 \text{ times}$$

Cost of sales to inventories is referred to as the inventory turnover ratio. The lower the ratio, the greater the possibility that the inventory is excessive and that it may contain some obsolete items.

$$\frac{\text{Cost of sales}}{\text{Inventories}} = \frac{\$525,000}{\$40,000} = 13.1 \text{ times}$$

Day's sales on hand indicates the average length in days in which inventory is held before it is sold. Two calculations must be made. The first calculation results in the average daily cost of sales.

$$\frac{\text{Cost of sales}}{\text{Number of days in a year}} = \frac{\$525,000}{365} = \$1,438.36 \text{ average daily cost of sales}$$

The second calculation measures the day's sales on hand.

$$\frac{\text{Inventories}}{\text{Average daily cost of sales}} = \frac{\$40,000}{\$1,438.36} = 27.8 \text{ day's sales on hand}$$

Total debt to total assets measures how much of the total funds are being supplied by its creditors. Total debt represents both current debt and long-term debt (including lease commitments). A high ratio indicates that a high level of leverage was used to generate higher earnings. Conversely, a low ratio reflects the low use of creditor funds.

$$\frac{\text{Total debt}}{\text{Total assets}} = \frac{\$89,000}{\$260,000} = 0.34 \text{ times}$$

Earnings before interest and taxes (EBIT) to interest measures a company's ability to meet its interest payments on both short- and long-term debt. This ratio will also indicate how far EBIT must decline before a company will have difficulty in meeting its interest requirements.

$$\frac{\text{Earnings before interest and taxes}}{\text{Interest}} = \frac{\$88,000}{\$10,000} = 8.8 \text{ times}$$

Profitability Ratios

Net income to net sales measures the profitability of every dollar of sales.

$$\frac{\text{Net income}}{\text{Net sales}} = \frac{\$50,000}{\$700,000} = 7.1\%$$

Gross margin percent indicates the margin of sales over the cost of sales.

$$\frac{\text{Gross profit}}{\text{Net sales}} = \frac{\$175,000}{\$700,000} = 25\%$$

Selling expenses to net sales measures the cost of selling a product.

$$\frac{\text{Selling expenses}}{\text{Net sales}} = \frac{\$30,000}{\$700,000} = 4.3\%$$

ALTMAN Z-SCORE MODEL: HOW RATIOS CAN BE USED TO PREDICT BANKRUPTCY

One interesting application of using ratios is the Altman Bankruptcy Predictor Model, commonly referred to as the Z-Score.[1] This model is a tool used to predict bankruptcy of a company and can be used to make critical decisions to avoid bankruptcy. These decisions are made as a result of this model, which uses a statistical technique known as discriminant analysis. Discriminant analysis is a multivariate technique that helps a company analyze the characteristics of two or more population groups, such as ratios, in an effort to identify and weigh these observations into their identified groups. These groups are considered corporations.

The Altman Z-Score Model uses five key ratios that objectively weigh and develop a total score used to predict a company's ability to survive. Each ratio is given a weighing factor based on the statistical sample that was taken to develop the mathematical equation referred to as the Z-Score (Z).

The Mathematical Equation

The equation is fairly straightforward as follows:

Z-Score Equation

$$Z = 1.2X1 + 1.4X2 + 3.3X3 + 0.6X4 + 1.0X5$$

Each of the five ratios has its own weighing factor. For example, X1, which represents the working capital divided by total assets, is assigned a factor, or a multiplier of 1.2. This multiplier is multiplied by the result of computing the ratio of working capital to total assets.

Each of the five ratios are explained in detail as follows:

X1—represents the ratio of working capital to total assets. This ratio measures the liquid assets of a company in relation to the overall capitalization of the company. Usually, when a company experiences consistent operating losses, it will also experience shrinking current assets in relation to the total assets of the company. This ratio is multiplied by the weighting factor of 1.2.

X2—measures the cumulative profits retained in the business over time. It is calculated by dividing total assets into retained earnings. This ratio is very closely related to the age of a company. For example, young companies usually have a low ratio because they have not had sufficient time to accumulate profits. Therefore, this ratio supports the premise that young companies often have a higher incidence of failure in their earlier years. This ratio is multiplied by the weighting factor of 1.4.

X3—is calculated by dividing total assets into a company's earnings before interest and taxes. This is a true measure of the productivity of a company's total assets, or the earning power of its assets. A multiplier of 3.3 is used in this ratio.

X4—the book value of a company's total liabilities is divided into the market value of its equity. The equity is the combined market value of all shares and types of stock, with liabilities representing both short and long term. When market values are not available, book values may be substituted. This ratio reflects at what point a company's assets can decline in value before the liabilities exceed the assets and the company reaches a point of insolvency. The multiplier of 0.6 is used.

X5—this ratio measures the ability of a company's assets to generate sales. It also reflects how well the management deals with competitive pressures. It is calculated by dividing total assets into net sales and uses the multiplier of 1.0.

It is interesting to note that four of the ratios use total assets as the denominator. This emphasizes the importance of total assets in measuring the performance of a company. Also, you will note that X3 has the highest weighting (multiplier) factor of 3.3. This indicates how important it is for companies to manage its assets in being able to generate earnings. This is no surprise to most managers, but is clearly emphasized in this ratio.

Ratio Interpretation

When analyzing the final score (Z), the following interpretation should be used.

Scores above 3.0 = Company is healthy.

Scores between 1.8 and 3.0 = Can be considered neutral since the company is neither heading for bankruptcy nor is it healthy.

Scores below 1.8 = Indicates a strong possibility of bankruptcy, or in the state of bankruptcy, and needs immediate attention, and major actions must be taken.

It is obvious that the higher the score, the healthier the company, and the lower the probability of failure. It is best to use the components of the Z-Score over a period of time and use corrective actions when one or more ratios appear to be out of line. Also, developing competitive Z-Scores would put your own company's Z-Score into perspective.

Applications of Z-Score

The Z-Score has many applications, some of which apply to interested parties outside the company, such as bankers and credit analysts. Nevertheless, the main application appears to be internally driven. Generally, the following applications have been recognized:

- Used by financial institutions to review the creditworthiness of loan applications
- Used to determine the financial health of a company when companies consider merging or reorganizing
- Used to evaluate the company's performance over time as to its financial health and the utilization of its assets
- Used as a tool for determining investment opportunities by investment managers and overall investors as to the potential of a company's future
- Used as a means for establishing legal procedures when it becomes obvious that bankruptcy will occur

It is through such techniques as the Z-Score that managers can protect their company from failures, for when parts or all of these ratios reflect downturns, immediate actions can be taken by managers to turn around a company's results. Such issues as growing too fast, inventory and receivables issues, overall working capital status, cash availability, product line eliminations, or plant closings can be isolated and often corrected by the use of the Z-Score.

CAUTIONS IN USING RATIOS

As discussed in chapter 2, caution should be taken before any conclusions are drawn regarding ratio results. These cautions are summarized as follows:

- Be sure to use several time periods to develop a trend.
- Be sure data are comparable, such as similarity in the nature of the business, similar accounting data, and so on.

- Develop key ratios that represent the "pulse" of the business.
- Also use ratios that are not necessarily financial in nature, for example, market share percentage or employee productivity.
- When using industry data, recognize that very few industries are alike and that ratio results may vary due in part to industry differences.
- Never draw conclusions from one ratio without relating it to other sets of data.

Remember, ratios are only tools and are not clear-cut solutions to all financial problems.

DECISION-MAKING STRATEGIES

- Develop ratios that are unique to each segment of the business.
- Group ratios into performance, managing, and profitability categories.
- Establish formal procedures for monitoring key ratios.

NOTE

1. Altman, Edward I. "Financial Ratios Discriminant Analysis and the Prediction of Corporate Bankruptcy," *Journal of Finance,* September 1968, pp. 589–609.

4

SHAREHOLDER VALUE AND ITS IMPACT ON ROI PERFORMANCE

Shareholder value is an important measurement to a shareholder.[1] It is an objective that company managers must pursue, since shareholders measure management's performance by how well they are able to increase their dividends and the appreciation of their stock price. The shareholders are able to assess the future value of their investments in the decision to invest based on what future they see given the anticipated return and risk.

Small business owners as well as large companies will be able to benefit from this concept by using it as a supplement to the traditional accounting and cash flow techniques. By acting as a supplement, operating managers will be able to achieve higher return on investment values through the utilization of resources as outlined in the planning process.

Shareholder value, or the economic value of the company, can be defined as the sum of the cash flows in the future in today's current value of the dollar. It provides a different analysis of the measurement of a business by the shareholder, that is, an economic measurement as compared to traditional accounting based on measures of business performance such as accounting earnings and traditional return on investment ratios.

The cash flows are based on both current and future cash inflows and outflows. Most other evaluations, such as return on equity and earnings per share, do not reflect the components that create value. For example, the risk of the business, the time value of money, and expectations by the investor strongly relate to stock prices and are external barometers of the value of a company. This method also puts more accountability on how value is created and a far greater concern for managing a company's assets.

Other decisions derived from shareholder value include a better link between the operations and strategy of a business with a company's financial results; a willingness to redirect and utilize the resources of a company more effectively; getting managers to act like owners; providing a basis for employee compensation; and the ultimate result of creating higher market value of the company.

CREATING SHAREHOLDER VALUE

The shareholder value is reflected by investors in equating the market value of a company in terms of the amount of financial securities, such as debt instruments and equity securities, that are issued to investors. Therefore, we can say that the shareholder value of the company is equal to the market value of the equity securities. For example, if the market value of debt were $240,000 and the market value of the equity were $750,000, then the market value of the company would be $990,000.

One way in which shareholder value can be increased is to increase shareholder equity and decrease the value of the debt. For example, if the shareholder equity were to be increased to $800,000, and the debt decreased to $200,000, then the shareholder value would be $1,000,000, an increase of $10,000 over the previous shareholder value of $990,000. This can be accomplished by a more efficient allocation of resources by managers, thus resulting in higher equity and higher shareholder value.

TWO METHODS USED FOR MEASURING SHAREHOLDER VALUE

There are two commonly used measures of computing shareholder value. While both measures are value based, one deals with the long term, and the other deals in the short term. Both measures (shareholder value and economic value added—EVA) use the results of the operations of the company, since they represent the true cash flow of a company, and eliminate the effects of traditional accounting, which can be misleading.

Method One: Using Shareholder Value to Measure Long-Term Value

This method measures the long-term value of a company and is based on the principal of discounted cash flow (see chapter 20 for a full discussion on discounted cash flow). This method is used to evaluate long-term

TABLE 4-1 Calculation of Free Cash Flow	
Operating income before interest and taxes	$900,000
Add: Other operating income	50,000
Less: Taxes paid in cash on operating income	(330,000)
Income after taxes (excluding interest)	620,000
Less: Additions to plant and equipment (net of depreciation)	(120,000)
Less: Additions to operating capital	(110,000)
Less: Other investment additions	0
Reinvestment capital	(230,000)
Free Cash Flow	$390,000

investment decisions such as capital projects and mergers and acquisitions.

The long-term evaluation is linked to investment decisions and uses free cash flow for an operation or capital project. These cash flows are expressed in today's dollar. They represent the after-tax cash generated from the operations of the company for a period after the money has been reinvested. They do not include cash flows generated from financing sources. Reinvestment is defined as changes in cash flow from capital expenditures, disposal of capital equipment, changes in accounts receivable and inventory less account payables (operating capital), and investments in mergers and acquisitions.

Table 4-1 illustrates how free cash flow is calculated. This forecast is presented in future dollars and should be discounted back into today's dollar value using present value tables as shown in Appendix A.

How Market Value Is Determined

The shareholder (or economic) value of a company is determined by how well it identifies investments that investors can expect to see in the future—higher returns in excess of the market rate required.[2] In the absence of such results, companies can expect to see a decline in a company's value through the erosion of the company's debt and/or equity. Therefore, a company that produces goods and services that are in market demand will generate higher profits, as well as higher cash flows, and will show higher equity values. In theory, if a company earns more than the market return investors need to stay invested in the company, the market value of the company will exceed the book value of the assets used within the company.

Using a simple equation, it can be demonstrated whether the investor will place a premium or discount to the book value of the assets invested in the business.

Market
Value
Equation

$$\text{Market value of the company} = \frac{\text{Corporate rate of return} \times \text{assets at book value}}{\text{Expected market rate}}$$

Assume that a company has a rate of return of 12%, and that the expected market rate by investors is 20%. Using these facts, a company will return $0.60 per $1 of assets as follows:

$$\frac{12\% \times \$1}{20\%} = \$0.60 \text{ per } \$1 \text{ of assets invested}$$

You can see that an investor loses $0.40 per $1 of assets because a company can only earn 12% on its assets, whereas the investors demand 20%. This will drive down the market value of a company. If the company can earn 25% on all its investments, however, then higher value results as follows:

$$\frac{25\% \times \$1}{20\%} = \$1.25 \text{ per } \$1 \text{ of assets invested}$$

In this scenario, every dollar of assets invested in the business by the company results in $1.25 in the market's evaluation of the company.

An Alternative Long-Term Evaluation Method

Another long-term evaluation is found in an index developed by Alfred Rappaport called the long-term value index (LVI).[3] It provides a rough estimate of the confidence that investors have in management's ability to create a long-term competitive advantage in the business. It is computed as follows:

Long-Term
Value Index
Equation

$$\text{LVI} = \frac{(1 - \text{Sum of dividends for next 5 years})}{\text{Current stock price}} \times 100$$

Assuming that a company's recent stock price is $75, and the total dividends for the next five years are $10, then the LVI is 86.7%, as follows:

TABLE 4–2   Example of Increasing EVA

	Current Business	+	Investment Addition	=	Increase in EVA
Net earnings	$ 50,000		$ 20,000		$ 70,000
Total assets	260,000		120,000		380,000
Return on assets	19.2%		16.7%		18.4%
Cost of capital	6.4%		6.4%		6.4%
Interest cost	16,640		7,680		24,320
Economic value added	$ 33,360		$ 12,320		$ 45,680

$$LVI = [1 - (\ \$10/\$75\ )] \times 100 = 86.7\%$$

With these assumptions, the market suggests that only 13.3% (1 − .867) of the value of the company will be attributable to dividends over the next five years. Whereas, beyond the five years, cash flows are expected to contribute about 87% of the stock's value.

Method Two: Using Economic Value Added (EVA) to Measure Short-Term Value

Economic value added (EVA) is a measurement that measures short-term values, that is, values added to or depleted from the shareholder value.[4] Unlike the first measurement discussed, namely, shareholder value, EVA deals with both earnings statement and balance sheet transactions and uses the traditional methods of accounting for computing cash flows.

The components of EVA include the earnings of the company, taxes paid by cash, capital assets on the balance sheets, and the cost of capital (see chapter 5). Anytime you can earn more than the cost of capital, you will add value to the company. Conversely, if you earn less than the cost of capital, you have decreased the value of the company.

Illustration

The impact on EVA can best be illustrated by showing two examples of hypothetical situations of how company efficiencies and capital investments can either decrease or increase EVA.

In Table 4-2, you will see that adding an investment that increases net

TABLE 4-3   Example of Decreasing EVA

	Current Business	+	Investment Addition	=	Increase in EVA
Net earnings	$ 10,000		$ 5,000		$ 15,000
Total assets	260,000		120,000		380,000
Return on assets	3.8%		4.2%		3.9%
Cost of capital	6.4%		6.4%		6.4%
Interest cost	16,640		7,680		24,320
Economic value added	($ 6,640)		($ 2,680)		($ 9,320)

earnings can reduce return on assets (net earnings/total assets), and result in higher EVA.

Conversely, adding an investment can increase net earnings and return on assets but can result in lower EVA, as shown in Table 4-3.

There are three ways of increasing EVA for a company. One way is to increase the operating efficiency of the company, thereby increasing the rate of return on the capital assets. A second way is when adding new investments, make sure that the capital invested returns more than the cost of capital. A third way occurs when capital is withdrawn from uneconomic activities; this capital should be below the cost of capital.

The EVA measurement is an excellent internal and single-period measure of creating value. Since this measurement is used for single-period analysis, it is not advisable to use this measure for long-term investment decisions such as for capital projects. Under these circumstances, the shareholder value method is advisable.

DECISION-MAKING STRATEGIES

- Use concepts to measure the value of capital projects and business units.
- Establish overall performance objectives using shareholder value and EVA techniques.
- Utilize concepts to determine the most effective utilization of resources.
- Use concepts for evaluating research and development projects.
- Determine value-added results during operating budget reviews.
- Include EVA techniques in tracking monthly performance.

NOTES

1. The ideas of shareholder value are based on the ideas presented in Ch. 11A, *Handbook of Budgeting,* 3rd ed., Robert Rachlin and H.W. Allen Sweeney, *1996 Cumulative Supplement* Copyright © 1996. Reprinted by permission of John Wiley & Sons, Inc., New York.

2. Gallinger, George W., and Jerry B. Poe, *Essentials of Finance: An Integrated Approach,* Englewood Cliffs, N.J.: Prentice-Hall, 1995, pp. 390–395.

3. Rappaport, Alfred, "Don't Sell Stock Market Horizon's Short," *Wall Street Journal,* June 27, 1983, p. 28.

4. Stewart, Bennett, III, *Stern Stewart Corporate Finance Handbook,* Stern Stewart Management Services, 1986, secs. 3–14, 8–13, 1986.

5

COST OF CAPITAL AND ITS APPLICATIONS TO ROI OBJECTIVES

Cost of capital serves as a standard for establishing acceptable ROI rates, as well as measuring whether actual ROI rates meet acceptable levels as in the case of operating divisions. It represents the interest or discount rate on the market value of cash flows used in measuring investments of a company. In addition, it represents the minimum rate at which investors expect to earn on their investment in the company. This required rate induces investors to provide all forms of long-term capital to the company.

It is recognized that other forms of establishing acceptable rates of return are available. For example, this rate can depend on the current experience of the company or industry standards; the risk factor of the investment and its relationship to market securities with similar risk factors; the availability of capital; the past performance of the company; government regulations in some cases; and expected potential. Although all of these are important, it is most important to ensure that a company earns more than its cost of capital.

HOW COST OF CAPITAL IS USED

Since investors expect to earn more on the investment they have in your company than on other, similar investments (e.g., securities, savings), it is important that company managers assure that the earnings generated on new investments are higher than the cost of capital to a company. There are three ways in which a company uses the cost of capital rate.

The first way, as previously discussed, is to assure that a new investment earns more than its average cost of capital. Investors will require a company to yield them more future earnings, or return on investment, than they can get on similar investments with the same risks. If this is not accomplished, investors will sell their equity position in the company, thus reducing the availability of much-needed capital in future years. Also, this could cause the price of the company's stock on the open market to decrease and further hamper its ability to acquire sufficient capital at an inexpensive rate.

A second use of cost of capital is to monitor the mix of capital acquired between debt and equity. As we discuss later in the chapter, each type of capital assumes a different cost and risk, thereby creating a need to protect the company's assets and financing capabilities.

A final use is to ensure that adequate ROI objectives are established on all new capital asset acquisitions, including assets acquired through leasing. This is necessary to ensure that a steady stream of future cash flows will continue to meet the needs for future capital investment opportunities at a rate sufficient to cover current and anticipated interest costs.

In evaluating new investments, it is important that the cost of capital meet several conditions. One condition is that the new investment incur the same historical risk typically undertaken by the company. In other words, a new investment cannot change the risk from what has previously taken place in other investments. Another condition is that any financing of new investments should not alter the financial risks of the company by either changing the mix of financing (e.g., debt versus equity) or exposing the company's assets to higher risk. Now that these conditions have been established, let us discuss two techniques used to measure cost of capital. They include the incremental cost method and the weighted average cost method.

INCREMENTAL COST METHOD

This technique says that any investment whose earning rate is above the cost of financing is a favorable investment. Therefore, at any interest rate, an investment would be justified if one could earn more than the cost of that borrowed capital. To illustrate the point, let us assume the following:

Net sales	$500,000
Net income	$ 50,000
Total assets	$250,000
Loan of $50,000 for 5 years at 15%	

From these facts, one can see that the ability to generate earnings on new capital is 20%, which is calculated as follows:

TABLE 5–1   Illustration of Incremental Earnings

Year	(1) Outstanding Balance	(2) Earnings Potential (1) × .20	(3) Interest at 15% (1) × .15	(4) Incremental Earnings (2)–(3)
1	$ 50,000	$10,000	$ 7,500	$2,500
2	40,000	8,000	6,000	2,000
3	30,000	6,000	4,500	1,500
4	20,000	4,000	3,000	1,000
5	10,000	2,000	1,500	500
Total	$150,000	$30,000	$22,500	$7,500

Incremental Cost Equation

$$\frac{\text{Net income}}{\text{Net Sales}} \times \frac{\text{Net sales}}{\text{Total assets}}$$

$$\frac{\$50,000}{\$500,000} \times \frac{\$500,000}{\$250,000}$$

$$10\% \times 2 = 20\%$$

Because the 20% represents the ability to generate earnings at that rate, it is now possible to compute the incremental earnings under the incremental cost method. To illustrate, we will use the preceding facts of a loan of $50,000 at 15% interest for 5 years, with equal installments of $10,000 each year. The results are shown in Table 5-1.

An easier way to compute the incremental earnings is to take the difference between the earnings potential rate (20%) and the interest rate (15%) and multiply the difference (5%) by the total outstanding balance of $150,000.

The total of $7,500 incremental earnings means that, by using $50,000 of capital for 5 years, a return of 15% can be expected ($7,500 divided by $50,000). In addition, because the earnings potential is 20%, the cost of capital, as well as any acquisition of new capital, should not exceed this amount.

Sources of Long-Term Debt

Debt financing may take many different forms and is for more than one year. It is an amount of money borrowed from a creditor and is usually accompanied by a formal document, or note, in which the borrower agrees to repay the borrowed principal plus interest in specified amounts on specified dates. The schedule of payments, the terms of interest, and the length of time are usually negotiated.

Debt financing may not always be available because of lenders' having doubts about the nature of your business; the future of your business in terms of its financial capability, the industry, the product, the markets, and so forth; or, in some cases, the ability of the management to operate the business effectively. In addition, the supply of money may be such that only preferred customers of lending institutions would have access to these funds. For example, when the money market is low, such financial institutions as banks limit the amounts they will lend to their customers and tend to select only borrowers with whom they have had a continuous and profitable relationship with very little risk involved. Other factors, such as the financial condition, stability, and liquidity of the company, will also play a major role in whether or not the banks will lend it the needed funds.

Debt sources are also available through many different types of financial institutions. Let us review some of these sources and the types of financing that are available.

Bank Financing

Banks, particularly commercial banks, are a major source of funds. They provide short-term loans such as commercial loans, lines of credit, inventory financing, and accounts receivable financing. They also provide both medium- and long-term loans in the form of unsecured term loans, financing of real estate and equipment, and leasing.

The criteria for bank loans will vary from period to period and from borrower to borrower. Nevertheless, there are generally accepted criteria that banks as well as other lending institutions look for in loan applications. They are the experience of the borrower in both prior loan agreements and business experience, forms of collateral that are available, and the potential ability of the borrower's business to repay according to the terms of the loan.

Commercial Finance Companies

When bank loans are denied, or when additional funds are needed over and above other finance sources, a source can be found in commercial finance companies. Unlike some banks, however, commercial finance companies usually require some form of collateral, such as accounts receivable and inventories. In addition, they also will be involved in equipment leasing and factoring. Because commercial finance companies usually deal in higher risk situations, their rates often are higher than bank rates.

Savings and Loan Companies

This source of funds deals primarily with loans on commercial, industrial, and residential real estate. The ability to repay the debt is usually the most important factor.

Other Sources of Financing

Other sources of funds involving debt include life insurance companies, factors, consumer finance companies, the Small Business Administration, and other governmental agencies, such as state and local industrial development administrations. Because these sources may not be available to all companies, it is important to seek assistance to see if you qualify for a particular type of loan agreement.

Calculating the Cost of Bonds

Bonds are instruments issued by companies agreeing to pay bondholders a specific amount of interest over a specified period of time. Most companies use bonds to generate large sums of money. Bonds are rated and the ratings are published in financial publications. These ratings assign classifications reflecting the risk of each type of security. In addition, long-term government bond rates can be used as a basis for calculating the cost of bonds.

Bonds are sold at greater than par, or face, value (premium) when the interest rate (coupon rate) is greater than those of similar instruments when considering risk. Bonds are also sold at less than par value (discount), which is below the prevailing interest rate for similar instruments also when considering risk.

Part of the costs of issuing and selling a bond is referred to as flotation costs, which result in reducing the net proceeds from premium, discount, or par value. To illustrate how the cost of bonds is calculated, assume the following facts for The Great Company, Inc.

Par, or face, value of bond	$1,000
Bond interest rate	10%
Flotation costs	$30
Years to maturity	10

By using the following formula, the company can approximate the cost of this security and use this rate for calculating the cost of long-term debt.

Long-Term
Debt
Equation

$$\frac{\text{Annual interest} + \dfrac{\text{Par value} - \text{Net proceeds}}{\text{Number of years maturity}}}{\dfrac{\text{Net proceeds} + \text{Par value}}{2}}$$

Substituting the facts in the above formula results in the following equation, which approximates the before-tax cost of debt.

$$\frac{\$100 + \dfrac{\$1,000 - \$970}{10}}{\dfrac{\$970 + \$1,000}{2}} = \frac{\$100 + \$3}{\$985}$$

or

$$\frac{\$103}{\$985} = 10.46\%$$

Since this amount represents the before-tax cost, the 10.46% must be converted to an after-tax cost basis. Using a 46% tax rate, the after-tax cost is 5.65% $(1 - .46 \times .1046)$. This amount represents the after-tax cost of the bonds and will be used to calculate the long-term-debt portion of the weighted average cost of capital.

Calculating the Cost of Preferred Stock

Many companies issue preferred stock as a way of generating equity capital. Preferred shareholders receive dividends at a specific rate before common shareholders, either in cash or as a percentage of par value. No adjustment is necessary for taxes since dividends are paid out of after-tax cash flows.

When preferred stock is issued using a cash or dollar amount, the stock will be referred to as X number of dollars per share on each share owned by the preferred shareholder. To illustrate this calculation, we assume the following facts:

Selling price or par value	$70
Dividend per share	$ 7
Flotation cost per share	$ 5

The proceeds received from each share of preferred stock are $65 ($70 – $5) after deducting the flotation costs. Dividing the dividend payment per share of $7 by the net proceeds of $65 results in a cost of preferred stock of 10.77%.

When the dividend is expressed as an annual percentage of the par value, such as 10%, the calculation is as follows, using the same set of facts as above.

Cost of Preferred Stock Equation

Dividend (.10 times $70)	
divided by	$ 7.00
Net proceeds ($70 - $5) equals	$65.00
Cost of preferred stock	10.77%

In either case, the same cost results, that is, 10.77%. This percentage would be used as part of the calculation for determining the weighted average cost of capital.

Calculating the Cost of Common Shareholders' Equity

The cost of common shareholders' equity is based on the expected returns discounted by the investor. This discount rate is based on the interest charged on risk-free securities and then adjusted for risk elements for both internal and external factors.

Risk-free securities are usually associated with U.S. Treasury bills, since it is unlikely that the Treasury will default on payments of principal and interest. Economists have estimated that the real rate of interest is 2%. Therefore, the difference between actual interest cost (nominal) and the real rate of interest represents the expected rate of inflation. For example, if the interest rate of U.S. Treasury securities is 7.75%, an estimated 5.75 (7.75% – 2%) represents the expected rate of inflation over the length of time (maturity). If the maturity date is 1 year, then the difference represents the expected inflation rate over a one-year period. If the maturity date is 5 years, then the expected rate of inflation is for the period covering five years.

The cost of shareholders' equity belongs to the shareholders, since they invest in a company with the expectation of receiving some future benefits. These benefits induce them to pay the price for the stock in anticipation of future dividends and capital appreciation. In analyzing both benefits, one will see that they come from future earnings per share and are the principal factors affecting the price of the stock in the long run. Therefore, the common shareholders' cost is measured by the inverse of the price-earnings ratios, or the earnings-price ratio.

The price-earnings ratio is a reflection of investor confidence. Investors will react in different ways depending upon their outlook. For example, when investors are optimistic about increasing future profits, they bid the price of the stock upward, thus raising the multiple. Conversely, when they are pessimistic about the future of earnings, or when they find more attractive alternatives, they tend to stay out of the market, and falling prices will reduce the price-earnings ratio.

As we have previously seen when reviewing the components of capital, one can identify the specific cost of most of the components, such as long-term debt and preferred stock. However, the common equity (common stock, capital in excess of par value and earnings retained in the business) presents a different problem and results in a different calculation. For example, it can be asked if earnings retained in the business have a cost. The answer is yes. This is so because shareholders view retained earnings as an opportunity cost—that is, when these earnings are retained in the business they cannot be used to earn money elsewhere. In theory, the retention of these funds is the same as if dividends were used to buy the company's stock. Therefore, it is part of the money that the shareholder has invested in the ownership of the company.

The cost of common equity is calculated as

Cost of Common Shareholders' Equity Equation

$$\frac{\text{Anticipated earnings at end of year 1}}{\text{Current net price per share}}$$

or as

$$\frac{\text{Dividends per share}}{\text{Current net price per share}} + \text{Expected annual rate of growth of dividends}$$

The cost of common shareholders' equity is calculated to be 6.25% given the following facts:

Anticipated earnings per share	$ 5
Net price per share	$80
Dividends per share	$ 2
Growth rate	3.75%

$$\frac{\$5}{\$80} = 6.25\%$$

or

$$\frac{\$2}{\$80} + 3.75\% = 6.25\%$$

The 6.25% cost of common shareholders equity will be used in the overall calculation of the weighted cost of capital.

THE WEIGHTED AVERAGE COST OF CAPITAL METHOD

This method encompasses all the components of capital, assigns given values for each component in accordance with contractual and calculated rates, and develops a weighted average cost. These components of capital include both internal funds, such as retained earnings, and external funds, such as debt and preferred and common stock. The calculations for each of the components have been previously made and are summarized as follows:

	Percentage Cost
Long-term debt	5.65%
Preferred stock	10.77%
Common shareholders' equity	
Common stock	6.25%
Capital in excess of par value	6.25%
Earnings retained in business	6.25%

Assuming that a company establishes a viable capital structure for its financing as follows, it is now possible to calculate the weighted average cost of capital as shown in Table 5-2.

Source of Capital	*Percentage Financing Desired*
Long-term debt	35%
Preferred stock	8%
Common shareholders' equity	57%
	100%

TABLE 5–2	Calculating the Weighted Average Cost of Capital		
Source	*Percentage Financing Desired*	*After-tax Percentage Cost*	*Weighted Cost*
Long-term debt	35%	5.65%	1.98%
Preferred stock	8%	10.77%	.86%
Common shareholders' equity	57%	6.25%	3.56%
Total	100%		6.40%

The weighted average cost of capital—in this case, 6.40%—is used as a base for determining the minimum required cutoff rate of return on new investments. In other words, management should not approve any new investments that are expected to yield less than 6.40%. Anything that yields less than 6.40% will yield losses, and any investment yielding more than 6.40% will yield profits. A sound management decision is to allow several percentage points over and above the weighted average cost of capital in case of errors in forecasting and unforeseen events. This decision will protect the investments' profitability in the long run. In this example, the minimum required cutoff rate would be rounded to 8.50%.

Since the components and rates of capital will change from time to time, it is important to recalculate the weighted average cost of capital each year to formulate a new ROI objective for the next year's budgeted new capital investments. As market conditions change, so will the interest rates and capital structures change.

DECISION-MAKING STRATEGIES

- Calculate cost of capital rate for the company.
- Assign cost of capital objectives to capital investment proposals and segments of the company.
- Determine the best method of financing (e.g., debt versus equity) to reduce the cost of capital rate.
- Develop strategies to increase the company's stock price.
- Look for other sources of capital, such as limited partnerships for such projects as research and development, to decrease the high cost of borrowing.
- Shift segments of the company's resources to areas that have higher profitability rates.

6

MANAGING WORKING CAPITAL TO INCREASE ROI RESULTS

Working capital is an integral part of the ROI calculation. In previous chapters, mention was made about the investment part of the ROI equation. Investments usually include monies spent for such assets as cash and marketable securities, accounts receivable, inventories, and fixed assets. In most definitions of investment, working assets (current assets) are part of the total invested in a business.

To acquire working assets requires the establishment of short-term obligations referred to as current liabilities. Therefore, working capital can be defined as current assets less current liabilities. The result represents working capital, or the liquidity that a company has at a given point in time. Current assets can be viewed as sources of cash receipts and current liabilities as cash disbursements. The results represent the liquidity of the company or the ability to convert current assets into cash in a relatively short period of time. Offsetting the cash generated by converting current assets into cash are current bills that must be paid, or current liabilities.

CURRENT ASSETS

As indicated, current assets are anticipated to be converted into cash within the current operating year. In addition to cash, it includes marketable securities, accounts receivable, and inventories. These are considered working assets, which are used to operate the business and usually are converted into revenues by either a direct sale or in support of the sales effort. For example, cash is used to pay for manufacturing or for buying inventory for sale. Inventory is needed to fulfill sales, which usually result in an accounts

TABLE 6–1   Working Capital for The Great Company, Inc.

Current Assets		Current Liabilities	
Cash in banks	$ 5,000	Accounts payable	$38,000
Marketable securities	7,000	Debt due within one year	4,500
Accounts receivable—net	80,000	Accrued expenses	10,000
Inventories	40,000	Income taxes payable	12,500
Prepaid expenses	5,500	Total	$65,000
Total	$137,500		
Working capital equals	$ 72,500		

receivable when goods are purchased on account. Marketable securities represent a temporary investment of excess cash, which is used to generate short-term income on idle cash.

WORKING CAPITAL

For The Great Company, Inc., the working capital is shown in Table 6-1. The importance of liquidity can be seen above by the following situation. Assume the company must pay 75% of the total accounts payable, or $28,500 (.75 × $38,000) by the end of the month. The company has liquid funds (cash and marketable securities) of $12,000, and the difference of $16,500 must be generated from collections of accounts receivable, selling inventories for cash, or both. Since the exact timing of these activities is not always feasible, it is important to manage working capital components so that adequate cash is available to meet current obligations.

For example, when a sale is made, an account receivable is established, whereby money owed the company by a customer will not be collected for several months. Tight control of accounts receivable will keep the liquidity of these accounts within the company's historical pattern and/or within industry standards.

In the case of inventories an even longer period is required for converting the inventory value into cash. Because inventory must be either manufactured or bought in advance of a sale, one will not convert the inventory for the length of the accounts receivable plus the period between paying for the inventory and the sale. This situation is illustrated in Figure 6-1.

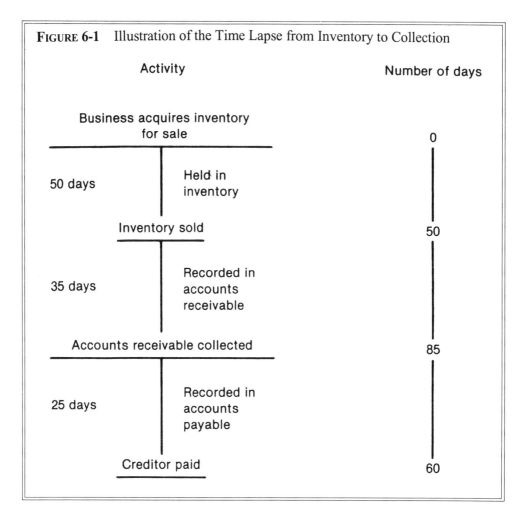

FIGURE 6-1   Illustration of the Time Lapse from Inventory to Collection

The figure shows that inventory was available for sale in period zero. It remained in inventory until it was finally sold 50 days later. When the inventory was sold, an account receivable was established and the customer paid 35 days later. This means that the time between the acquisition of inventory and the company's recovering the investment of its inventory was 85 days. Because the company did not pay the supplier for 25 days, however, the actual time from when cash was paid out for the inventory until it was recovered amounted to 60 days.

It is also obvious that for a period of 60 days this money was tied up in both inventories and receivables and could not be used for investment purposes elsewhere in the company. If the inventory investment had been recovered sooner, this money could have been used for other opportunities to generate profits and cash flow. At the current rate of interest, or at the rate for which opportunities were available, this could have amounted to a substantial loss of earnings.

Therefore, it is critical to ensure that inventory turnover and day's sales outstanding are not beyond the normal amount for your business. Every effort should be made to improve these relationships, to speed up inventory turnover, and to reduce the number of day's sales outstanding. Should these periods exceed the norm, critical cash shortages and lower return on investment may occur.

HOW INVESTING IN WORKING CAPITAL IMPACTS THE ROI EQUATION

Using Table 6-1 as an illustration, let's review how investing in any components of working capital changes the ROI results. Assuming the following facts using total assets as the investment base and assuming that additional sales generate additional earnings, Table 6-2 illustrates the impact on return on total assets.

Facts (based on data from Tables 2-1 and 2-2)

Additional 5% sales	$35,000
Profit margin before tax @ 25%	8,750
Net income @ 49% tax rate	4,463
Sales resulted in the following:	
Cash—10%	
Accounts receivable—90%	

Table 6-2 illustrates how investments in current assets affect the return on total asset rate. In this illustration, a 0.7 (19.2%-18.5%) percentage point decline resulted from an increase in sales. This highlights how important it is to manage working assets to assure that the company does increase profitability and maintain adequate liquidity. In a typical situation, substantial cash flows and profits would be generated from investments in fixed assets and would ultimately increase the return on total asset rate.

MANAGING WORKING CAPITAL THROUGH RATIOS

To manage working capital effectively, a series of key ratios can be developed. These ratios will put into perspective the relationship of working

---

TABLE 6–2   Impact of Generating Higher Sales on the Return
                   on Total Asset Rate

	Original Data	Revised Data
Cash in banks	$ 5,000	$ 8,500
Marketable securities	7,000	7,000
Accounts receivable—net	80,000	111,500
Inventories	40,000	40,000*
Prepaid expenses	5,500	5,500
Total current assets	137,500	172,500
Fixed and other assets	122,500	122,500
Total assets	$260,000	$295,000

Return on total assets

$$\frac{\text{Net income}}{\text{Total assets}} \quad \frac{\$\ 50,000}{\$260,000} = 19.2\% \qquad \frac{\$\ 54,463}{\$295,000} = 18.5\%$$

* Assume sold inventory was replenished at same cost and purchased on account.

---

capital to the ROI performance of the company. Guidelines must be established for each ratio based on both historical and industry standards. The following calculations will be made using the data for The Great Company, Inc.

Net sales to working capital. This ratio measures the turnover of working capital. The more a company can turn over its working capital, that is, to generate more sales, the more liquidity and profits it should generate.

$$\frac{\text{Net sales}}{\text{Working capital}} \qquad \frac{\$700,000}{\$72,500} = 9.66 \text{ times}$$

Net earnings to working capital. This ratio measures the ability of a company to use working capital to generate net earnings.

$$\frac{\text{Net income}}{\text{Working capital}} \qquad \frac{\$50,000}{\$72,500} = 69.0\%$$

Current assets to current liabilities. This ratio is referred to as the current ratio and indicates the ability of a company to meet its current obligations.

$$\frac{\text{Current assets}}{\text{Current liabilities}} \quad \frac{\$137,500}{\$65,000} = 2.12 \text{ times}$$

Quick ratio. This ratio is similar to the current ratio but places more emphasis on those liquid assets that can easily be converted into cash. The quick assets represent the current assets less inventories. Inventories cannot be included since they have not been sold and do not immediately present the opportunity to convert these assets easily into cash.

$$\frac{\text{Quick assets}}{\text{Current liabilities}} \quad \frac{\$97,500}{\$65,000} = 1.5 \text{ times}$$

Liquidity ratio. This ratio is a refinement of the quick ratio and deals with even more liquid assets, namely, cash and marketable securities.

$$\frac{\text{Cash and marketable securites}}{\text{Current liabilities}} \quad \frac{\$12,000}{\$65,000} = 18.5\%$$

In the following chapters (chapters 7 and 8) further strategies will be developed in managing the major components of working capital, namely, cash in banks and marketable securities, accounts receivable, inventories, accounts payable, and accruals.

DECISION-MAKING STRATEGIES

- Establish acceptable working capital levels based on historical patterns and/or industry standards.
- Monitor each of the components of working capital and set objectives.
- Establish a formal program of effectively managing the balance sheet with particular emphasis on working capital.
- Establish different return on investment rates for investments in working capital.

7

How Managing Cash
Improves ROI Performance

The first of the working capital components is cash and marketable securities. This current asset is part of the cash management program. This program typically involves these three major services in managing company's cash and the optimization and utilization of a company's available funds.

TYPICAL METHODS FOR MANAGING CASH

The process of maximizing cash utilizes an overall cash management program. This program typically involves these three major services:

- Collection
- Disbursement
- Control

Each of these services provides a company with the ability to manage cash by harnessing payments, speeding collections, and providing swift movement of funds. Let us briefly explore each process, but keep in mind that many innovative approaches are continually being offered by financial institutions and it is suggested that these topics be used primarily as guidelines for further discussion with your own financial institution.

Collection Services

This part of the cash management program is intended to "speed up" the collection of funds and be able to make funds available as soon as possible within the company. The following services can be used to accomplish this objective.

Lockbox services are the most commonly used service to establish convenient and economical mail-collection points for customers who pay by mail. Customers send remittances (checks) to designated post office boxes, where local banks collect these checks and deposit them as soon as possible for collection (in most cases, the same day). The key is to have lockboxes conveniently located to reduce the time from receipt of mail to actual deposit. The advantages of this service are that it:

- Reduces the time of internal mail processing and mail float (time between mailing by customer and actual deposit to bank account).
- Reduces internal staff requirements.
- Speeds the information flow of collections.
- Speeds the actual collection of funds.
- Provides quick notification of incoming receipts and balances available in the company's bank account.
- Speeds up the availability of funds for use within the company.

Some disadvantages of the lockbox service are that it:

- Does not allow immediate checking of accuracy of remittance.
- Is usually beneficial only for companies that have a high dollar face value of remittance due to substantial processing fees.

Preauthorized checks (PACs) are checks without signature issued by a payee with a prearranged agreement with a payor. This service is designed to accelerate the receipt of funds, usually through a high-volume fixed payment situation. Among the benefits of the service are that it:

- Reduces the time of mail float.
- Reduces the cost of billing.
- Allows for a more accurate cash forecasting mechanism.

Preauthorized debits are similar to PACs except that no checks are issued. This service is usually associated with an electronic-based system.

Wire transfers are designed to move funds quickly from one location to another without the loss of time inherent in the mail system. Two wire, or electronic, transfer systems that are available include the Federal Reserve system and various bank systems. High interest rates make wire transfers economical for many companies.

Depository transfer checks are an alternative to wire transfers whereby checks without signatures are drawn against the bank of deposit as a way of concentrating monies at a different location.

Disbursement Services

The object of using some form of disbursement services is to allow for more funds within the disbursement pipeline. Three commonly used methods include zero balance accounts, drafts, and remote disbursements.

Zero balance accounts are agreements with one or more banks whereby checks can be drawn against an account with no required balance, with the understanding that the company will transfer funds automatically to cover any overdrafts. In some cases, specified amounts must always be kept in a bank account and replenished to that amount when monies leave this account. This system's benefits are that it:

- Increases centralization and control of funds.
- Decentralizes the disbursing of funds.
- Creates float by issuing checks at local levels.
- Reduces or eliminates the need to keep balances in certain bank accounts.

Drafts are negotiable instruments that are used like checks but are drawn against a company rather than a bank. They are presented through the normal clearing system to the bank with the company name appearing on the front of the check. The company, not the bank, promises to pay, and the bank allows a company twenty-four hours within which to make payment following the presentation of the draft to the bank.

Remote disbursements create float by lengthening the time it takes a check to clear through the banking system after it is presented for payment. The slower mail and clearing processes inherent in this system allow for additional available monies within the cash pipeline of a company by giving the company additional time to use the cash value of checks before the checks are drawn against the company's account balance.

Two methods of remote disbursements are used. One method involves drawing checks on banks in remote geographic locations, such as a New York bank for a customer located in Los Angeles. A second method is to draw checks on remote Federal Reserve areas where presentation of payments are made less frequently.

Both methods are looked upon unfavorably by the Federal Reserve since it creates excessive float within the system. Your bank can be of help in further explaining the use of remote disbursements.

Control Services

These services establish an overall cash management system that provides information and controls cash. Control services include such systems as deposit reporting, balance reporting, forecasting, reconciliation, and funds management. These systems are often developed internally, but in some situations outside service organizations can provide them more effectively and/or at lower cost.

HOW TO DETERMINE HOW MUCH CASH IS NEEDED TO PAY OPERATING EXPENSES

It is important for a company to know the extent to which it can show declining liquidity before certain actions are necessary for improving its cash position. In other words, until what point will the company have enough cash to meet operating expenses? The following illustration can be used to meet this test.

Calculate Operating Expenses

Using The Great Company, Inc., Statement of Income (Table 2-1), the following represents the operating expenses of the company for that period of time.

Operating Expenses

Cost of sales	$525,000
Selling expenses	30,000
Administrative expenses	25,000
General expenses	15,000
Interest expense	2,000
Total operating expenses	$597,000

Calculate the Number of Days' Coverage

Using the total operating expenses as calculated above and the cash in banks and marketable securities amount from the Balance Sheet of The Great Company, Inc. (Table 2-2, in chapter 2), the following calculation is made.

Expenses per day (total operating expenses divided by 365)	$ 1,636
Cash in banks and marketable securities	12,000
Number of days' coverage (cash in banks and marketable securities less debt due within one year divided by expenses per day)	

$$\frac{\$12,000 - \$4,500}{\$1,636} = 4.6 \text{ days}$$

The results show that The Great Company, Inc., can show declining liquidity up to 4.6 days before certain actions, such as borrowing additional short-term funds, would be necessary to improve its cash position.

HOW TO DETERMINE THE CASH CYCLE

Every company has various time periods that begin when cash is disbursed to purchase raw materials and end when cash is collected from the sales of finished goods inventory or services. This period is referred to as the cash cycle and is used to calculate the cash turnover and annual minimum cash requirements.

The cash cycle determines how long the cash funds of a company are tied up before actual cash is received from the goods and/or services. This is important because the longer cash is tied up, the less cash is available for other expenditures such as replenishing sold inventories, operating costs, expansion, purchasing of fixed assets, and other cash requirements. If the delay is overly long, a company may need to defer such actions and may incur additional interest costs through additional borrowings.

For example, if The Great Company, Inc., were to reduce its cash operating expenses by 15%, then $89,550 (.15 × $597,000) would be freed up to apply to other operations of the company. In theory, if these cash funds were to be invested either in additional working capital investments or by putting the money in the bank at 8.5% interest, the company would earn $7,612 (.085 × $89,550) before tax on these funds.

To determine the cash cycle, let's assume the following facts.

Cash Inflows	*Cash Outflows*
Payment from customers— 40 days	Payment to creditors— 30 days
Average collection period— 50 days	Average payment period— 33 days
	Average age of inventory— 71 days

The cash cycle is calculated by adding the average age of inventory (71 days) to the average collection period (50 days) and subtracting the average payment period (33 days) as follows:

$$71 \text{ days} + 50 \text{ days} - 33 \text{ days} = 88 \text{ days}$$

This means that the company would be tied up 88 days or approximately three months from the time raw materials were purchased until monies were collected from the sale of the finished goods. Any reduction in the number of days that monies are tied up represents additional return on investments. Any increase in this number of days represents additional costs in the form of lost earnings (opportunity costs) or of higher interest costs on additional borrowings.

How to Determine the Cash Turnover

Using the results of the cash cycle, we can compute the cash turnover, which indicates the rapidity with which cash moves within the company. The higher the rapidity (turnover rate), the less cash is needed to meet the requirements of the company and the less likelihood that the company will be short of cash.

The cash turnover for The Great Company, Inc., is computed by dividing the number of days in a year (365) by the cash cycle (88 days). The calculation results in a cash turnover of 4.15 times, as follows:

$$\frac{365}{88} = 4.15 \text{ times}$$

On the average, cash turns over 4.15 times a year for this company. If the company can reduce the cash cycle by 8 days, from 88 days to 80 days, the average cash turnover would be increased from 4.15 times to 4.56 times. This would have a major impact on the minimum cash balance that the company would need to operate the business effectively.

HOW TO DETERMINE THE MINIMUM OPERATING CASH BALANCE

If The Great Company, Inc., establishes an objective of maintaining a minimum cash balance of 2% of its sales revenues, then the average cash balance will be $11,940 based on 2% of the $597,000 operating expenses previously calculated. Considering the company's balance for cash in banks ($5,000) and marketable securities ($7,000), it is carrying an adequate amount of cash to meet its stated objectives. Should the objective and/or operating expenses change, then the minimum operating cash balance would also change.

HOW THE BAUMOL MODEL IS USED FOR CALCULATING THE OPTIMUM AMOUNT OF CASH

The Baumol Model is based on the concepts employed in the economic order quantity (EOQ), since it treats cash as an inventory item with the expectation that settling cash transactions can be predicted with certainty.[1] This concept, as in the EOQ concept, trades off the opportunity cost of holding cash balances rather than the cost of securing cash. It is a mathematical model that calculates the optimal cash order size while minimizing the cost of ordering and holding costs. The more cash a company has on hand, transactions to acquire cash become less frequent. The higher the cash balances of a company, however, the higher the holding costs due to foregoing opportunities for the inventory of cash in profit producing investments.

The mathematical model for calculating the economic conversion quantity (ECQ), or the optimal cash order size in which to convert marketable securities to cash is:

The Economic Order Quantity Equation

$$ECQ = \sqrt{\frac{2 \times \text{conversion cost} \times \text{demand for cash}}{\text{Opportunity cost per period}}}$$

Remember that marketable securities are used in a company as a reservoir to replenish each transaction and should measure the cost of converting marketable securities into cash. Also included is the cost of holding cash as compared to holding marketable securities.

This model makes some assumptions as follows: the financial officer is totally aware of the demand for cash during a specific period; there is a fixed cost of acquiring cash to replenish the cash balances, and is done quickly; the opportunity cost is equivalent to the interest that is foregone on an investment and is risk free; all cash flows are considered certain; the outflows of net cash happen at a constant rate; trends of seasonality and cyclicality are not considered; and that interest rates are even in time periods with nonchanging rates.

Conversion costs. Includes the fixed cost of placing and receiving a cash order, such as paperwork, follow-up and communications costs, and is stated as dollar conversion amount.

Opportunity Cost or Holding Cost. Represents the amount of interest that would be foregone over a specific period of time by maintaining funds in noninterest cash accounts, as compared to investing these funds in interest-bearing marketable securities.

Average cash investment. Represents one half of the ECQ.

Number of transactions. This amount is needed to replenish levels of cash to the levels of ECQ and is calculated by dividing the total demand for cash for a specific period by the ECQ cash amount.

Cost of transactions. Calculated by multiplying the dollar cost per transaction by the number of transactions.

Total cost represents the following:

$$\text{Total cost} = (\text{conversion cost} \times \text{number of transactions}) + (\text{opportunity costs} \times \text{average cash investment})$$

Illustration

Let us assume that the financial officer of a company expects the demand for cash for the next six months to be $650,000. It is estimated that each transaction costs $20. The estimated opportunity cost for the six months is 10%, or 0.0488 (1.10) 6/12 − 1. With these given facts, the economic conversion quantity (ECQ), or the optimal cash replenishment level is $23,082 calculated as follows:

$$\text{ECQ} = \sqrt{\frac{2 \times \text{conversion cost} \times \text{demand for cash}}{\text{Opportunity cost per period}}}$$

$$= \sqrt{2 \times \$20 \times \$650,000 \div 0.0488}$$

$$= \$23,082$$

The average cash investment is $11,541 ($23,082 ÷ 2). Since $23,082 is received every time the cash account is replenished, there will be 28.2 ($650,000 ÷ $23,082), or approximately 28 transactions during this six-month period; or 1.08 transactions per week. Ordering costs are $560 (28 × $20). The total cost of managing cash is as follows:

$$\text{Total cost} = (\$20 \times 28) + (0.0488 \times \$11,541) = \$1,123$$

In summary, the Baumol Model determines the economic conversion quantity (ECQ), which in this illustration was calculated to be $23,082. This amount represents the optimal cash order size that minimizes the total cost, that is, both the conversion and opportunity cost.

This chapter has highlighted the importance of managing cash as an integral part of managing working capital. Cash management ultimately affects the return on investment calculation and assists in effectively using ROI as a measurement tool for operating the business.

DECISION-MAKING STRATEGIES

- Establish collection procedures to speed the collection of funds.
- Create a disbursement system that will harness the disbursement of funds in keeping with creditors' policies.
- Develop a cash management program for controlling and monitoring the flow of cash.
- Determine what cash levels are needed for operating expenses.

NOTE

1. Baumol, William J. "The Transactions Demand for Cash: An Inventory Theoretic Approach," *The Quarterly Journal of Economics,* 66:4 (November 1952), pp. 545–556 © 1952 by the President and Fellows of Harvard College.

8

Managing Accounts Receivable and Current Liabilities

Two major elements of working capital are presented in this chapter. The first major element is the management of a company's accounts receivable, which involves maintaining an effective credit and collection policy. It also involves monitoring certain key ratios surrounding the managing of accounts receivable.

The second major element is current liabilities, which represent a source of short-term financing. This is discussed later in the chapter.

Guidelines for Managing Accounts Receivable and Its Impact on ROI

Managing accounts receivable begins with an effective credit and collection policy. This policy affects the amounts of accounts receivable that will appear on a company's balance sheet. Maintaining lower accounts receivable balances will contribute substantially to higher cash balances and in turn less need to borrow funds. Ultimately, the freeing up of funds will generate more investment opportunities and, if allocated wisely, higher return on investment rates.

The Elements of an Effective Credit and Collection Policy

The following elements are necessary to maintain a credit and collection policy that will provide a company with an adequate flow of funds through collections. These elements include:

- Reviewing reasonable credit limits for each customer.
- Providing reasonable payment terms and credit policies.
- Timely and aggressive follow-up with customer billings.
- Offering discounts to customers that make economic sense to both company and customer.
- Requesting other forms of advance payment, such as deposits, partial shipments, and letters of credit.
- Maintaining policies for past-due accounts in keeping with industry and economic standards.
- Reviewing ratio relationships to trigger necessary actions.
- Penalties for making payment on time, or late charges.
- When payment is due, or the collection period.
- Conditions of nonpayment such as personal guarantees by officers of customers, collateral, and collection and attorney fees if legal action is necessary to collect a bad debt.

Evaluating Varying Credit Policies

To establish an effective credit and collection policy, an analysis needs to be developed that measures the impact of economic gains at varying levels of credit. This analysis will measure the amount of risk of expanding credit sales, either maintaining the same level or reducing the level of sales. Using this as a basis for discussion, the following facts are presented to illustrate this concept.

The Great Company, Inc., is contemplating revising its credit standards, and management is asked to present an analysis of what credit standard will offer the greatest benefit and less risk to the company. Four proposals are presented as shown in Table 8-2. It is estimated that the daily average credit sales amounted to $1,630 ($700,000 ÷ 365 × .85). This resulted in daily sales of $1,918 ($700,000 ÷ 365), and 85% of these sales were on credit (.85 × $1,918).

Based on the facts in Table 8-1, the economic benefits level of increasing credit sales by 10% is 16% (economic benefit ÷ estimated average daily credit sales). Although actual dollars increase from the current level ($1,630) to $1,712 and $1,793 at credit sales increases of 5% and 10%, the percentage remains almost the same as a percentage of the estimated average daily credit sales (16.1% versus 16%). Therefore, based on these facts, the company should increase credit sales by 10%, since at this level the company maximizes the percentage economic benefit, and further increases may create greater risk.

TABLE 8-1   Analysis of Proposed Credit Standards

Line no.	*Proposed Credit Standards*			
	Lower credit sales by 5%	*Maintain current level*	*Increase credit sales by 5%*	*Increase credit sales by 10%*
1. Estimated average daily credit sales	$ 1,549	$ 1,630	$ 1,712	$ 1,793
2. Estimated average collection period—days	25	30	35	35
3. Estimated Accounts Receivable—Line 1 × 2	$38,725	$48,900	$59,920	$62,755
4. Estimated daily bad debts .8% on credit sales*—line 1 × 4 (.8%)	12	13	14	14
5. Estimated daily cost of carrying A/R at 12% annual interest—line 3 ÷ 365 × .12	13	16	20	21
6. Other daily costs	1	1	1	1
7. Total daily costs—lines 4, 5, and 6	26	30	35	36
8. Daily Contribution Margin @ 18%—line 8 × 1	279	293	308	323
9. Economic benefit—line 8–7	$ 253	$ 263	$ 273	$ 287
Percent of average daily credit sales—line 9 ÷ 1	16.3%	16.1%	15.9 %	16.0%

* Assume no significant increase in bad debts percent.

TABLE 8-2   Cost of Additional Investments in Accounts Receivable
at 18% ROI Rate

Line no.	Proposal I	Proposal II	Proposal III	Proposal IV
1. Turnover rate assumed	14.6	12.2	10.4	10.4
2. Investment in A/R	$38,725	$48,900	$59,920	$62,755
3. Average A/R investment— line 2 ÷ 1	2,652	4,008	5,762	6,034
4. a. Incremental investment from Proposal I to II		1,356		
b. Incremental investment from Proposal II to III			1,754	
c. Incremental investment from Proposal III to IV				272
5. Cost of incremental investment in A/R @ 18%		$ 244	$ 316	$ 49

Evaluating Effect of Additional Investment in Accounts Receivable

Using the data from Table 8-1, an evaluation can be made of the cost of carrying additional investments in accounts receivable. An additional calculation must be made to determine the turnover rate for each of the proposals. This is done by dividing the average collection period into 365, the number of days in a year. In addition, the company requires an 18% after-tax return on its investment rate. This will be used in the calculation in Table 8-2, which illustrates this analysis.

The cost of the incremental investment in accounts receivable at 18% return on investment indicates that Proposal III ($316) has the highest cost, since it represents an amount that could have been earned on another risk-free investment, or referred to as the opportunity cost. Table 8-2 would lead one to choose Proposal IV on an incremental basis using Proposal I as the base.

Ratios Used to Manage Accounts Receivable

Certain key ratios are necessary to manage accounts receivable. These ratios are used to indicate how accounts receivable relate to the sales and working capital of a company. The Great Company, Inc., financial statements will be used to illustrate each calculation.

Accounts receivable to working capital measures the impact of receivables on the liquidity of a company. It is calculated as follows:

$$\frac{\text{Accounts receivable—net}}{\text{Working capital}} \qquad \frac{\$80,000}{\$72,500} = 110.3\%$$

When comparing this ratio with other time periods, further analysis would determine how much was due to changes in net sales; the timing of these net sales, that is, early or late in the calendar/fiscal year; and an aging of customer receivables to determine the extent, if any, of past-due accounts.

Net sales to accounts receivable—net measures the turnover of a company's accounts receivable or how often the accounts receivable change in relation to the net sales of the company. A higher turnover rate is favorable since it indicates monies due the company are being collected at a faster rate, which makes cash available more quickly. The Great Company, Inc., had a turnover of 8.75 times, as shown below.

$$\frac{\text{Net sales}}{\text{Accounts receivable}} \qquad \frac{\$700,000}{\$80,000} = 8.75 \text{ times}$$

Average collection period is an important ratio since accounts receivable balances have a high correlation to a company's sales. It will indicate how long it takes a company to collect its receivables from customers. It is calculated as follows:

$$\frac{\text{Accounts receivable}}{\text{Net sales}} \times 365 \qquad \frac{\$80,000}{\$700,000} \times 365 = 41.7 \text{days}$$

Increases in the number of days have an additional cost to the company in that a company must finance the added days in receivables at the current interest rate. For example, a yearly interest rate of 12% can be translated to a 1% interest cost per month on the outstanding accounts receivable. Over a period of time, this can amount to a substantial loss in both cash flow and net earnings. The return on investment rate would also be negatively affected.

GENERAL GUIDELINES FOR MANAGING CURRENT LIABILITIES

The final element of working capital is current liabilities. They represent a source of short-term financing and are made up principally of accounts payable and accruals. Both of these accounts generally increase or decrease in relation to sales volume. For example, in a manufacturing company as sales increase, additional purchases *will* be required to replenish the sold inventory. If the company required additional labor and generated higher earnings, accrued expenses will be higher and reflected in higher accrued salaries, wages, and taxes.

The managing of current liabilities plays an important role in generating cash flows from operations. Several guidelines are recommended to assist in accomplishing this objective:

- Develop internal programs to pay creditors only on due dates.
- Try to negotiate extended terms of payments.
- Evaluate taking discounts versus what might be earned in other activities of the company.

In all cases, caution should be taken not to jeopardize the sources of supply.

EVALUATING THE IMPACT OF CASH DISCOUNTS

Cash discounts are given by creditors to encourage customers to pay early. Since cash has greater value when received earlier, a creditor is willing to give a customer an incentive to pay within a short period of time. Thus, creditors offer their customers special credit terms for early payment.

A typical credit term would be 2/10 net 30, or 2% discount if paid within 10 days and the invoice amount paid beyond the 10 days, but payable within 30 days. There are many other terms that are offered with varying percentage discounts and time periods for calculating the discount period. It may be advantageous to accept discounts offered when paying bills. The discount is not always an advantage to a company, however, and it may in fact be better to forego the discount in favor of borrowing funds at the current interest rate (see Table 8-3).

To illustrate how to evaluate the impact of credit terms, let us assume that two suppliers have the following credit terms: supplier A has terms that are 2/10 net 50; supplier B has terms of 3/10 net 80.

TABLE 8-3 Calculating the Cost of Foregoing the Cash Discount

Formula

PD = Stated percentage cash discount

ND = Number of days that a cash discount can be delayed

365 = Number of days in a year

$$\frac{PD}{1-PD} \times \frac{365}{ND}$$

Calculation

　　Supplier A: 2/10 net 50

$$\frac{.02}{1-.02} \times \frac{365}{50-10} = \frac{.02}{.98} \times \frac{365}{40} =$$

$$.0204 \times 9.125 = 18.62\%$$

　　Supplier B: 3/10 net 80

$$\frac{.03}{1-.03} \times \frac{365}{80-10} = \frac{.03}{.97} \times \frac{365}{70} =$$

$$.0309 \times 5.214 = 16.11\%$$

Cost of Foregoing the Cash Discount

The formula and calculations for determining the cost of foregoing the cash discount are shown in Table 8-3. If the company can borrow funds at 17%, it would be advisable to forego the cash discount from supplier B, since the cost of financing is cheaper than borrowing money at 17% interest costs. In the case of supplier A, the cash discount should be taken since the cost of foregoing the cash discount is more (18.62%) than the cost of financing (17%).

Effect of Extending Credit Terms

It is sometimes possible to extend the credit terms offered by the supplier without affecting the credit rating and/or credit relationship between the customer and the supplier. Using the data for supplier A and extending the terms from 2/10 net 50 to 2/10 net 60, the effect is shown in Table 8-4. By extending the credit terms, the cost of foregoing a cash discount is reduced. In this case, an extension of ten additional days (from 50 days to 60 days)

TABLE 8-4	Effect of Extending Credit Terms—Supplier A
Extended terms 2/10 net 60	*Original terms 2/10 net 50*
$\dfrac{.02}{1-.02} \times \dfrac{365}{60-10} = 14.89\%$	$\dfrac{.02}{1-.02} \times \dfrac{365}{50-10} = 18.62\%$

reduces the cost 3.73 percentage points (18.62%–14.89%). Using the same 17% cost of borrowing, the decision would now be to forego the cash discount, since the cost of financing is now cheaper than the interest costs.

THE IMPACT OF SHIFTING FUNDS ON ROI

An important part of the decision-making process is knowing how to allocate the resources of the company to maximize returns. During the planning stage, estimates are developed by operating managers requesting funds for investing in either current assets, fixed assets, or working capital. Based on these projections, it is possible to estimate the profitability, cost of financing, return on investment rates, and certain key operating ratios.

Table 8-5 illustrates how to compute the estimated earnings on assets and the estimated costs on liabilities and shareholders' equity. Some of the rates were developed in chapter 5, where the components of cost of capital were calculated and other rates were arbitrarily chosen. The balance data were taken from the Balance Sheet of The Great Company, Inc. (Table 2-2).

Table 8-5 shows that the total assets earn an average 10.6%, while the liabilities and shareholders' equity have an average cost of 6.8%. An excess of 3.8 percentage points results (.106–.068), or a net profitability of $9,915 ($27,550–$17,635).

Key operating ratios can also be calculated as follows:

$$\frac{\text{Current assets}}{\text{Total assets}} \quad \frac{\$137,500}{\$260,000} = 52.9\%$$

$$\frac{\text{Current liabilities}}{\text{Total assets}} \quad \frac{\$65,000}{\$260,000} = 25\%$$

$$\frac{\text{Current assets}}{\text{Current liabilities}} \quad \frac{\$137,500}{\$65,000} = 2.115 \text{ times}$$

TABLE 8-5   Computing Earnings and Costs of Balance Sheet Components

	Amount	Percent	Estimated Earnings
Current assets	$137,500	4.0	$ 5,500
Fixed and other assets	122,500	18.0	22,050
Total	$260,000		$27,550
Average earnings percentage		10.6%	

	Amount	Percent	Estimated Costs
Current liabilities	$ 65,000	8.0	$ 5,200
Long-term debt	24,000	5.5	1,320
Shareholders' equity	171,000	6.5	11,115
Total	$260,000		$17,635
Average cost percentage		6.8%	

$$\text{Working capital} = \text{Current assets} - \text{current liabilities}$$
$$\$137,500 \quad - \quad \$65,000 \quad = \$72,500$$

$$\frac{\text{Net profitability}}{\text{Total assets}} \quad \frac{\$9,915}{\$260,000} = 3.8\%$$

$$\frac{\text{Net profitabiilty}}{\text{Shareholders' equity}} \quad \frac{\$9,915}{\$171,000} = 5.8\%$$

Let's assume that the company shifted $21,000 of current assets to fixed assets and $2,000 of long-term debt to current liabilities. Table 8-6 reflects the results of these changes.

The revised key operating ratios are calculated as follows:

$$\frac{\text{Current assets}}{\text{Total assets}} \quad \frac{\$116,500}{\$260,000} = 44.8\%$$

TABLE 8-6	Effect of Shifting of Funds on the Earnings and Costs of Balance Sheet Components		
	Amount	*Percent*	*Estimated Earnings*
Current assets	$116,500	4.0	$ 4,660
Fixed and other assets	143,500	18.0	25,830
Total	$260,000		$30,490
Average earnings percentage		11.7%	
			Estimated Costs
Current liabilities	$ 67,000	8.0	$ 5,360
Long-term debt	22,000	5.5	1,210
Shareholders' equity	171,000	6.5	11,115
Total	$260,000		$17,685
Average cost percentage		6.8%	

$$\frac{\text{Current liabilities}}{\text{Total assets}} \qquad \frac{\$67,000}{\$260,000} = 25.8\%$$

$$\frac{\text{Current assets}}{\text{Current liabilities}} \qquad \frac{\$116,500}{\$67,000} = 1.739 \text{ times}$$

$$\text{Working capital} = \text{Current assets} - \text{current liabilities}$$
$$\$116,500 \quad - \quad \$67,000 \qquad = \$49,500$$

$$\frac{\text{Net profitability}}{\text{Total assets}} \qquad \frac{\$12,805}{\$260,000} = 4.9\%$$

$$\frac{\text{Net profitabiilty}}{\text{Shareholders' equity}} \qquad \frac{\$12,805}{\$171,000} = 7.5\%$$

Both Tables 8-5 and 8-6 can be summarized and conclusions drawn as shown in Table 8-7.

TABLE 8-7   Summary of the Impact of Shifting Resources

	Table 8–5	Table 8–6	Change
Average estimated earnings	$27,550	$30,490	$ 2,940
Average estimated costs	17,635	17,685	50
Average estimated profitability	9,915	12,805	2,890
Current assets/total assets	52.9%	44.8%	(8.1%)
Current liabilities/total assets	25.0%	25.8%	.8%
Current assets/current liabilities	2.115 times	1.739 times	(.376 times)
Working capital	$72,500	$49,500	($23,000)
Return on total assets	3.8%	4.9%	1.1%
Return on shareholders' equity	5.8%	7.5%	1.7%

PROFITABILITY AND RISK CONCLUSIONS

Based on Table 8-7, the following profitability and risk conclusions can be drawn from shifting $21,000 of current assets to fixed assets and $2,000 of long-term debt to current liabilities.

- *Higher profitability* resulted due to more monies being invested at higher rates.
- Decrease in current assets to total assets (8.1%) usually *increases profitability and risk.*
- Decrease in current liabilities to total assets usually *decreases both profitability and risk.*
- Current ratio (current assets/current liabilities) decreased, thereby *increasing risk.*
- Decline in working capital ($23,000) *increases risk.*
- Both return on total assets and shareholders' equity increased, reflecting *improved profitability.*

In summary, the shift of these resources overall resulted in an increase in profitability and an increase in risk. A company must measure whether the additional profits warrant assuming additional risks. Estimates and weighting factors can be developed to put both elements of profitability and risk into perspective.

This chapter has highlighted the importance of managing the various components of working capital that play a vital role in the liquidity and profitability of a company. Both objectives lead to well-managed organizations with the ability to prosper and grow during healthy and lean economic periods.

DECISION-MAKING STRATEGIES

- Develop a credit and collection policy to meet both company and industry standards.
- Measure the cost of accounts receivable with the cost of money to assist in establishing credit and collection policies.
- Set standards for key ratios in controlling accounts receivable and inventory.
- Determine the economics of taking cash discounts with other alternative investment opportunities.
- To assist in formulating a credit policy, calculate the cost of extending credit terms.
- Measure the effect of revenues on the ROI rate in an effort to maximize resources.
- Review for new sources of raw materials as well as accessibility.

9

INVENTORY MANAGEMENT—
KEY TO HIGHER RETURNS

This chapter focuses on the techniques needed to control levels of inventory. You will be taken through ratios for controlling inventory, techniques for managing inventory, and major decisions that are necessary to maintain low levels of inventory. Ultimately, this will lead to higher return on investment rates with additional cash available to promote growth opportunities.

FACTORS THAT INFLUENCE THE
LEVEL OF INVENTORY

It is important to recognize what factors influence the level of a company's inventory so as not to tie up much needed funds in excessive inventory. These factors are:

Sales levels. The most obvious factor is the level of sales activity. The more sales that are generated, the more inventory is needed. In addition, the turnover of inventory will also play a major role as measured by the inventory turnover ratio (see Ratios for Controlling Inventory pages 95–96).

Length of time to produce a unit. Generally speaking, the longer it takes to produce a unit, the more inventory must be available. For example, if a product takes 30 days to produce, there must be at least 30 days' inventory to meet sales orders if a company's policy is to service a customer immediately. There are exceptions, however, depending upon the industry and nature of the product.

Access to raw materials. We have been discussing inventory from a finished goods basis, that is, inventory that is available for sale and needs no further production to put it in a salable state. Raw materials are equally important since they provide the basis for which finished goods inventory is produced. The size of the raw material inventory depends on many factors:

- The time period from ordering to delivery
- Availability from suppliers in relation to demand
- Ability to negotiate reasonable payment terms with suppliers
- Economic outlook on both price and supply
- Transportation problems, such as labor disputes
- Storage capacity
- Physical life of raw materials
- Obsolescence risk

Finished goods' life. In most companies finished goods have a defined life. That is, in a given time frame, the finished units no longer have the same economic value as originally intended within the marketplace. This economic value can relate to such elements as perishability, fashion design, style changes, obsolescence, or innovation and new technology.

These are just some of the factors that influence the level at which a company should maintain inventory balances.

KEY ELEMENTS IN MANAGING INVENTORY

There are three basic areas necessary for managing inventory: monitoring quantities, materials purchasing, and protection against loss. These elements are discussed in more detail below as a guideline for developing an effective inventory management program.

Monitor Inventory Quantities

Excessive inventories create drains on cash flow, as well as declining profits. Therefore, it is essential that inventory be monitored and controlled by the use of some of the following barometers.

- Study historical patterns of the company's inventory turns and compare company performance to industry standards.
- Monitor inventory levels to see if they are increasing faster than actual or anticipated sales volume is increasing.

- Determine if there is a lack of storage facilities with no depreciable increase in sales volume.

Develop a More Effective Materials Purchasing Program

A materials purchasing program is a major factor in controlling total inventory. The following guidelines are suggested to accomplish this objective.

- Study alternative ways of acquiring materials, such as group buying, buying and/or co-op services, buying versus making, and subcontracting a complete product or components of the product.
- Speed the process of receiving shipments from suppliers to reduce purchases.
- Look for technical changes for cost reductions.
- Design products that can have universal parts.
- Look for cheaper substitutes of raw materials without affecting the quality of the product.
- Try to negotiate fixed prices from suppliers, particularly where prices may increase, as in commodities.
- Develop special dating and return policies with suppliers.
- Be aware of special prices such as end-of-season runs, overstock specials, and special factory deals.

Protect Against Loss

A company should discourage loss to protect the value of its inventory and, ultimately, profits and cash flow. Loss can occur in different ways. A program of loss prevention calls for the following measures.

- Protect against flammable and combustible incidents by storing in accordance with required standards.
- Try to have a security program that discourages theft, pilferage, and embezzlement.
- Protect against inventory that is subject to spoilage and limited shelf life.

RATIOS FOR CONTROLLING INVENTORY

The following ratios are used as a means of controlling and monitoring inventory. These ratios must be compared to historical patterns as well as to industry standards.

Inventory turnover measures the efficiency of a company to move inventory.

$$\frac{\text{Net sales}}{\text{Inventory}} \quad \frac{\$700,000}{\$40,000} = 17.5 \text{ times}$$

Inventory to total assets measures the percentage of inventory in relation to the total assets of the company.

$$\frac{\text{Inventory}}{\text{Total assets}} \quad \frac{\$40,000}{\$260,000} = 15.4\%$$

This ratio also points out how effective a company is in controlling inventory as a percentage of the total assets.

Inventory to current assets measures how much of the current assets are tied up by inventory. This can change depending upon the seasonality, the timing of when the ratio is computed, and economic conditions.

$$\frac{\text{Inventory}}{\text{Current assets}} \quad \frac{\$40,000}{\$137,500} = 29.1\%$$

Inventory to working capital measures the dependency of working capital on the inventory value of the company. Since inventory accounts for a large portion of the working capital in a manufacturing company, this ratio must be reviewed as part of an effective inventory management program.

$$\frac{\text{Inventory}}{\text{Working capital}} \quad \frac{\$40,000}{\$72,500} = 55.2\%$$

INVENTORY MANAGEMENT TECHNIQUES

Whether to carry large quantities of supplies inventory, raw materials, or finished goods is a question all companies ask periodically. The answers to these and other questions are sometimes found in inventory management techniques such as ABC analysis, just-in-time inventory, and inventory models such as economic order quantity (EOQ), production order quantity, back-order inventory, and quantity discounts. Each of these techniques and models provide management with the ability to control, monitor, and evaluate levels of inventory.

TABLE 9-1   Calculating Annual Dollar Volume for 19X3

Item Stock Number	Annual Unit Volume	Unit Cost	Annual Dollar Volume
#101	1,020	$25.60	$26,112
#310	459	28.00	12,852
#210	1,122	3.00	3,366
#211	763	3.40	2,594
#102	1,328	1.50	1,992
#312	1,432	1.05	1,504
#209	1,348	.86	1,159
#103	916	.18	165
#213	971	.16	155
#212	841	.12	101
	10,200		$50,000

ABC Analysis

ABC analysis provides management with three classifications of inventory on hand based on annual dollar volume.[1] This concept is based on the works of Vilfredo Pareto, an 18th-century Italian economist. He stated that there always exist a critical few and trivial many, or significant items in any group generally provides a small percentage of the total group. Or to put it another way, it means that 80% of any output usually comes from 20% of the input. This is commonly called the Pareto Principle, or the 80–20 rule.

This principle can apply to many situations, such as: most people probably get 80% of their days' results completed in 20% of their time; 80% of a company's sales probably is generated from 20% of its customers; 80% of a customer's impression of your company is probably found by the first 20% of the person's contact with you; 80% of your profits come from 20% of your products; and 80% of your inventory dollar value come from 20% of your inventory.

Therefore, this principle is basically a formula for setting priorities. It will illustrate where to concentrate your effort by highlighting what 20% of the inventory needs to be dealt with to maximize the highest return.

The first step is to determine the annual dollar volume by measuring the annual demand of each inventory item times the cost of each inventory item. Table 9-1 illustrates how annual dollar volume was calculated, using an estimated dollar amount of inventory for 19X3 based on an actual amount

TABLE 9-2   ABC Classification

Class of Inventory	Level of Volume	% of Annual Dollar Usage	% of Total Inventory Items
A	High	75–80%	14–16%
B	Medium	15–16%	30–35%
C	Low	5–7%	50–60%

for 19X2 as shown on The Great Company, Inc., of $40,000. The Great Company, Inc., makes ten items for sale with estimated annual unit volume, unit cost, and annual dollar volume.

You will note that using estimated annual unit volume and unit costs, annual dollar volume was generated for each stock item. The total annual dollar volume for 19X3 was $50,000.

The three classifications for ABC analysis is Class A, Class B, and Class C. Each of these classes represents percentages of annual dollar usage and a percentage of total inventory items. This is summarized in Table 9-2.

Using the guidelines as shown in Table 9-2 for ABC analysis, Table 9-3 breaks down the total inventory in its different classes and percentages thereof.

You will see from Table 9-3 that Class A provides 14.5% of the number of items stocked, but 78% of the annual dollar volume. Class B provides 31.5% of the items stocked and 15.9% of the annual dollar volume. Class C, or low levels of volume items, results in 54% of the number of items stocked but only 6.1% of the annual dollar volume.

The advantage of such an analysis provides a company with the ability to establish policies and controls for each of the classifications. Such policies include:

- Spending more time to develop purchasing resources and supplier development for items in Class A than for individual items in Class C.
- Items in Class A should have tighter controls in terms of security and accuracy of inventory records as compared to items in Class B and C.
- More time should be spent on forecasting of Class A items than other times.

TABLE 9-3 ABC Calculation

Item Stock Number	Percent of Number of Items Stocked	Percent of Annual Dollar Volume	Class
#101	10.0%	52.3%	A
#310	4.5	25.7	A
#210	11.0	6.7	B
#211	7.5	5.2	B
#102	13.0	4.0	B
#312	14.0	3.0	C
#209	13.2	2.3	C
#103	9.0	.3	C
#213	9.5	.3	C
#212	8.3	.2	C
	100.0%	100.0%	

JUST-IN-TIME INVENTORY

Just-in-time inventory is a management system that is part of a manufacturing approach that estimates how much inventory is necessary to keep the production line running efficiently. The basic idea associated with this system is that necessary inventory items be available for production at the right time and at the required quantities. This method does not allow for having backup inventory to be used during the production process. Therefore, inventory levels needed for the production process is greatly reduced.

This management system works more effectively for companies that have a repetitive production process and requires a close relationship with suppliers. Any delays encountered by a supplier can cause additional production costs and possibly a loss of sales. Allowing for inventory to be available by suppliers at the right quantity and at the right time results in lower inventory levels and, ultimately, higher return on investment rates.

INVENTORY COSTS

There are many costs associated with inventory. These costs include carrying costs, ordering costs, set-up costs, and stockout costs. These costs play an important role in evaluating the investment in inventory since they represent a major cost of operating a business.

Carrying costs. Carrying costs represent the costs associated with the holding of inventory items over a period of time. They are sometimes referred to as "holding costs." Such costs include the cost of storage and handling, or housing costs; obsolescence, pilferage, deterioration, and scrap; taxes and insurance; ordering costs; set-up costs; the cost of investing; and stockouts.

Storage and handling costs. These are costs associated with the housing of inventory, such as warehouse space, depreciation on building and handling equipment, wages and salaries paid to workers, and utilities. These costs can be expressed as a per unit cost or as a percentage of the total inventory value in a given period.

Obsolescence. Associated with declining values of inventory that make inventory less salable due to technology or changes in style.

Pilferage costs. Loss of inventory value due to stealing by employees or outsiders.

Deterioration and scrap costs. Represents the declining of inventory value due to spoilage, breakage, and scrap from producing the product.

Taxes and insurance. Taxes include taxes on buildings, business taxes, and personal property taxes. Insurance includes the cost of insuring the buildings, insurance on inventory such as for fire, theft, and natural disasters.

Ordering costs. Represents the costs of supplies, human resource support, processing of orders, forms, and so on.

Set-up costs. Costs associated with preparing or setting up a machine or process to manufacture an order.

Cost of inventory investment. These are costs of funds invested in inventory, such as the cost of money (rate of interest), and are based on the amount of risk associated with manufacturing or acquiring inventory. This cost is measured using return on investment techniques such as weighted cost of capital (see chapter 5).

Stockouts. These are costs that results from the inability of a company to fill orders because of greater demand than availability of salable inventory. Stockouts can occur at different stages of inventory, such as raw materials that cause additional costs because of production delays, costs incurred in reordering, and the additional handling when inventory is received. During the work-in-process stage additional costs are incurred when production needs to be rescheduled and from possible work stoppages. Stockouts caused by unavailable finished goods inventory may result in lost business and, ultimately, lost profits and lower return on investment rates.

HOW INVENTORY IS MANAGED USING THREE TYPES OF INVENTORY MODELS

The three inventory models discussed are considered independent demand models and respond to two basic questions about inventory. The first question needed by companies that maintain inventory is, when should an order for inventory be placed? The second question is, how much should be ordered? With answers to these questions, a company can begin to manage its inventory and thus play an important role in higher return on investment rates. To illustrate how inventory is managed through different types of models, three different models are explored. They include the economic order quantity (EOQ) model, the production order quantity model, and the back-order inventory model.

Economic Order Quantity (EOQ) Model

This inventory model makes many assumptions. It assumes that the demand for a specific item is known with certainty and that orders to replace used inventory is done instantaneously. It also assumes that lead times for placing and receiving of an order are similar for each order. Another assumption is that inventory is received in one shipment and at the same time. No quantity discounts are possible. And it assumes that the costs of carrying a unit of inventory, such as set-up costs, ordering costs, and the costs of carrying the inventory, are constant no matter what the inventory level. Therefore, shortages or stockouts can be avoided through the use of the EOQ model.

Discussions center on independent models and do not discuss the more complex inventory models that deal with probabilities and random variables.

Using the definition of ordering and carrying costs, the following variables are needed to complete the calculation to determine the optimal number of units per order.

Economic
Order
Quantity
Equation

Q = Number of units per order
D = Annual per unit inventory demand
S = Cost per order for placing and receiving an order (set-up costs)
C = Annual carrying or holding cost per unit
A = Annual working days
EOQ = Economic order quantity

To determine the annual set-up costs the following equation is necessary:

$$\frac{D}{Q} \times S$$

The annual per unit inventory demand is divided by the number of units per order, and the sum is multiplied by the set-up costs. To determine the annual carrying costs per unit, the following equation is necessary:

$$\frac{Q}{2} \times C$$

The number of units per order is divided by 2, and the result is multiplied by the annual carrying costs per unit.

To determine the optimal order quantity, the following equation is used:

$$EOQ = \sqrt{\frac{2DS}{C}}$$

Illustration

To illustrate the optimal number of units per order, let's assume the following facts:

Annual demand	5,000 units
Set-up costs	$30 per order
Carrying costs	$3 per unit

$$EOQ = \sqrt{\frac{2DS}{C}}$$

$$= \sqrt{\frac{2(5,000)\,(30)}{3}}$$

$$= \sqrt{100,000}$$

$$= 316.2 \text{ units}$$

From this set of data, two additional pieces of information can be determined. This includes the number of orders needed to be placed during the year (N) and the expected time between orders (T). Using the above facts, these two sets of information are calculated as follows:

$$N = \frac{\text{Demand (D)}}{\text{Economic order quantity (EOQ)}}$$

$$= \frac{5,000}{316.2} = 15.8 \text{ orders per year}$$

$$T = \frac{\text{Number of annual working days}}{\text{Orders per year}}$$

$$= \frac{230}{15.8} = 14.6 \text{ days between orders}$$

Production Order Quantity Model

Since this model is ideal within the production environment, it is referred to as the production order quantity model and uses many of the same variables as the EOQ model. This model, unlike the EOQ model, assumes that inventory flows in a continuous manner or that inventory accumulates over a period of time. Additional variables are necessary, such as the daily production rate as well as the daily demand rate.

Illustration

To illustrate how to calculate the optimum number of units per order, we use the same data as the EOQ model with two additional variables as follows:

p = Daily production rate

d = Daily demand rate

Q = Optimum number of units per order

Assuming that the daily production rate (p) is 25 units, and the daily demand rate (d) is 20 units, the following formula is used:

Production
Order
Quantity
Equation

$$Q = \sqrt{\frac{2DS}{c[i - (d/p)]}}$$

$$= \sqrt{\frac{2(5,000)\,(30)}{3[1 - (20/25)]}}$$

$$= \sqrt{\frac{300,000}{3(.20)}}$$

$$= \sqrt{500,000}$$

$$= 707.1 \text{ units}$$

The 707.1 units calculated above represent the optimum number of units per order, compared to 316.2 units under the EOQ model. The difference of 390.9 units represents the difference of using the assumption of instantaneous receipt of inventory (EOQ model) versus the production order quantity model where inventory is perceived to flow continuously.

Back-Order Inventory Model

In the two previous models, no allowance was given for stockouts, or shortages of inventory caused by higher demand versus inventory in stock. This not only happens in situations where inventory is produced or bought, but when a company has high-priced items that they do not wish to inventory, such as jewelry and automobiles, where every design and model is not kept in inventory.

Illustration

The back-order inventory model assumes that back ordering is acceptable, as well as is planned shortages. Using the same set of data as the EOQ model, several variables need to be introduced in computing optimum amounts of units back ordered.

$$B = \text{Yearly per unit cost of back ordering}$$

$$Qb = \text{Back ordered amount}$$

Using the data from the EOQ model and assuming that the yearly per unit cost (B) is \$14, the following illustration is presented. **Note:** Two equations are necessary to arrive at the amount of back-ordered inventory. The first equation determines the number of units per order with per unit back-order costs included in the equation as follows:

Back Order Inventory Equation

$$Q = \sqrt{\left(\frac{2DS}{C}\right)\left(\frac{C+B}{B}\right)}$$

$$= \sqrt{\left(\frac{2(5,000)\,(30)}{3}\right)\left(\frac{3+14}{14}\right)}$$

$$= \sqrt{100,000\left(\frac{17}{14}\right)}$$

$$= \sqrt{121,429}$$

$$= 348.5 \text{ units per order}$$

The second equation determines the number of back-ordered units necessary between the stocking period.

$$Qb = Q\left(\frac{1-b}{B+C}\right)$$

$$= 348.5\left(1 - \frac{14}{17}\right)$$

$$= 61.5 \text{ units to be back ordered}$$

ROI DECISIONS IN INVENTORY CONTROL

Successful businesses spend a great deal of time controlling inventory levels. In addition, since inventory contributes a sizable percentage to the overall investment of a company, proper control is essential to keep inventory levels at a minimum level for effective and less costly operations. Too often, businesses measure inventory by means of turnover ratios. While this yardstick measures the speed at which inventories are passed through the business, the effect on profits is often completely ignored. The standard premise that the faster the turnover, the higher the return is not necessarily a true and accurate statement.

As we saw in earlier chapters, return on investment can be increased by changes in the turnover rate, of which inventories are a major part. For example, Table 2-2, the Balance Sheet for The Great Company, Inc., reflects an inventory amount of $40,000, which represents over 15% of the total assets for the company. Therefore, it is suggested that inventory objectives should include maximizing return on investment in inventories. Like all measurable yardsticks, however, this method of inventory control does not strive for perfection but merely is a sound and practical approach. As with any practical approach, we must face the realities involved in the evaluation process, such as the inventory control process.

Utilizing the basic equation of net income divided by investment, we can apply this principle to test the effectiveness of additional inventory on the return on investment equation. This is done by estimating the incremental net income and incremental inventory amounts and applying them to the formula. Simply, if $100,000 additional inventory generates net income of $10,000, the incremental return on investment is 10%. You can reach the conclusion of what additional inventory investments and net income will have as an increment, as well as the effect on the company, by applying this increment to the overall amounts. The effect on the total company is shown in Table 9-4.

TABLE 9-4   Impact of Added Inventory on the Total Company's Return
on Total Assets

Assets	19X2*	Added Inventory	Revised Total Assets
Inventories	$ 40,000	$10,000	$ 50,000
Other current assets	97,500	—	97,500
Other noncurrent assets	122,500	—	122,500
Total assets	$260,000	$10,000	$270,000
Net income	$ 50,000**	$ 2,500***	$ 52,500
Return on total assets	19.2%	25.0%	19.4%

*See Table 2–2
**See Table 2–1
***Estimated net income from the sales of these inventories.

You can see that an additional $10,000 of inventory that is anticipated to generate $2,500 additional net income has very little impact on the overall return on asset rate of 19.2%, even though the estimated return on total assets was anticipated to be 25%. Where more substantial inventories are added and more earnings anticipated, a more dramatic change would occur. Particularly where inventories are added rapidly and sales either lag or remain at an even level, higher inventories and lower net income would result, thus creating lower return on total assets.

This exercise highlights the need to control inventory levels using return on investment techniques. It will put heavy emphasis on quantitative results and is not to be construed as a panacea for all inventory problems. It will also not resolve issues of avoiding stock-outs and being able to service all of your customer needs.

DECISION-MAKING STRATEGIES

• Establish an inventory policy and methods for controlling inventory levels.
• Determine the cost of carrying excessive inventory with the cost of acquiring funds.

- Maintain low levels of inventory without affecting reasonable delivery dates.
- Try to negotiate extended terms from your suppliers without jeopardizing relationships with them.

NOTE

1. Heizer, Jay, and Barry Render, *Production and Operations Management,* Fourth Edition, pp. 575–577. Adapted by permission of Prentice-Hall, Inc., Upper Saddle River, N.J.

10

CASH FORECASTING AND DETERMINING A COMPANY'S CASH NEEDS

Every company must provide the necessary cash for operating the business in both the short term and the long term. This cash is needed to ensure that the business will operate smoothly and that sufficient funds will be available to meet both current and future obligations. It is also a major contributor to ROI results. Generally, short-term cash forecasts are for one year or less, whereas long-term forecasts are for more than one year. But if a business requires shorter or longer periods, it is acceptable to change the time limits between long- and short-term forecasts. Let us explore some of the reasons for forecasting cash needs.

REASONS FOR CASH FORECASTING

The following reasons should be used merely as guidelines for pointing out the importance of cash forecasting. Some of these points may not apply immediately if your company is new but will apply at some time during the company's life.

Expansion

In order to expand, large sums of monies must be available. The demands for monies in providing for expansion will play an important part in your future plans. In order to know how much and when monies are available, a

TABLE 10-1	Impact of Sales Increases on Additional Money Requirements		
Operating Sources	*Current Level of Activity*	*Additional Monies @ 20%*	*Reasons for Increases*
Sales revenues	$700,000	$140,000	More sales
Depreciation	5,000	200	Additional machinery
Total cash sources	705,000	140,200	
Operating Uses			
Wages and operating expenses	70,000	14,500	Additional labor
Working capital	72,500	13,500	Additional inventory
Purchase of fixed assets	15,500	3,200	Additional machinery
Total cash uses	158,000	31,200	
Net cash use	$547,000	$109,000	Approximately 20%

cash forecast is necessary. Knowledge of advance monies will also assist you in making the best deal for additional funds, such as the equity and long-term capital markets.

Expansion requires additional monies for such items as working capital, capital assets, expenses, etc. For example, a 20% increase in sales revenues may require 20% more monies. Table 10-1 illustrates the impact of a 20% increase in growth in revenues and the need for additional monies. Note that additional monies would be required in wages and operating expenses, working capital, and, in this case, perhaps additional machinery. In reality, some differences may occur in each of the account balances. They are presented here merely to illustrate what might occur and the effect of sales growth on the need for more monies. Some of these monies are not all cash, and therefore the term "monies" is used to reflect the use of both cash and related funds.

Control

A cash forecast will assist a company in setting up centralized control mechanisms that will enable the company to know the amounts of cash available in the cash system, how much additional cash will be needed in what time period, and when to expect both receipts and disbursements of cash. This is discussed later in the chapter.

Payments

A cash forecast will highlight anticipated payments of loans, including interest payments, bonuses, major creditors, and dividends. It will indicate when these payments are to be paid and whether sufficient funds are available. Having this knowledge on hand can provide a company with the tools for shifting funds on a temporary basis to meet the demands of current payments. By using this technique, temporary shortages of cash may be avoided.

Investments

A cash forecast will point out how much and in what period cash will be in excess, in other words, how much and when excess cash can be invested in short-term securities. These short-term securities will generally yield high short-term interest, which can be used to generate additional income. This becomes part of a company's cash management program.

Borrowings

Irregularity in the flow of cash is inherent in any operating business and may require temporary borrowings. From time to time, shortages of cash will result, especially to support working capital requirements. Seasonality may create a cash shortage that is temporary. Therefore, money may need to be borrowed temporarily to meet cash requirements caused by buildups of working capital such as receivables and inventories.

Requirements from Lending Institutions

Lending institutions will require that a company prepare a cash forecast in support of any loan application. This enables the lending institution to determine the company's needs as well as its ability to pay back the loan. A cash forecast is as vital to the operations of a business as are the typical financial statements issued by companies.

CASH FORECASTING TECHNIQUES

There are many techniques for forecasting the cash requirements of a company. We deal with three methods. The two that are more commonly used are the cash receipts and disbursements method and the adjusted net income method, or the source and application of funds method. The third method is the percentage method, which utilizes percentage relationships and applies them to forecasting balances in future years.

Cash Receipts and Disbursements Method

This method is used for short periods of time, such as days, weeks, months, and quarters. It allows a company to forecast its cash inflows and outflows, or cash receipts and cash disbursements, in periods that are closer to reality. The basic problem with this method lies in its estimating of cash inflows or receipts. Errors in estimating receipts will invalidate any of the projections, particularly, as will be seen, the projecting of any short-term loan requirements.

Estimating Cash Receipts

In cases where a company has no historical base, it must use the best educated guess available; however, there are sources where data may be obtained that would be of value in the estimation process. For example, market consultants, federal government statistics, trade organizations, local chambers of commerce, local colleges or universities, libraries, and local governmental agencies can provide data to help a company in estimating the potential market and, ultimately, what receipts the company can expect during the length of the forecast.

For companies with historical data, a simple analysis, as shown in Table 10-2, will provide some basis for cash to be received, assuming that sales forecasts are reasonably accurate. In this situation, all sales are expected to be collected within a three-month period. One can see that applying the percentage for each month times the total sales estimate will give a company an estimate of collections for up to three months. Using the monthly average as a base will provide an overall average, but the percentages for individual months are preferred.

Using Table 10-2, we can develop an illustration of how cash receipts can be computed using this technique, as shown in Table 10-4. Assume that The Great Company, Inc., is projecting net sales for the next year of $840,000, which are arbitrarily broken down by month as shown in Table 10-3. The

	Estimated Collections from Sales			
Month	Current Month	1 Month Later	2 Months Later	3 Months Later
January	6%	67%	20%	7%
February	5	70	19	6
March	7	70	16	7
April	4	75	18	3
May	5	69	21	5
June	3	68	22	7
July	8	61	20	11
August	7	69	16	8
September	5	72	15	8
October	3	74	14	9
November	4	70	19	7
December	6	67	18	9
Monthly average	5.3%	69.3%	18.2%	7.3%

TABLE 10-2   Collection Pattern of Sales

company is estimating the cash receipts for the months of September, October, and November. We will assume that the data in Table 10-2 will represent the collection pattern for the entire year. Also, that the percentages in the column titled "Current Month" will represent cash sales, and these percentages will be used for calculating for the three months in question.

Table 10-4 illustrates how cash receipts are calculated using the data for these months, as shown in Table 10-2. The net sales data were taken from Table 10-3. Since it takes three months to collect the total of accounts receivable fully, the months of June, July, and August are presented to reflect the cash received from collections for the forecasted months of September, October, and November. Let us review how the month of June resulted in the amounts for later months.

Net sales for the month of June are collected as follows:

Cash sales	3%
1 month later	68
2 months later	22
3 months later	7
Total collected	100%

TABLE 10-3   Projected Net Sales by Month for The Great Company, Inc.

Month	Projected Net Sales	% to Total
January	$ 63,000	7.5%
February	62,160	7.4
March	72,240	8.6
April	57,120	6.8
May	60,480	7.2
June	63,840	7.6
July	70,560	8.4
August	69,720	8.3
September	75,600	9.0
October	82,320	9.8
November	84,840	10.1
December	78,120	9.3
Total	$840,000	100.0%

TABLE 10-4   Estimate of Cash Receipts

	Jun	Jul	Aug	Sep	Oct	Nov
Net Sales	$63,840	$70,560	$69,720	$75,600	$82,320	$84,840
Cash Sales	1,915	5,645	4,880	3,780	2,470	3,394
%	3%	8%	7%	5%	3%	4%
Collections of A/R						
1 Month Later	—	$43,411	$43,042	$48,107	$54,432	$60,917
%	68%	61%	69%	72%	74%	70%
2 Months Later	—	—	14,045	14,112	11,155	11,340
%	22	20	16	15	14	19
3 Months Later	—	—	—	4,469	7,761	5,578
%	7	11	8	8	9	7
Cash received from collections				$70,468	$75,818	$81,229

Applying these percentages, the net sales for the month of June were spread over three months as follows:

June:	$(.03 \times \$63,840) =$	$ 1,915
July:	$(.68 \times \$63,840) =$	43,411
August:	$(.22 \times \$63,840) =$	14,045
September:	$(.07 \times \$63,840) =$	4,469
Total collected		$63,840

A similar calculation is made for the months of July through November. Since we are projecting only the months of September through November, the calculations are not projected beyond this period. As a result, the total cash received from collections for these months are as follows:

	Cash Sales	Collection of A/R	Cash Received from Collections
September	$3,780	$66,688	$70,468
October	2,470	73,348	75,818
November	3,394	77,835	81,229

In addition, other cash receipts would be projected, such as sale(s) of assets, interest income, or dividend income.

Estimating Cash Disbursements

The next step is to forecast cash disbursements. Cash disbursements represent payments to creditors and employees for goods and/or services received. Some purchases will be made for cash, while others will be paid over a short period of time from the accounts payable account.

It is important to forecast each item as accurately as possible. Many of these payables are fixed in nature, such as rent payments, interest payments, insurance premiums, and loan repayments. On the other hand, many disbursements are controllable in that they can be increased or decreased to a great degree as the need arises. They include payroll, machinery purchases, certain administrative costs, and advertising.

Therefore, it is generally accepted that cash disbursements are considered more controllable than cash receipts. As a result, certain disbursements can be planned to meet the availability of cash so that borrowings are not necessary. For example, when monies are currently unavailable, the purchase of a piece of machinery may be deferred one or more months.

Table 10-5 illustrates the preparation of estimating cash disbursements. Since some disbursements are paid with cash, it is necessary to provide some amounts for cash purchases. In addition, an estimate must be developed as to when accounts payable are paid, such as one month later, two months later, and so on. This is based on historical patterns of payments from the accounts payable records.

Let us assume that The Great Company, Inc., estimates that purchases of raw materials and office supplies represent 65% of the estimated net sales. In addition, cash purchases represent 2% of net sales, 80% one month later, and 18% two months later. The cash disbursements for the months of September, October, and November can now be transferred to Table 10-6 in the appropriate categories under the heading "Cash Disbursements" to arrive at the cash budget.

Determining the Cash Budget Using the Cash Receipts and Disbursements Method

Both cash receipts, Table 10-4, and cash disbursements, Table 8-5, have been calculated. Table 10-6 is a sample cash budget form to be used for developing a cash budget using this method. If receipts exceed disbursements, thus resulting in a positive figure, the company can expect enough funds to keep operations running smoothly. If disbursements exceed receipts, thus resulting in a negative figure, then a shortage of cash may result, unless the beginning cash balance is sufficient to cover the excess of disbursements over receipts. In any case, there is a cash drain on the business, and consideration must be given to remedying the situation.

Table 10-7 summarizes the bottom portion of Table 10-6, which will determine whether The Great Company, Inc., will have to borrow or have excess cash to invest during the months of the forecast.

To illustrate this concept further, we will assume that the company requires a minimum desired cash balance of $9,000 and that its beginning cash balance (including marketable securities) is $8,000. With these facts, Table 10-7 is presented. The table summarizes the cash budget for the months of September, October, and November. A cash shortage ($835) resulted in the month of September and may require an additional short-term loan. The months of October and November reflect excess cash on hand, which can be used for such expenditures as capital expenditures, investments,

TABLE 10-5   Estimate of Cash Disbursements

	Jun	Jul	Aug	Sep	Oct	Nov
Purchases (.65 × net sales)	$41,496	$45,864	$45,318	$49,140	$53,508	$55,146
Purchases for cash (.02)	830	917	906	983	1,070	1,103
Accounts payable payments:						
1 Month later (.80)		33,197	36,691	36,254	39,312	42,806
2 Months later (.18)			7,469	8,256	8,157	8,845
Payroll costs				6,000	6,000	6,000
Other factory expenses				300	300	300
Tax payments						10,000
Purchases of machinery				7,200	5,000	
Utilities				300	300	300
Rent				400	400	400
Insurance premiums				60	60	60
Mortgage payments				200	200	200
Other administrative costs				150	150	150
Selling expenses				3,000	3,000	3,000
Advertising				5,000	6,000	8,000
Loan repayments				1,500	1,500	1,500
Pension contributions				500	500	500
Shipping				200	200	200
Other (list)						
Total cash disbursements				$70,303	$72,149	$83,364

and dividends, and expenditures in other areas where cash is needed for expansion and growth. Additional surplus cash should be invested in an effort to generate a higher return than would ordinarily be expected.

Remember that this forecast is based on internal requirements that the company maintain a minimum desired cash balance of $9,000. It is suggested that consideration be given to determine whether this amount can be reduced to avoid the need to borrow short-term for the month of September.

TABLE 10-6   Cash Budget Form

The Great Company, Inc.
Cash Budget Form
Period _____

Period
____ ____ ____ ____

Cash Receipts
Cash sales
Cash received from collections
Sale(s) of assets
Other income (List)
Total cash receipts
Cash Disbursements
Payroll costs
Other factory expenses
Tax payments
Purchases of machinery
Utilities
Rent
Insurance premiums
Mortgage payments
Other administrative costs
Selling expenses
Advertising
Loan repayments
Pension contributions
Shipping
Other (List)
Total cash disbursements

Cash receipts (Table 10–4)
Less: Cash disbursements (Table 10–5)
Net cash receipts over cash disbursements
Add: Cash balance at beginning of month
Cash balance at end of month
Less: Desired cash balance
Required short-term loans
Available cash on hand

TABLE 10-7   Summary of Cash Budget for The Great Company, Inc.

	September	October	November
Cash receipts (Table 10–4)	$70,468	$75,818	$81,229
Less: Cash disbursements (Table 10–5)	70,303	72,149	83,364
Net cash receipts over cash disbursements	165	3,669	(2,135)
Add: Cash balance at beginning of month	8,000	8,165	11,834
Cash balance at end of month	8,165	11,834	9,699
Less: Desired cash balance	9,000	9,000	9,000
Required short-term loans	$ 835	—	—
Available cash on hand	—	$ 2,834	$ 699

It also may be possible to have differing desired cash balances for each month of the forecast, such as $8,000 for September, $8,500 for October, and $9,000 for November. If this is possible, more monies can be planned for other expenditures, which will have the potential of generating higher earnings, thus, higher return on investment rates.

Adjusted Net Income Method

The second method of cash forecasting is the adjusted net income method, also referred to as the source and application of funds method or the "statement of changes in financial position." This method deals with the sources and applications of funds as they flow throughout the company and is designed to reflect changes in the company's balance sheet from one period to another. Since the concept deals with the funds of the company, particular emphasis is given to the working capital of the company as discussed in chapter 6.

Like the cash receipts and disbursements method, it enables a company to see how items of the balance sheet will affect the cash balance at some future date and to determine whether it can generate enough funds internally or whether it must borrow funds from other sources and, if so, how much. However, this method measures the changes in accounts during a specified period that is usually longer than the period used for the cash receipts and disbursements method. The results reflect a complete analysis of both cash inflows and cash outflows. They will include not only working capital changes but also changes in nonworking capital accounts.

In chapter 6, it was pointed out that working capital represents the working funds of a company and is computed by subtracting current liabilities from current assets. Using the hypothetical balance sheet of The Great Company, Inc. (Table 2-2 in chapter 2), the calculation results as follows:

Adjusted Net Income Equation

Current assets less current liabilities = working capital
$137,500   – $65,000   = $72,500

The difference of $72,500 represents the working capital of the company.

In preparing the balance sheet, it must always be in balance. Total assets must equal total liabilities and shareholders' equity. Or, a further refinement of balance sheet categories states that:

Current assets + fixed assets + other noncurrent assets

equals

Current liabilities + long-term debt + shareholders' equity

Applying the same figures, we get the following results:

$137,500 + $118,000 + $4,500 = $65,000 + $24,000 + $171,000

These results are said to be in balance. Let us rearrange the equation, however, to keep working capital segregated from the other parts of the balance sheet. By doing this, we now have the following:

Current assets – current liabilities

equals

Long-term debt + shareholders' equity – fixed assets – other noncurrent assets

or

$137,500 – $65,000 = $24,000 + $171,000 – $118,000 – $4,500

The left-hand side of the equation represents working capital, and therefore the right-hand side of the equation must also equal working capital. Sources and applications of funds can be computed by reflecting changes in either side of the equation. For example, if long-term debt increases and fixed assets decrease, this would represent a source of funds, since net working capital would increase. On the other hand, if long-term debt decreases and fixed assets increase, net working capital would decrease, representing an application of funds.

The Percentage Method

The third method for forecasting the cash needs of a company, the percentage method, is less commonly used than techniques that use funds statements and receipts and disbursements schedules. Nevertheless, it is a method that provides a shortcut to determining future money requirements. Keep in mind that these future requirements may include generating more cash from operations, selling of assets and/or segments of businesses, debt or equity financing, or other forms of financing. Whatever the situation, it will require raising the necessary funds to meet future needs.

This shortcut method involves the estimating of future accounts for each segment of the balance sheet. This is done by estimating future levels based on the percentage relationship of each balance account to net sales. The method involves these steps:

Step 1. Use the current balance sheet as a base. Year-end balance sheet figures are preferred and should represent the same time period as Step 2.

Step 2. Determine the percentage relationship for each item of the balance sheet to the total yearly net sales.

Step 3. Estimate next year's projected net sales revenues based on average yearly sales increases over several years, judgmental decisions on the estimate of net sales revenues for next year, industry forecasts translated into your own company's growth pattern, estimated net sales budget, or a combination of the above.

Step 4. Multiply the percentage of net sales as calculated in Step 2 by the new estimate of next year's net sales as calculated in Step 3. This represents the new projected balance and will be used to calculate additional financing that is needed.

Step 5. The final step is to balance all the items of the balance sheet and use the difference to represent additional funds required for the future.

Illustration

Using Table 10-8, let us go through each of the five steps and calculate a future year's projection, for example, year 19X3. The starting point for Table 10-8 will be the balance sheet previously used (Table 2-2) for the year ended 19X2. The explanations for each column are as follows:

Column 1 represents the year-end balance sheet for 19X2.

Column 2 represents the relationship of each item in column 1 as a percentage of the total net sales dollars for 19X2 of $700,000. The following list explains exceptions and/or adjustments necessary for completing column 3.

TABLE 10-8   The Great Company, Inc.
Balance Sheet
Projection for Year 19X3

| | Column | | |
	1	2	3
Assets			
Current assets			
Cash in banks	$ 5,000	.7%	$ 5,880
Marketable securities, at cost that approximates market	7,000	1.0	8,400
Accounts receivable—net of allowance for doubtful accounts	80,000	11.4	95,760
Inventories	40,000	5.7	47,880
Prepaid expenses	5,500	.8	6,720
Total current assets	$137,500	19.6	$164,640
Fixed assets—net of accumulated depreciation	118,000	16.9	141,960
Other assets	4,500	.6	5,040
Total assets	$260,000	37.1	$311,640
Liabilities			
Current liabilities			
Account payable	$ 38,000	5.4%	$ 45,360
Debt due within one year	4,500	n/a	4,500
Accrued expenses	10,000	1.4	11,760
Income taxes payable	12,500	1.8	15,120
Total current liabilities	65,000	—	76,740
Long-term debt	24,000	n/a	24,000
Total liabilities	$ 89,000	—	$100,740
Shareholders' equity			
Common stock	$ 40,000	n/a	$ 40,000
Capital in excess of par value	10,000	n/a	10,000
Earnings retained in business	121,000	n/a	127,958
Total shareholders' equity	$171,000	—	$177,958
Additional funds needed	—	—	32,942
Total liabilities and shareholders' equity	$260,000	—	$311,640

- It is assumed that additional investments in fixed assets are necessary to support increased sales. In this example, the additional net fixed assets needed to support a dollar of sales increase would be 16.9¢. However, this assumes no excessive capacity in manufacturing facilities and that additional land would not have to be acquired. Where there is sufficient capacity to support additional sales revenues, no entry would be made and an "n/a," or "not applicable," would be appropriate with a footnoted explanation.
- Debt due within one year, long-term debt, common stock, and capital in excess of par value will not be affected by sales growth. In some cases, this may not be true; for example, dividends may rise with levels of sales, assuming net earnings rose in proportion to increased sales revenues. In this example, an estimate can be made as to how much additional dividends may be required and adjusted on the balance sheet estimate accordingly. Others would be handled the same way and explained with a footnote.
- It is estimated that additional sales revenues will result in a 7.1% increase in net income. This is based on historical data and management's projection of next year. This means that sales revenues increase $140,000 ($840,000–$700,000), which represents an additional $9,940 in net income for year 19X3 ($140,000 × .071).
- Dividends are usually awarded at 30% of net income. This is the policy of The Great Company, Inc., and its board of directors. Using this as a guideline, the additional dividends would be $2,982 ($9,940 × .30).
- Retained earnings would change with increased sales revenues. The increase to the retained earnings account would be the additional net income ($9,940) less additional dividends ($2,982) or an addition to retained earnings of $6,958 ($9,940 – $2,982).

Column 3 represents additional dollars for 19X3 based on 19X3 net sales revenues of $840,000 times column 2. For example, the line titled "Cash in banks" is estimated to be $5,880 and represents an increase of $880 ($5,880 – $5,000).

Interpretation

It is anticipated that based on an additional increase in net sales revenues of $140,000 ($840,000 – $700,000), an additional $32,942 of monies will be needed in 19X3. As you can see, the balance sheet is now in balance for 19X3; that is, total assets equal the total of total liabilities and shareholders' equity.

It may be worthwhile to note that because the percentage method is a rather simple way of determining future funds, additional analysis will be required to validate fully the accuracy of the forecast. The percentage method is merely a quick, or shortcut, method of forecasting funds and should be used only with that limitation in mind.

STATEMENT OF CASH FLOWS

Financial statements issued by business enterprises usually provide an additional report called the statement of cash flows (SCF) based on the operations of that enterprise for that specific period. This statement follows the format as outlined by the Financial Accounting Standards Board (FASB) and specifically refers to FASB #95.

The primary purpose of this statement is to provide the necessary information relating to the cash receipts and cash payments of a company during a specific period of time. It is an additional reported statement along with the balance sheet and the statement of earnings.

The information provided from this statement is designed to help investors, creditors, and other interested parties to:

- Analyze the ability of a company to generate positive future net cash flows.
- Be able to determine a company's ability to meet both current and future obligations, such as the payment of dividends and the need for external financing.
- Determine the reasons for differences between net income and related cash receipts and disbursements.
- Assess the financial position of both cash and noncash investing and related financing transactions during a given period.

To assist in providing the above information the statement of cash flows reports the cash effects for a given period of a company's operations, its investing transactions, and its financing transactions that affect a company's financial position but do not directly affect cash flows for that given period. The statement explains the change of cash and cash equivalent during that period. Cash equivalent refers to short-term and highly liquid investments that are readily convertible to identifiable amounts of cash and that are near their maturity (less than three months) and present insignificant risk of changes in value due to interest rate changes. Examples of these items commonly considered cash equivalents are Treasury bills, commercial paper, money market funds, and federal funds sold. Cash purchases and sales of those investments are part of a company's cash management activities rather than part of operating, investing, and financing activities, which are not reported in the statement of cash flows.

Classification of Cash Receipts and Cash Payments

The statement of cash flows is classified into three categories: operating, investing, and financing. Operating activities include all cash inflows (receipts) and cash outflows (payments) that involve the delivering or producing of goods for sale as well as the providing of services. Investing activities include all cash inflows and cash outflows, such as the acquisition and disposition of long-term productive assets (plant, property, and equipment), or securities that are not considered cash equivalents. It also includes the lending of money and the collection on loans. Financing activities represents cash inflows and cash outflows from the acquiring of resources and the returning of resources to the owners of the company. This also includes resources from creditors and the repaying of those amounts borrowed.

Cash inflows from operating activities. Cash inflows from these activities include receipts from the sale of goods or services, including receipts from the collection or sale of accounts, as well as short- and long-term notes receivable from customers arising from those sales; cash receipts from the sale of loans, debt, or equity instruments that are part of a company's trading portfolio; return on loans such as interest; returns on equity securities such as dividends; and other cash receipts that are not defined as inventory or financing activities. They include such items as proceeds from settlements of lawsuits and refunds from suppliers.

Cash outflows from operating activities. Includes cash payments to suppliers to acquire inventory (raw or finished goods) for resales; cash payments to other suppliers and employees for other goods and services; the payments of taxes to governmental agencies as well as duties, fines, and other fees and penalties; payments of interest to lenders and other creditors; and other cash payments that arise from settling lawsuits, charitable cash contributions, customer cash refunds, and other payments that are not defined as investing or financing activities.

Cash inflows from investing activities. These activities include the receipts from collections or sales of loans and other debt instruments (other than cash equivalents) purchased by the company; receipts from the sale of equity instruments of other companies and from returns on investment (interest) in those instruments; receipts from the sale of property, plant, and equipment; and receipts from other productive assets.

Cash outflows from investing activities. Cash payments (disbursements) for loans made by the company and disbursements for the acquisition of other entities' debt instruments; the purchase of equity instruments (available for sale or held to maturity) of other companies; and the purchase of property, plant, equipment, and other productive assets.

Cash inflows from financing activities. Represents the proceeds from issuing equity instruments, and proceeds from issuing short- and long-term debt such as bonds, mortgages, and notes.

Cash outflows from financing activities. Cash payments from dividends or other distribution to owners; the repurchase of a company's stock; and other principal payments to creditors who have extended long-term credit such as capital lease obligations.

Statement of Cash Flow Presentations

The statement of cash flows can be presented in several ways. This is so because the operating activities have the option of using the direct or indirect method. Nevertheless, the FASB has expressed a preference for the direct method of presenting net cash flows from the operating activities.

Table 10-9 illustrates a typical statement of cash flows as discussed in detail previously. You will notice that cash flows from operating, investing, and financing activities are shown, which provides the reader with information on the company's cash balance from the beginning of the year to the end of the year due to various cash receipts and payments.

Direct versus Indirect Method

The cash flow from operating activities can be presented using either the direct or indirect method with FASB preference given to the direct method.

The direct method derives its net cash from operating activities through the components of operating cash receipts and payments compared to adjusting or converting net income for items that do not affect funds. When using this method, a separate schedule that reconciles net income to net cash flow must be provided. Table 10-10 illustrates the direct method.

TABLE 10-9   The Great Company, Inc.
                       Statement of Cash Flows
                       for the Year Ended December 31, 19X2

Net cash flows from operating activities		$xxx
Cash flows from investing activities:		
Purchase of property, plant, and equipment	$(xxx)	
Sale of equipment	xx	
Collection of notes receivable	xx	
Net cash used in investing activities		(xx)
Cash flows from financing activities:		
Sale of common stock	xxx	
Repayment of long-term debt	(xx)	
Reduction of notes payable	(xx)	
Net cash provided by financing activities		xx
Effect of exchange rate changes on cash		xx
Net increase in cash		$xxx
Cash and cash equivalents at beginning of year		xxx
Cash and cash equivalents at end of year		$—
Schedule of noncash financing and investing activities:		
Conversion of bonds into common stock		$xxx
Property acquired under capital leases		xxx
		$xxx

The indirect method derives its net cash from operating activities by adjusting net income for revenues and expense items that do not result from cash transactions. It is easier to prepare because it focuses on the difference between net income and cash flows. The net income beginning balance is taken directly from the income statement. Table 10-11 illustrates the indirect method.

- Forecast needed funds for capital investments and working capital requirements.
- Invest in available short-term cash needs.
- Anticipate short-term cash needs.
- Improve collections of funds from customers.
- Monitor and analyze cash receipts and cash disbursements at least monthly.

TABLE 10-10   The Great Company, Inc.
Statement of Cash Flows—Direct Method
for the Year Ended December 31, 19X2

Cash flows from operating activities:		
Cash received from customers	$xxx	
Cash paid to suppliers and employees	(xx)	
Dividend received from affiliate	x	
Interest received	x	
Interest paid (net of amount capitalized)	(xx)	
Income taxes paid	(xx)	
Insurance proceeds received	x	
Cash paid to settle lawsuit	x	
Net cash provided by operating activities		$ xx
Cash flows from investing activities:		
Proceeds from sale of facility	xx	
Payment received on note for sale of plant	xx	
Capital expenditures	(xxx)	
Payment for purchase of Company Z, net of cash acquired	(xx)	
Net cash used in investing activities		(xx)
Cash flows from financing activities:		
Net borrowings under line-of-credit agreement	x	
Principal payments under capital lease obligation	(x)	
Proceeds from issuance of long-term debt	xx	
Proceeds from issuance of common stock	xx	
Dividends paid	(xx)	
Net cash provided by financing activities		xx
Net increase in cash and cash equivalents		xxx
Cash and cash equivalents at beginning of year		xx
Cash and cash equivalents at end of year		$xxx
Reconciliation of net income to net cash provided by operating activities:		
Net income		$ xx
Adjustments to reconcile net income to net cash provided by operating activities:		
Depreciation and amortization	$ xx	

(continued)

TABLE 10-10 *(continued)*

Provision for losses on accounts receivable	xx
Gain on sale of facility	x
Undistributed earnings of affiliate	(x)
Payment received on installment note receivable for sale of inventory	xx
Change in assets and liabilities net of effects from purchase of Company Z:	
Increase in accounts receivable	(xx)
Decrease in inventory	xx
Increase in prepaid expenses	(x)
Decrease in accounts payable and accrued expenses	(xx)
Increase in interest and income taxes payable	x
Increase in deferred taxes	xx
Increase in other liabilities	x
Total adjustments	xx
Net cash provided by operating activities	$xxx

TABLE 10-11   The Great Company, Inc.
Statement of Cash Flows—Indirect Method
for the Year Ended December 31, 19X2

Cash flows from operating activities:	
Net income	$ xx
Adjustments to reconcile net income to net cash provided by operating activities:	
Depreciation and amortization	$ xx
Provision for losses on accounts receivable	xx
Gain on sale of facility	x
Undistributed earnings of affiliate	(x)
Payment received on installment note receivable for sale of inventory	xx
Change in assets and liabilities net of effects from purchase of Company Z:	
Increase in accounts receivable	(xx)

(continued)

TABLE 10-11 *(continued)*

Decrease in inventory	xx	
Increase in prepaid expenses	(x)	
Decrease in accounts payable and accrued expenses	(xx)	
Increase in interest and income taxes payable	x	
Increase in deferred taxes	xx	
Increase in other liabilities	x	
Total adjustments		xx
Net cash provided by operating activities		xxx
Cash flows from investing activities:		
Proceeds from sale of facility	xx	
Payment received on note for sale of plant	xx	
Capital expenditures	(xxx)	
Payment for purchase of Company Z, net of cash acquired	(xx)	
Net cash used in investing activities		(xxx)
Cash flows from financing activities:		
Net borrowings under line-of-credit agreement	xx	
Principal payments under capital lease obligations	(xx)	
Proceeds from issuance of long-term debt	xx	
Proceeds from issuance of common stock	xx	
Dividends paid	(xx)	
Net cash provided by financing activities		xx
Net increase in cash and cash equivalents		xxx
Cash and cash equivalents at beginning of year		xx
Cash and cash equivalents at end of year		$xxx

DECISION-MAKING STRATEGIES

- Forecast needed funds for capital investments and working capital requirements.
- Invest in available short-term cash needs.
- Anticipate short-term cash needs.
- Improve collections of funds from customers.
- Monitor and analyze cash receipts and cash disbursements at least monthly.

11

HOW TO APPLY ROI TECHNIQUES FOR IMPROVING MARKETING PERFORMANCE

The importance of developing marketing segments can be seen by the impact it has on return on investment results. In previous chapters, we mentioned that all activities of a company, including marketing, reflect on the ROI performance.

There are many different ways of segmenting a company. These segmentation techniques highlight how decisions can be reached by evaluating and establishing guidelines for segments of the company. Before the technique of marketing segmentation is discussed, a brief discussion of some overall company segmentation concepts is presented.

TRADITIONAL CONCEPTS SEGMENTS WITHIN THE STRUCTURE OF A COMPANY

There are seven traditional concepts of segmenting a company into manageable parts. They usually follow the organizational structure of the company and can be used for setting objectives, for managing, and for controlling the business segment.

1. Accountability segments are segments of a business for which managers have the responsibility and authority to manage an operation. The accountability center head generally has full control and responsibility for meeting budgetary performance. An example of an accountability head would be a general manager of an operation or division (also known as a responsibility center).

2. Cost segments are those where output is measured in terms of predetermined costs. In manufacturing, standards would be developed for each manufacturing segment meeting certain predetermined levels of production. Production cost standards would then be established and operating results measured against these objectives.

3. Expense segments are those functions measured along organizational structures. For example, the legal and accounting departments represent expense segments. Managers are responsible for budgeting related to their specific department's expenses.

4. Revenue segments are those segments of the company in which performance is measured in terms of sales revenues. The sales department is typical of this segment, where sales are measured by product, geographic area, salesperson, and product line (which are discussed further later in the chapter).

5. Profit segments are an approach that measures the earnings of the business by evaluating those segments that have both revenue and expense responsibility without the effects of investment. The profit segment is also referred to as the accountability segment. Every business has its own definition of "accountability" and "responsibility," however, and its own concept of how the terms relate to the duties of its managers.

6. Investment segment is a concept that takes into consideration the elements of both earnings and investment in an effort to achieve the necessary support to produce earnings in that business segment.

7. Return on investment combines both profitability and investment. This was explored in earlier chapters of the book.

Two Analytical Approaches to Segmentation

Several other segmentation concepts are used and provide a more analytical approach to segmenting a company. They are designed to strengthen the earnings of a company and assist in determining how resources are best used.

1. Rule of three divides an organization into three parts. When dealing with operating divisions, an organization may be divided into those operations absolutely necessary to retain; those that are better to retain (due to economic benefits) than dispose of; and those that could be divested given poor performance or shifts in the direction of a company's business. Another variation would be to divide human resources into three categories: key individuals absolutely necessary to retain; those who are better to retain; and those who could be terminated given certain budgetary restraints.

2. Pareto's law is an accepted rule of thumb that says that 80% of any output usually comes from 20% of the input. (Example: a small portion of the product line will generally account for the majority of sales.) Using this guideline, a company can allocate resources to obtain the highest maximum return on investment rate. This method will also assist in identifying where the greatest opportunities for improvement in performance lie. During the planning and budgeting preparation, management must determine what 20% of the company it anticipates will contribute 80% of overall company objectives. When this is known, final company and/or division objectives can then reflect elimination and/or trimming down of product-line activity.

HOW TO MEASURE MARKETING PERFORMANCE USING RETURN ON MARKETING ASSETS

Too often, sales segments of a company are measured on sales performance only, and very little recognition is given to the amount of investment dollars that are tied up in the business. Therefore, it is possible to assign an investment base to a sales segment and establish a true accountability center for measuring performance. The concept to be used will be referred to as return on marketing assets. It illustrates how evaluating marketing segments relates to the overall company objectives.

Return on marketing assets follows the ROI concept by applying ROI principles to evaluating the marketing side of the business. To illustrate this marketing concept further, the two major components of ROI previously discussed will be used, namely, the profitability rate and the turnover rate. However, some changes in the elements have to be made to accommodate evaluating only the marketing segment of the business.

Return on marketing assets is defined as:

Return on Marketing Assets Equation

$$\frac{\text{Marketing Contribution}}{\text{Net Sales}} \times \frac{\text{Net Sales}}{\text{Marketing Assets}}$$

Marketing Contribution

Marketing contribution results from taking net sales by marketing territory, less cost of sales and selling expenses used by the marketing territory to sell the product. The following is a list of selling expenses that are typically part of the operations of a sales territory. They are by no means the only expenses but represent a sampling.

Typical Branch Expenses

- Salespersons' salaries and employee benefits
- Salespersons' commissions
- Manager's override
- Travel and entertainment
- Advertising and promotion
- Telephone and other communications expenses
- Rent
- Insurance and taxes
- Utilities
- Repairs and maintenance
- Office supplies
- Postage
- Depreciation
- Miscellaneous

Illustration

Using Tables 2-1 and 2-2 of The Great Company, Inc., a new statement is developed by marketing territory based on actual results for net sales, expenses, and marketing assets. These data are available or can be constructed from accounting records.

An explanation is in order for determining marketing assets by sales territory. Both accounts receivable and inventories are assets that are generally controllable by the sales territory. Since most net sales are generated by the sales territory, accounts receivable is a function of net sales by sales territory. Net sales are generated by selling inventories and can be isolated by product line and sales territory. Therefore, for the purpose of this illustration, both accounts receivable and inventories will be considered marketing assets. If other assets exist that are directly controllable by the sales territory, such as a company-owned branch office, these would also be included in the marketing asset calculation. Table 11-1 illustrates how a typical statement by marketing segment can be presented.

Using the Return on Total Asset Calculation

You will note that all of the data that affect a territory's return on investment are included, such as net sales from sales volume and sales mix; marketing

TABLE 11-1   The Great Company, Inc.
                  Profitability by Marketing Territory—Year 19X2

	North	West	East	South	Total
Net sales	$180,000	$140,000	$210,000	$170,000	$700,000
Cost of sales	150,000	100,000	160,000	115,000	525,000
Gross profit	30,000	40,000	50,000	55,000	175,000
% to sales	16.7%	28.6%	23.8%	32.4%	25.0%
Selling	6,000	7,500	12,000	4,500	30,000
% to sales	3.3	5.4	5.7	2.6	4.3
Marketing contribution	24,000	32,500	38,000	50,500	145,000
% to sales	13.3	23.2	18.1	29.7	20.7
Other expenses					
General expenses					15,000
Administrative expenses					25,000
Depreciation					5,000
Other expense					2,000
Income before income taxes					98,000
Income taxes					48,000
Net income					50,000
Profitability rate					7.1%
Marketing Assets					
Accounts receivable	26,000	20,000	24,000	10,000	80,000
Inventories	10,000	8,000	11,000	11,000	40,000
Total	$36,000	$28,000	$35,000	$21,000	120,000
Turnover rate	5.0	5.0	6.0	8.1	5.8
Other assets					140,000
Total assets					$260,000
Turnover rate					2.7
Return on marketing assets	66.7%	116.1%	108.6%	240.5%	120.8
Return on total assets					19.2%

TABLE 11–2   The Great Company, Inc.
Summary of Return on Marketing Assets

	Marketing Contribution Percent	×	Marketing Turnover Rate	=	Return on Marketing Assets
North	13.3%		5.0		66.7%
West	23.2		5.0		116.1
East	18.1		6.0		108.6
South	29.7		8.1		240.5
Total marketing territories	20.7%		5.8		120.8
Return on total assets					19.2%

contribution resulting from net sales less territory expenses and cost of sales; and marketing assets for each territory. As you will recall from a previous chapter, the return on total asset calculation was computed as follows:

$$\frac{\text{Net sales}}{\text{Total assets}} \times \frac{\text{Net income}}{\text{Net sales}} = \text{Return on total assets}$$

$$\frac{\$700,000}{\$260,000} \times \frac{\$50,000}{\$700,000} = 19.2\%$$

$$2.7 \times .071 = 19.2\%$$

This can be broken down by marketing territory as shown in Table 11-2. You will note that each territory contributes a higher rate of return than the overall company. This is due to assets that do not directly contribute any sales dollars but are necessary for the survival of the business, such as capital assets, cash, and the like. In order to compensate for this, either higher objectives must be established for the sales territories or other areas of the company must be reduced to a more productive basis. Assuming this has already been done, let us illustrate how the overall return on total assets can be increased by establishing certain revised objectives for the sales territories.

Applying the Assumptions

- Increase net sales by price increases on selected products and changing sales mix to sell more higher-priced products.
- Reduce selling expense by instituting a more effective cost control program.
- Reduce receivables by tighter screening of customers and offering discounts for cash payments.
- Reduce inventories by disposing of obsolete and slow-moving products.

Applying these assumptions to the data for 19X2 results in Table 11-3 for the following year 19X3. Note that applying the assumptions increases the return on marketing assets from 120.8% to 228.8%, and the return on total assets from 19.2% to 41.8%. Comparisons made between the years 19X2 and 19X3, shown in Table 11-4, indicate the effect of setting higher objectives in the sales territories on the overall corporate objective.

EFFECT ON INDIVIDUAL ASSUMPTIONS

Sometimes it is not feasible to change at the same time all the factors that may result in higher rates of return. The previous example reflects all assumption changes that resulted in a 22.6 percentage point increase in return on total assets. Changes in individual assumptions can be considered separately to show how each change affects the ROTA rate, net sales, marketing contribution, and marketing assets. Table 11-1 data will be used for illustration purposes.

Net Sales

Assuming net sales were increased by 20%, or $140,000, while the profitability rate was maintained at 7.1%, the following results:

$$\text{Profitability rate} \times \text{Turnover rate} = \text{Return on total assets}$$

$$\frac{\$59,640^*}{\$840,000} \times \frac{\$840,000}{\$260,000} = 22.9\%$$

$$7.1\% \times 3.23 = 22.9\%$$

$$^*\$840,000 \times .071$$

TABLE 11-3   The Great Company, Inc.
              Profitability by Marketing Territory—Year 19X3

	North	West	East	South	Total
Net sales	$225,000	$165,000	$330,000	$120,000	$840,000
Cost of sales	140,000	110,000	220,000	90,000	560,000
Gross profit	85,000	55,000	110,000	30,000	280,000
% to sales	37.8%	33.3%	33.3%	25.0%	33.3%
Selling	5,590	6,930	11,520	4,300	28,340
% to sales	2.5	4.2	3.5	3.6	3.4
Marketing contribution	79,410	48,070	98,480	25,700	251,660
% to sales	35.3	29.1	29.8	21.4	30.0
Other expenses					
General expenses					15,000
Administrative expenses					10,000
Depreciation					20,000
Other expense					2,000
Income before income taxes					204,660
Income taxes					100,242
Net income					104,418
Profitability rate					12.4%
Marketing Assets					
Accounts receivable	24,000	18,000	22,000	10,000	74,000
Inventories	10,000	9,000	8,000	9,000	36,000
Total	$34,000	$27,000	$30,000	$19,000	$110,000
Turnover rate	6.6	6.1	11.0	6.3	7.6
Other assets					140,000
Total assets					$250,000
Turnover rate					3.4
Return on marketing assets	233.6%	178.0%	328.3%	135.3%	228.8
Return on total assets					41.8%

| | | | Percentage Point |
	Year 19X2	Year 19X3	Change
TABLE 11-4 The Great Company, Inc. Return on Marketing Assets and Return on Total Assets—19X2 versus 19X3			

Return on Marketing Assets

	Year 19X2	Year 19X3	Change
North	66.7%	233.6%	166.9
West	116.1	178.0	61.9
East	108.6	328.3	219.7
South	240.5	135.3	(105.2)
Total	120.8	228.8	108.0

Return on Total Assets

Total company	19.2%	41.8%	22.6

This calculation shows that for a 20% increase in net sales with the profitability rate unchanged, return on total assets will increase from 19.2% to 22.9%, or 3.7 percentage points.

Marketing Contribution

Let us assume that marketing contribution is increased $106,660 ($251,660 - $145,000), or 73.6%. This represents the increase of marketing contribution from year 19X2 (Table 11-1) to year 19X3 (Table 11-3). To illustrate the change, the net sales figure of $700,000 (Table 11-1) will be used.

$$\text{Profitability rate} \times \text{Turnover rate} = \text{Return on total assets}$$

$$\frac{\$104,418^*}{\$700,000} \times \frac{\$700,000}{\$260,000} = 40.2\%$$

$$14.9\% \times 2.69 = 40.2\%$$

*Reflects revised net income as per Table 11-3

Results indicate an increase of 21 percentage points (.402 − .192) due to an increase of marketing contribution of $106,660.

Marketing Assets

To reflect the effect of lowering marketing assets, the data in Table 11-3 will be used. The other data of net sales and net income will be taken from Table 11-1.

$$\text{Profitability rate} \times \text{Turnover rate} = \text{Return on total assets}$$

$$\frac{\$50,000}{\$700,000} \times \frac{\$700,000}{\$250,000} = 20.0\%$$

$$7.1\% \times 2.8 = 20.0\%$$

A decrease of $10,000 in marketing assets results in an increase of .8 percentage points $(.200 - .192)$ in return on total assets.

These are just a few of the various ways by which sales management can reflect changes in return on total assets. Changes in sales volume, sales mix, and asset utilization must be fully evaluated by management in order to ensure the highest maximization of return on assets to the company. As just illustrated, the return on asset rate can vary substantially by influencing certain decisions relating to the marketing organization.

DECISION-MAKING STRATEGIES

- For measuring and maximizing return on investment performance, an organization must be divided into meaningful segments.
- Apply return on investment techniques to marketing segments of the business for measuring and establishing return on investment objectives.
- Review new distribution channels for speed and cost effectiveness.
- Determine market reaction to your marketing strategy.
- Review marketing segments to be sure that the proper marketing mix is being maintained.
- Where feasible, measure the impact of your advertising and promotion program.

12

PRICING STRATEGIES AND THEIR IMPACT ON THE PROFITABILITY RATE

Establishing the right price for a product or service is a major management function. It is a function that has an impact throughout the organization and is especially noticed when calculating the profitability rate, a major component of the return on investment equation. Pricing strategies are so vital to a business that they are considered among its most important functions. The ultimate survival of the business depends on effective pricing strategies.

The ability to maximize both volume and price is unquestioned. Every business, in order to survive in the marketplace, must market its goods and/or services in such a way that revenues exceed costs and that the remainder generates a fair and reasonable ROI.

KEY FACTORS AFFECTING PRICING

Management must understand that pricing is a complex subject and that it responds to many factors. For example, the marketplace in which a company operates will determine at what price and at what volume levels customers will respond. A company's ability to keep unit costs as low as possible will aid in setting pricing guidelines. You must have the capability of manufacturing and selling the product at different economic levels. You must also be aware of what profits are needed to sustain growth and to move in the direction anticipated for the long term.

Outside influences cannot be ignored. They are at times equally or more important in establishing a pricing structure. For example, costs of manufacturing and distribution, governmental regulations, plant capacity, governmental regulations, capital investments, legal implications, financial liquidity, technological changes, competitive conditions, and current economic conditions will play a key role in pricing decisions.

INFLUENCES ON PRICING DECISIONS

In setting prices, several major influences must be considered. Other influences unique to a specific business, however, cannot be ignored.

The buyer generally has the options from whom to buy, how to buy, what to buy, and what price to pay. Given our competitive society, the buyer is sometimes in a very strong position to dictate how the seller reacts. Therefore, it is important that the seller always examine the pricing policies through the eyes of the customer. Put yourself in the customer's shoes by determining how you would react to a specific price if you were the customer. By doing this, you will understand more about how you should price your product.

Know how your competition will react to a certain pricing policy. It is important to know as much as possible about the competition, including its volume, costs, plant capacity, method of distribution, technology, key personnel, credit terms, and profitability. This will help in determining your pricing policy, including how much to charge for special volume users.

CHECKLIST OF PRICING STRATEGIES

Part of the management function is to establish the most effective and profitable pricing strategy. This means being able to price the product and/or service in keeping with the objectives and/or life cycle of the product at different stages. For example, a new product reaching a new selective audience has a different strategy than attracting buyers for other products as a loss leader. Also, gaining entry into new markets will differ from pricing in keeping with industry leaders.

Each pricing strategy is designed to accomplish a different objective. These objectives will change as the marketplace changes and with changes in the life cycle of the product. A brief review of the various pricing strategies is presented. By no means is this the definitive discussion on pricing. The order in which these pricing strategies are presented has no relation to the importance or priority of the strategy. What follows is merely a listing of pricing strategies.

High-price strategy is a technique whereby higher than usual prices are established on selected products. This can create an image for the buyer that the product is of higher quality as compared to those of competitors. This can be effective in the long run only if the product is, in fact, of higher quality than those of your competitors.

Volume strategy accepts low-margin products with profits being generated from high volume. This is referred to as a "low-margin, high-volume" philosophy.

Psychological pricing is pricing just below the round dollar amount, designed to create in customers' minds the impression that the product is priced lower than it is. For example, $9.95, $25.99, and $99.99 appear to be lower than $10, $26, and $100.

In-and-out pricing. Products are normally priced high, but price reductions occur when that segment of the market that is sought after becomes saturated. This strategy is effective only when there is limited or no competition and when substitutes for the product are almost nonexistent.

Typical pricing strategy is generally established by the marketplace in that it is a price that is accepted by the customer as being a fair price. We see this strategy in the pricing of certain items, such as chewing gum and cigarettes.

Entry pricing occurs when pricing is used to establish a position in a specific market. Using this strategy requires pricing below the existing competitive price level.

Elasticity pricing is a strategy whereby a drop in price causes a sharp increase in demand. A product and/or service is said to be elastic because it springs up and down in price. A decreasing price causes the total value of sales to increase. The sensitivity to price changes (elasticity) exists when one or more of the following conditions exist.

- The product is considered a luxury.
- The price is considered a major portion of the family's disposable income, such as the price of a house or auto.
- Substitutes for the product are readily available, such as concentrated orange juice versus fresh-squeezed orange juice.
- The product has long-lasting quality, such as with home appliances.

Cost-plus pricing involves developing a pricing structure from the bottom up, usually using percentages to build the total price. This type of pricing strategy is used heavily by governmental agencies.

Phase-out pricing This strategy is used when a company is anticipating phasing out a product and/or product line. The strategy dictates setting a high price to discourage both new customers and continuing sales of the product. In many cases, such a product has reached the downside of the life cycle and appeals to a few select markets and/or customers.

Loss-leader pricing is a strategy used effectively by retail establishments that want to attract buyers for other products. It is also used to complement other high-margin products, such as inexpensive razors with razor blades to fit that specific brand of razor sold at profitable prices.

You can see the complex nature of establishing a pricing strategy. Each strategy must be evaluated periodically to make sure it meets the objective of how a company wants to market the product and/or service in an effort to maximize ROI rates.

FOUR PRICING TECHNIQUES

There are four commonly used pricing techniques. They include markup pricing, contribution pricing, margin pricing, and return on investment pricing. Within each of the pricing techniques, there are variations such as incremental cost and conversion cost methods relating to the markup techniques. Where feasible, we will show the technique's effect on the profitability rate.

Markup Pricing—An Overall Approach

An approach commonly used is called markup pricing. Although many businesses use this approach, it makes no provision for the impact of fixed costs on profit. Because it applies the same amount of fixed costs regardless of volume levels, it treats fixed costs as a variable expense. In addition, since profits are considered variable in relation to volume, it does not allow the opportunity to cost a product based on volume. The calculation is made as follows:

Step 1. Determine the cost of acquiring the product for sale. It may be the cost of manufacturing the product or of purchasing the finished or subassembled parts.

Step 2. To the results of Step 1, add the costs associated with obtaining the volume, such as selling, advertising, promotion, sales salaries, commissions and overrides, and travel and entertainment costs.

Step 3. Determine the desired profit as a dollar amount or as a percentage

TABLE 12-1   The Overall Markup Technique

	Variable Unit Costs	Fixed Unit Costs	Total Unit Costs
Production costs	$40.00		$ 40.00
Selling and distribution costs	20.00		20.00
Fixed costs		$20.00	20.00
	$60.00	$20.00	80.00
Desired profit			20.00
Selling price			$100.00

TABLE 12-2   Statement of Income Using the Overall Markup Technique

Unit volume	10,000 units
Unit selling price	$100.00
Net sales ($100 × 10,000 units)	$1,000,000
Less: Variable costs ($60 × 10,000 units)	600,000
Fixed costs ($20 × 10,000 units)	200,000
Profit (desired $20/unit)	$ 200,000
% of net sales	20%

of total costs in Steps 1 and 2. This desired profit is added to the total costs to determine the selling price.

Table 12-1 illustrates the overall markup technique and how the selling price is determined. If a company sold 10,000 units, the hypothetical statement of income shown in Table 12-2 would result.

As you have just observed, the markup pricing method establishes the lowest basic price given a desired level of profit. This method requires determining and identifying different types of costs and adding a desired markup in order to arrive at a selling price. It is sometimes referred to as the total cost method, or full costing, and can be expressed in terms of a formula, as can other markup methods. The formula for this technique can be expressed as:

$$SP = TC + MU(TC)$$

TABLE 12-3   Statement of Income Using the Total Cost Method

Unit volume	10,000 units
Unit selling price	$75.00
Net sales ($75.00 × 10,000 units)	$750,000
Less: total costs ($60.00 × 10,000 units)	600,000
Profit	$150,000
% of net sales	20%

and can be illustrated by using the following per unit data:

SP = Selling price
MU = Markup percent—25%
DM = Direct material—$30 per unit
DL = Direct labor—$20 per unit
OH = Overhead—$10 per unit
TC = Total cost—$60 per unit

Total Cost Method

This method also recoups all costs of the product and adds a desired profit margin (markup) to arrive at a selling price. It is one of the easiest methods to use but can be misleading because of the way overhead costs are allocated. The calculation is as follows:

Total Cost Method Equation

$$SP = TC + MU(TC)$$
$$= \$60 + .25(\$60)$$
$$= \$60 + \$15$$
$$= \$75$$

Using the new selling price of $75, a hypothetical statement of income is presented in Table 12-3.

Incremental Cost Method

This method uses only direct material costs and direct labor costs and puts the emphasis on products that absorb more overhead costs. It also empha-

TABLE 12-4	Hypothetical Statement of Income Using the Incremental Cost Method
Unit volume	10,000 units
Unit selling price	$62.50
Net sales ($62.50 × 10,000 units)	$625,000
Less: Direct costs ($50 × 10,000 units)	500,000
Profit	$125,000
% of net sales	20%

sizes the incremental costs involved in producing additional sales units. The formula is:

Incremental Cost Equation

$$SP = (DM + DL) + MU(DM + DL)$$

The calculation is:

$$SP = (DM + DL) + MU(DM + DL)$$
$$= (\$30 + \$20) + .25(\$30 + \$20)$$
$$= \$50 + \$12.50$$
$$= \$62.50$$

Table 12-4 illustrates the hypothetical statement of income using the incremental cost method and the new selling price of $62.50 per unit.

Conversion Cost Method

This method emphasizes the conversion costs (direct labor plus overhead) and shifts the emphasis to products that have high material costs. In using this method, it is very important to allocate overhead clearly and rationally, since overhead will play a major role in determining the selling price. The formula for this method is as follows:

$$SP = (DL + OH) + MU(DL + OH)$$

TABLE 12-5   Statement of Income Using the Conversion Cost Method

Unit volume	10,000 units
Unit selling price	$37.50
Net sales ($37.50 × 10,000 units)	$375,000
Less: Direct labor and overhead costs	
($30.00 × 10,000)	300,000
Profit	$ 75,000
% of net sales	20%

The calculation is:

Conversion Cost Equation

$$\begin{aligned} SP &= (DL + OH) + MU(DL + OH) \\ &= (\$20 + \$10) + .25(\$20 + \$10) \\ &= \$30 + \$7.50 \\ &= \$37.50 \end{aligned}$$

Table 12-5 illustrates the hypothetical statement of income using the conversion cost method and the new selling price of $37.50.

Note that using the same data for each method results in the following different prices:

Method	Selling Price
Total cost	$75.00
Incremental cost	$62.50
Conversion cost	$37.50

A company can see that in using the same markup of 25%, there is a wide variation of selling price, from a low of $37.50 to a high of $75. If a company wanted to sell a product to receive the highest profit, it would choose the $75 price as calculated using the total cost method. On the other hand, if a company could not even sell a product(s) at the lowest price of $37.50, then it would have to adjust the markup objectives downward, reduce product costs, or a combination of both.

Although the preceding approaches are acceptable to many companies, a more advisable approach is to deal with price, volume, and cost relationships. The following suggested method, contribution pricing, will deal with these relationships.

Contribution Pricing

Under the contribution pricing technique, the best price is the one that generates the highest profits, or contribution. It relies on using only direct costs, such as for material, labor, and overhead, and brings into focus the impact on profits at different levels of volume and selling price. The key is to determine the best mix of selling price with the number of units you plan on selling, or what combination of volume and price levels will provide you with the greatest amount of contribution. The result, or contribution, will provide monies toward meeting your overhead costs and still add an adequate or desired profit to the business.

Let us look at an illustration that shows how the price, volume, and cost relationships reflect the decision to establish the most favorable price for a product using the following hypothetical data:

Current selling price	$100.00
Current unit sales	10,000 units
Sales dollar volume	$1,000,000
Direct costs per unit	$60.00
Overhead and other costs	$150,000

Given these facts, the contribution and income before income taxes are calculated as follows:

Net sales	$1,000,000
Direct costs	600,000
Contribution	400,000
Overhead and other costs	150,000
Income before income taxes	$250,000

Assuming that you can sell 10% more units at $95 per unit, and 15% more units at $90 per unit, what is the effect on both contribution and income before income taxes? The data are shown in Table 12-6.

You can see that in both cases—a reduction in price of $5 and $10, with increased volume of 10% and 15%, respectively—the projected income does not exceed the income before income taxes of $250,000 as originally calculated. Table 12-7 illustrates the contribution and income before income taxes for each of the selling price levels. There is, however, a more favorable combination, which is to use a $95 selling price with an increase in volume of 15%, or 11,500 units. The results are shown in Table 12-8.

Assuming that a 15% unit volume increase can be attained at the $95

TABLE 12-6   Impact of Selling More Units at Lower Prices

	Projected Selling Price	
	$95.00	*$90.00*
Projected unit sales	11,000	11,500
Projected sales dollars	$1,045,000	$1,035,000
Projected direct costs	660,000	690,000
Projected contribution	$ 385,000	$ 345,000
Overhead and other costs	150,000	150,000
Projected income before taxes	$ 235,000	$ 195,000

TABLE 12-7   Comparisons at Different Selling Price Levels

	Selling Price Levels		
	$100.00	*$95.00*	*$90.00*
Contribution	$400,000	$385,000	$345,000
Income before income taxes	$250,000	$235,000	$195,000

TABLE 12-8   Impact of Using a $95 Selling Price with 15% Higher Volume

Projected unit sales	11,500 units
Projected selling price	$95.00
Projected dollar sales	$1,092,500
Projected direct costs	$ 690,000
Projected contribution	$ 402,500
Overhead and other costs	$ 150,000
Projected income before income taxes	$ 252,500

selling price, other factors must be taken into consideration in establishing a selling price:

- Can you manufacture or obtain the additional 1,500 units? What is internal or supplier capacity?

TABLE 12-9	Calculating the Contribution Percentage for Pricing	
		Per Unit
Selling price		$100.00
Direct Costs		
Materials	$30.00	
Labor	20.00	
Overhead	10.00	60.00
Contribution		$ 40.00
Percentage of selling price		40%

- What will be the additional financial burden of adding 1,500 units? Are there sufficient working capital funds available?
- Are sufficient storage facilities available to house the additional units?
- Are additional personnel needed in manufacturing, distribution, selling, and administration to support the additional volume? If so, at what cost?
- Is additional raw material available and, if so, at what price? How quickly can it be delivered?
- Will the market support that additional volume? What is the capacity of the marketplace?
- How will the competition react to your aggressiveness in reducing price? Can you afford to lower your price even further if necessary?
- How quickly can you produce or acquire these additional units?
- Is the product's life cycle on the rise or is it declining? What is the estimated life of the product in question?

Using a Contribution Percentage in Determining Prices

In using the contribution pricing approach, it is possible to use a contribution percentage in the pricing calculation. But, it is important to make sure that you review this percentage periodically to be satisfied that it is sufficient to cover all costs of the company, such as interest costs on all borrowed capital, and yet still provide an adequate profit. Using the previous data, we are able to calculate the contribution percentage as shown in Table 12-9.

If the selling price of $100 were not given, and if it were determined that direct costs were to be 60% of the selling price ($60 ÷ $100), then the following calculation would give you the projected selling price:

TABLE 12-10	Comparison Using the Contribution Method		
Selling Price	*$100.00*	*$95.00*	*Change*
Units sold	10,000	11,000	1,000
Sales dollars	$1,000,000	$1,045,000	$45,000
Direct costs	600,000	660,000	(60,000)
Contribution	$ 400,000	$ 385,000	($15,000)
Contribution per unit	40.00	35.00	(5.00)
Overhead and other costs	150,000	150,000	—
Income before income taxes	$ 250,000	$ 235,000	($15,000)

Contribution Pricing Equation

$$\frac{\text{Direct costs}}{\text{Direct cost percentage}} \text{ or } \frac{\$60}{0.60} = \$100 \text{ selling price}$$

This results in the following:

Projected selling price	$100
Projected direct costs	60
Projected contribution	$40
% of selling price	40%

Knowing your projected direct costs and what percentage they should be of the selling price in order to provide a sufficient profit is an excellent tool for pricing a product in the short run. Because costs change frequently, this percentage must be reviewed periodically and therefore is not useful for long-term pricing strategies.

Use of Contribution in Determining Break-Even

The contribution percentage can be used in determining the break-even in units at a specific selling price. As opposed to using the number as a percentage, it is referred to on a per unit basis. For example, in a previous illustration, it was stated that by reducing the selling price to $95 from $100, 10% more would be sold. Table 12-10 shows the comparison of two selling prices, $100 and $95, and units sold of 10,000 and 11,000, respectively. In addition, the contribution per unit has been added to the data.

The question to be answered is: If you want to maintain an income before

TABLE 12-11   Impact of Using a $95 Selling Price to Generate a $250,000
                Income Before Income Taxes

Selling Price	$100.00	$95.00	Change
Units sold	10,000	11,428.6	1,428.6
Sales dollars	$1,000,000	$1,085,716	$485,716
Direct costs	600,000	685,716	$ 85,716
Contribution	$ 400,000	$ 400,000	—
Overhead and other costs	150,000	150,000	—
Income before income taxes	$ 250,000	$ 250,000	—

income taxes of $250,000, how many additional units must you sell at a selling price of $95? In the formula that follows, X equals the number of additional units that must be generated to earn an income before income taxes of $250,000:

*Contribution
Pricing in
Break-even
Equation*

$$X = \frac{\text{Overhead and other costs} + \text{Desired profit}}{\text{Contribution per unit}}$$

$$X = \frac{\$150,000 + \$250,000}{\$35}$$

$$X = 11,428.6 \text{ units, or } 1,428.6 \text{ additional units}$$

The proof is shown in Table 12-11.

Impact of Changing Direct Costs

What would be the result if material costs were reduced 20% but labor costs increased 10%? The per unit direct costs would be $56, as shown in Table 12-12.

The income before income taxes would result as shown in Table 12-13.

Establishing the Optimum Selling Price

Many companies have the option to establish different prices, with antici-pated sales reacting to the different price levels. For example, in most

TABLE 12-12   Impact of Changing Direct Costs

	Original	Revised	Change
Materials	$30.00	$24.00	$6.00
Labor	20.00	22.00	(2.00)
Overhead	10.00	10.00	—
Total	$60.00	$56.00	$4.00

TABLE 12-13   Impact on Profits of Changing Direct Costs

Selling Price	$100.00	$95.00	Change
Units sold	10,000	11,000	1,000
Sales dollars	$1,000,000	$1,045,000	45,000
Direct costs	600,000	616,000	(16,000)
Contribution	$ 400,000	$ 429,000	$29,000
Overhead and other costs	150,000	150,000	—
Income before income taxes	$ 250,000	$ 279,000	$29,000

situations, lowering the price would mean more units sold. On the other hand, raising prices would generally not generate higher sales. Therefore, given this very general theory, it is possible to estimate the most profitable price level taking into consideration fluctuating volume levels and fixed costs.

Let us assume that you have the option to sell your product at the following price levels with estimated sales volume at each level:

Price Levels	Estimated Sales Volume	Estimated Sales Dollars
$ 90.00	12,000	$1,080,000
95.00	11,000	1,045,000
100.00	10,000	1,000,000
105.00	9,000	945,000
110.00	8,000	880,000

Note that the estimated sales dollars range from $880,000 to $1,080,000. This $200,000 range resulted from a range in price of $20 per unit ($110–$90) and a 4,000-unit range in sales volume (12,000 – 8,000). Keep in mind that these figures must represent realistic estimates in order for the analysis to be valid. The following hypothetical cost data correspond to each of the estimated sales volume levels:

Estimates Sales Volumes	Variable Cost Per Unit— $60.00	Overhead and Other Costs	Total Costs	Per Unit
12,000	$720,000	$150,000	$870,000	$72.50
11,000	660,000	150,000	810,000	73.64
10,000	600,000	150,000	750,000	75.00
9,000	540,000	150,000	690,000	76.67
8,000	480,000	150,000	630,000	78.75

Note that, whereas the total costs increase with additional sales volume ($630,000 to $870,000), unit costs decrease ($78.75 to $72.50) because overhead or fixed costs are spread over more units sold. Combining both revenues and costs results in the following contribution:

Estimated Sales Volume	Price Levels	Estimated Sales Dollars	Total Costs	Contribution	Per Unit
12,000	$ 90.00	$1,080,000	$870,000	$210,000	$17.50
11,000	95.00	1,045,000	810,000	235,000	21.36
10,000	100.00	1,000,000	750,000	250,000	25.00
9,000	105.00	945,000	690,000	255,000	28.33
8,000	110.00	880,000	630,000	250,000	31.25

Based on contribution, both sales volume levels of 10,000 units and 8,000 units result in the same contribution of $250,000. However, on a per unit basis, the sales volume level of 8,000 units with a selling price of $110 is more favorable. This assumes that this volume and price level can be reasonably attained in the marketplace.

In summary, the use of the contribution pricing approach allows management to see how variations can create changes in units sold, selling price, and desired profits. Finding the right pricing, cost, and volume combination is not difficult but requires realistic estimates and lots of trial and error. Remember that the data used are not constant over time and must be reviewed and revised to reflect changing trends.

Margin Pricing Approach

Another pricing approach is to establish an acceptable margin rate based on sales dollars. This approach will assist in identifying what price must be charged to attain a desired margin. Margin pricing affords the luxury of simulating different variations to determine various selling prices that will result in different margin returns. In addition, it allows a company to vary cost data and to reflect different price ranges. Let us illustrate this approach by assuming a hypothetical business situation.

You are responsible for determining the price of a new product. Based on historical data, you need to generate a 30% margin return based on sales dollars. In addition, selling, administrative, and general expenses average around 20% of sales dollars. The following per unit cost data have been developed for you to use in calculating the selling price under this approach.

Direct material (DM)	$30.00
Direct labor (DL)	20.00
Selling, general, and administrative expenses (O/H)	10.00
Total per unit cost	$60.00

Using these data, the following calculation results:

Total per unit	$60.00
Margin desired	30%
Selling, general, and administrative expenses	20%
Remainder	50%

or

$$\frac{\$60.00}{0.50} = \$120.00 \text{ selling price}$$

The proof of this is:

Selling price	$120.00
Less direct costs	60.00
Less selling, general, and administrative costs	24.00
	$36.00
Percentage of selling price	30%

You must now determine whether $120 is an acceptable price in the marketplace. If it is not, you can lower the margin expectations, reduce costs, or a combination of both. For example, by lowering your margin return expectations from 30% to 20%, the selling price becomes $100:

$$\frac{\$60}{0.60} = \$100$$

Other similar analyses can be developed under this approach.

Return on Investment Pricing Approach

This approach determines the price needed to achieve a desired return on investment. As in other approaches, the pricing accuracy is only as good as the estimates used. The ROI approach should be used with caution because of the sensitivity of sales volume estimates and the effect they have on the estimated selling price.

Given a situation where a new product requires a substantial investment, it is often necessary to ensure the business of a satisfactory ROI. Using this premise, the following data will be used for illustration purposes:

Investment	$750,000
Fixed costs	$150,000
Variable costs	$60 per unit
Estimated units sold	10,000 units
Desired ROI (after taxes)	20%
Payback desired	5 years

The formula that can be developed for computing the selling price under this approach is:

ROI Pricing Equation

$$P = \frac{(ROI)(I/PB) + FC + VC(US)}{US}$$

P = Price
ROI = Desired return on investment
I = Investment
PB = Desired payback period, in years
FC = Fixed costs
VC = Variable costs per unit
US = Estimated units sold

or

$$P = \frac{(0.20)(750,000/5) + \$150,000 + \$60.00(10.000)}{10,000}$$

$$P = \frac{(0.20)150,000 + \$150,000 + \$600,000}{10,000}$$

$$P = \frac{\$30,000 + \$150,000 + \$600,000}{10,000}$$

$$P = \frac{\$780,000}{10,000} = \$78$$

The question that you now must answer is whether you can sell 10,000 units at a $78 selling price per unit over the next five years. If you cannot do this, you must accept a lower ROI, reduce the costs, or a combination of both. When you do either of these alternatives, you must rework the calculation to arrive at a different selling price. When your revised estimate of how many units you can sell is equal to or exceeds the estimated units sold in the preceding formula, in this case 10,000 units, then you can anticipate reaching the desired ROI.

TRANSFER PRICING TECHNIQUES

Knowing how much to charge another part of the organization for products transferred is an important issue.[1] It impacts upon the segments' profitability and return on investment rate and decisions thereof. Under various circumstances, different transfer pricing techniques can be used. These are discussed later.

Dilemmas arise during the transfer pricing process. They include one

TABLE 12-14	Transfer Pricing Techniques Profit Center Concept	
Market Based	*Nonmarket Based*	
Prevailing market prices	Opportunity cost	
Adjusted market price	Marginal cost	
Negotiated prices	Cost plus	
Contribution margin		

internal division profiting from selling to another internal division at their expense. In addition, the evaluation of the selling and receiving divisions can be distorted and can create differences in performance standards if comparisons are made between divisions. This holds true whether it is a profit or cost center. Table 12-14 is a summary of transfer pricing techniques.

Let's review the market-based techniques under the profit center concept.

Prevailing market price— represents transactions of significant quantities that were sold at arm's length such as quoted and printed prices.

Adjusted market price—similar to the prevailing market price, but adjusted for such expenses as selling and bad debts, since these costs would not be incurred when selling internally.

Negotiated prices—similar to the adjusted market price, since discounts for internal transfers of products are negotiated and therefore reflect the adjusted market price.

Contribution margin—under this technique the contribution margin (see chapter 17) is allocated between the division supplying the product and the division receiving the product.

Illustration

To illustrate, let's use the following facts:

Market price	$12
Variable costs—Division A	$4
Variable costs—Division B	$2
Division A sells to Division B	

Transfer
Pricing
Equations

To determine the transfer price of Division A, the contribution per unit must be calculated for the overall company for this particular product as follows:

Market price	$12
Less: Variable costs—Division A	(4)
Variable costs—Division B	(2)
Contribution margin per unit	$6

The $6 contribution margin per unit is then divided between Division A and B and is based on their respective variable costs as follows:

Variable costs for Division A is divided by total variable costs multiplied by the contribution margin per unit

or

$$\frac{\$4}{\$6} \times \$6 = \$4 \text{ contribution margin per unit for Division A}$$

Therefore, the transfer price for Division A is $8 as follows:

Transfer price	$8
Less: Variable costs	4
Contribution margin per unit	$4

The contribution margin per unit for Division B is $2 as follows:

Market price	$12
Less: Variable costs	(2)
Transfer price	(8)
Contribution margin per unit	$2

Notice that while the total company (Divisions A and B) results in a contribution margin percent of 50% ($6/$12), the individual divisions vary substantially. Division A has a contribution margin percent of 33⅓% ($4/$12), and Division B 16.7% ($2/$12), or a total of 50%.

This simple illustration highlights how divisional performance can change through the use of transfer pricing.

Cost Center—Nonmarket Based

Nonmarket-based transfer pricing techniques are based on a cost definition.[2] This includes opportunity cost, marginal cost, and cost plus.

Opportunity cost—represents benefits that are foregone as a result of not using other alternatives. An example is the return on investment on other possible project alternatives.

Illustration

To illustrate, let's assume the following facts for a company that manufactures two products, R and S:

Market price—Product R	$15
Variable cost—Product R	$6
Product S cannot be sold in the open market, but must be transferred to Division B	
Division A (before transfer)—variable costs for Product S	$5
Division B—additional variable costs	$4
Market price—Division B for Product S	$18

The above facts are summarized in Figure 12-1.

The total contribution margin for Product R is $1,400, with division A receiving the entire contribution because it manufactures and sells the product to the external market. The contribution margin for Product S is $1,800 ($2,800 − $1,000), which includes the ($1,000) loss from Division A and a profit of $2,800 from Division B.

If management is making an economic decision as to the profitability of Division A versus Division B, it would prefer to produce only Product R, since it makes a profit of $1,400, whereas Product S generates a loss of $1,000. It is therefore preferable to produce more units of Product R as opposed to producing Product S, which generates a loss. A solution to this dilemma is to establish a transfer price that is equal to the sum of the variable cost incurred by Division A on Product S and the opportunity cost of Product R.

The opportunity cost of Product S represents the contribution margin per unit of $5 that Division A does not generate when it produces Product S with manufacturing facilities that could be used to produce Product R. Figure 12-2 illustrates this point.

The company decision to continue producing Product S is based on the contribution margin. As long as the contribution margin of $1,800 is greater than any other opportunity, the decision to continue producing Product S is a sound decision.

FIGURE 12-1   Summary of Products R &S

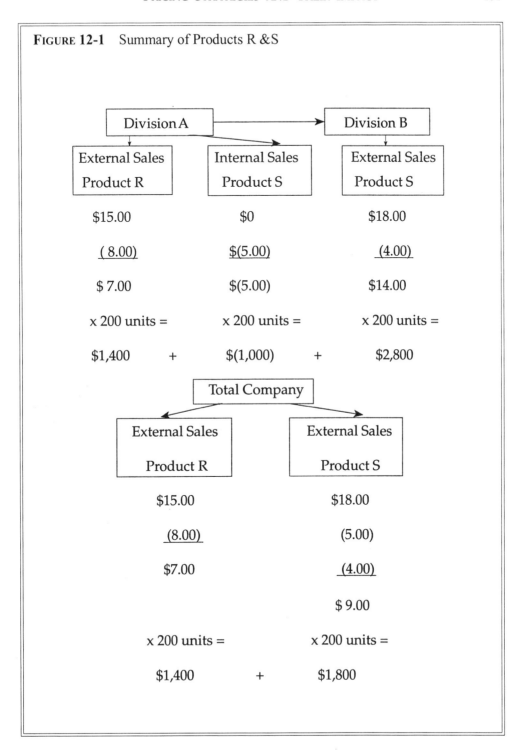

FIGURE 12-2   Illustration of Opportunity Cost Transfer Pricing

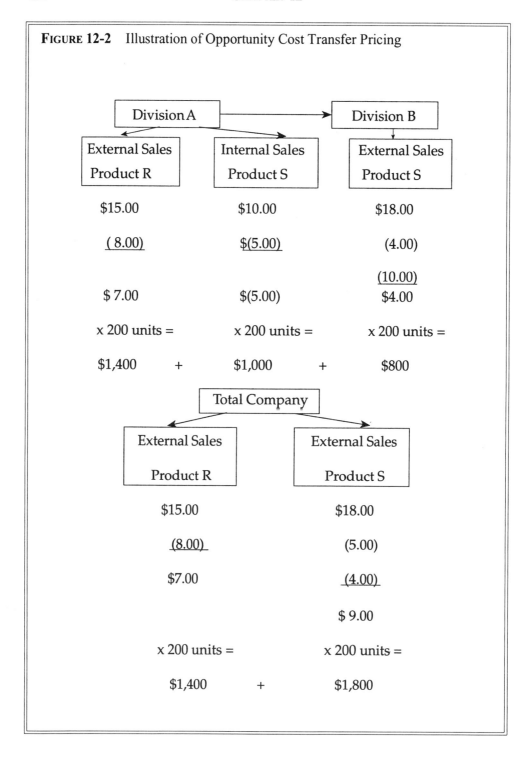

Marginal cost—see marginal approach discussed earlier in the chapter.

Cost plus—see markup approach to pricing discussed earlier in the chapter.

To be effective, a transfer pricing technique should promote profit maximization, have the ability to evaluate performance, and be a technique that is easy to understand. In any transfer pricing technique, the decision maker should consult experts to understand the tax effects of transfer pricing. This is true when transferring both domestic and international costs.

DECISION-MAKING STRATEGIES

- Establish different pricing strategies to coincide with marketing objectives and product/service life cycle.
- Measure impact of differing selling prices on profits and return on investment.
- Where pricing creates higher volume, determine the impact on storage and distribution facilities.
- Determine the effect of elasticity of price on supply and demand.
- If the selling price is dependent upon the production costs, develop a strategy to meet this reality.
- Tie pricing strategies into acceptable levels of return on investment.

NOTES

1. Benke, Ralph L. Jr., and James Don Edwards, *Transfer Pricing: Techniques and Uses,* Montvale, N.J.: ImA Foundation for Applied Research, Inc., © 1980, Ch. 3. Reprinted by permission.

2. Ibid., Ch. 4. Reprinted by permission.

13

How Cost Control Can Be Used to Achieve Higher Profits and ROI

At some point all businesspeople have asked themselves the questions "How much is it costing me to run my business?" and "How much can I afford to spend?" Answering these questions is an essential part of most business decisions. In fact, the answers are probably among the most important sets of numbers that a business needs in its day-to-day operations. For example, managers of a business need to know how much profit a product and/or product line is generating, how to evaluate managers' performance as they operate under certain cost standards, and, most of all, ways to improve profitability through cost control and generating efficiencies of scale.

As indicated in Chapter 12, pricing plays an important role in profitability and return on investment, as does cost control. Since "cost" is defined as an outlay of expenditure of monies needed to acquire goods or services, or in support of a function(s) in performing business activities, the end results are measured in terms of profits (revenues less costs). This profit becomes a key element in the ROI equation.

How Controlling Your Costs Increases ROI

Effective cost control requires constant review of costs to identify those areas that need corrective action. The key is to identify problem areas and to be able to isolate and direct all attention to those areas so that prompt action is taken not only to resolve the problem but to ensure that it does not arise again. Avoiding waste, labor inefficiencies, and administrative ex-

TABLE 13-1	Cost Savings Illustrated		
	Original	*Revised*	*Change*
Selling price	$10.00	$10.00	—
Cost of product	6.00	5.94	$0.06
Other costs	3.00	2.97	0.03
Income before income taxes	$ 1.00	$ 1.09	$0.09
Percentage of selling price	10.0%	10.9%	0.9%

penses disproportionate to the company's size contributes to the profit side of your company. The sensitivity of the costs of your products to profitability is easily demonstrated by the following illustration:

Selling price	$10
Cost of product	6
Other costs	3
Income before income taxes	$1
Percentage of selling price	10%

The illustration shows that for every unit sold a dollar will result in income before income taxes, or a 10% return for every unit sold.

Saving just 1% of the total cost of $9 ($6 + $3), or $0.09, would increase income before income taxes from 10% to 10.9%, as shown in Table 13-1. This 9% increase in profits, from $1 to $1.09, occurs without a sales price increase or higher volume. One can see that cost savings add substantially to the profitability of the product as well as to the company.

How to Identify a Cost Problem

One of the most important elements of controlling costs is the identification of the costs needing correction. There are many ways to establish guidelines that will enable you to recognize that costs are "out of line." They include industry averages, historical performance, percentages, and standards.

Industry Averages

A useful way of determining whether your costs are within standard guidelines is to use industry averages. These averages can be obtained from trade associations, certain firms that report specific financial data by industry, annual reports, 10Ks, or any other available source. Many of these data are available as percentages of sales for each of the major expense classifications. In some cases, data are broken down by the size of the business in such terms as number of employees, sales volume, and assets employed. Comparing your percentages to industry averages will provide some guidance as to where you need to spend some time in analyzing and controlling costs.

Historical Performance

Probably the easiest and most beneficial approach is to observe trends in historical performance. Be careful to use comparable periods before drawing any conclusions. For example, it is best to compare like months or like seasons, since certain expenses would affect the percentage relationships given different levels of volume. In addition, be sure that you are taking into consideration the same number of working days if sales are dependent on working days. One way to solve this problem is to use the same period, such as a thirteen-week quarter. With holidays falling out on different days, using a thirteen-week quarter will generally give you the same amount of working days from like quarter to like quarter.

Percentages

Another way of recognizing excessive costs is to develop a statement that shows percentage relationships between each expense category and net sales. You must recognize, however, that certain costs will increase with higher volumes but will remain at a constant percentage. These costs are variable and increase in the same proportion with volume. For example, in the statement of income shown in Table 13-2, cost of sales dollars increased $150,000 ($375,000 to $525,000) from 19X1 to 19X2 due to higher sales volume but the percentage relationship remained at 75%. In other words, every sales dollar required $0.75 of costs, thus leaving $0.25 to recover all the other costs and still generate an adequate profit.

In reviewing the cost of sales, it is important to determine whether you are in a competitive market with your pricing and whether your costs of producing the product are in line with sales prices of your competitors. You can draw several conclusions from analyzing the cost of sales. When comparing cost of sales as a percentage of net sales, the following rules apply:

TABLE 13-2   The Great Company, Inc.
Statement of Income
19X1 versus 19X2 (in $1,000s)

	19X1		19X2	
	$	*%*	*$*	*%*
Net sales	500	100.0	700	100.0
Cost of sales	375	75.0	525	75.0
Gross profit	125	25.0	175	25.0
Other Operating Expenses				
Depreciation	5	1.0	5	0.7
Salaries—management	20	4.0	25	3.6
Salaries—sales	8	1.6	9	1.3
Salaries—other	7	1.4	8	1.1
Rent	3	0.6	4	0.7
Interest	1	0.2	2	0.3
Bad debts	1	0.2	1	0.1
Advertising	3	0.6	4	0.7
Employee benefits	2	0.4	3	0.4
Payroll taxes	2	0.4	3	0.4
Utilities	2	0.4	3	0.4
Travel and entertainment	2	0.4	3	0.4
Shipping	1	0.2	2	0.3
Telephone	1	0.2	2	0.3
Insurance	1	0.2	1	0.1
Supplies	1	0.2	1	0.1
Other	1	0.2	1	0.1
Total other operating expenses	61	12.2	77	11.0
Income before income taxes	64	12.8	98	14.0

- High cost of sales and competitive prices. *Conclusion*—the cost of purchasing materials is too high.
- Low cost of sales and high prices. *Conclusion*—the high prices are creating the favorable low cost of sales, and no problem exists in the cost of purchasing.

Also note that although other operating expenses increased from $61,000 to $77,000, the percentage to net sales decreased from 12.2% to 11% due to fixed costs being spread over more volume, thus reducing the percentage relationship. One can see this in the salary accounts, which are fixed regardless of sales volume. A more favorable analysis would be to measure fixed expenses in total dollars from period to period to avoid the false conclusion that certain fixed expenses as a percentage of net sales are decreasing. In fact, this may not be true. Over long periods, however, a conclusion may be reached even using percentages when comparing these figures to industry averages.

Standards

Another method of controlling costs is to establish standards for each element of expense. A format similar to that of a statement of income can be compiled using realistic standards as to what the elements of the statement of income would look like in a future period if everything materialized as planned. From a practical point of view, however, there will be differences in certain cost elements as well as in revenue projections. By analyzing the major unfavorable variances, you will begin to uncover areas that need explanation and control.

CONTROLLING MANUFACTURING COSTS

Because manufacturing expenses account for a large portion of the total costs, it is important to concentrate on controlling these costs. The manufacturing cost of a product breaks down into three basic components: direct materials, direct labor, and manufacturing overhead or burden.

Direct Materials

Direct materials represent those that are used to manufacture a product and that ultimately become part of that product. They also can be identified and traced to a specific finished product. Direct materials can be raw materials, any finished components, or other materials used for the overall completion of the product, such as paint. Most companies know how many direct materials are required to product a unit. Therefore, the important factors are the controlling of material requisitions and the elimination of waste. Consideration should also be given to looking for cheaper substitute materials or components as a way of saving costs.

Direct Labor

Direct labor represents the amount of labor and cost needed to convert the materials used into a finished product. Labor standards are established for each operation so that an overall labor cost can be developed. In addition, such devices as time-and-motion studies and rate charts, as well as previous experience, will provide data for accurately establishing these standards. Problem areas that increase labor costs and therefore need controlling are excessive time spent in loitering, inefficient floor layout, tardiness, improper scheduling, absenteeism, poor quality standards, and uneven flow of production lines.

Manufacturing Overhead

These are costs of manufacturing the product other than direct materials and direct labor. They are indirectly used in the manufacturing process and therefore are sometimes called indirect costs because they are not part of the finished product. For example, maintenance, machine supplies, janitorial service, telephone service, clerical support, and property insurance support the manufacturing process. Many of these expenses are difficult to control because they do not coincide with volume levels. But guidelines can be established for controlling these costs. Let us look at these guidelines and some possible solutions.

Labor. The best way to control labor costs is through proper training and development of your employees. This includes using the right employees for jobs that are in keeping with their qualifications and responsibilities.

Supplies. Such costs can best be controlled by keeping tight control on requisitioned supplies. Know how long certain supplies should last for their given functions, and always know why they are being requested and how valid the request may be. In addition, always check for possible salvage value of supplies that are being replaced, and look for use in other parts of the company.

Tools. Always order tools that are projected to have long lives. Maintain and repair tools properly to ensure longer life. A major factor in controlling tool costs is to establish policies and procedures against loss and theft.

Utilities. Always practice light, power, heat, air-conditioning, and water conservation. Where possible, a utility conservation program should be established that will inform and remind employees of such conservation measures as turning off lights, keeping windows and doors closed when heat or air-conditioning is on, turning off unused equipment, and keeping room temperatures at an acceptable level.

Other. Other steps such as proper maintenance programs, fire protection, safety, pollution control, and housekeeping will assist in controlling costs and thus increase profits.

CONTROLLING SEGMENTS OF THE BUSINESS

Expenses can be more easily controlled by breaking down the business into controllable segments. These segments can take the form of profit centers and cost centers. These centers can be controlled by careful analysis of the activity in each. Even though you may operate a single product operation or a single location, this type of analysis could be valuable even if you establish only several cost centers.

Profit Centers

Establishing profit centers divides the business into business units responsible for generating income and cost expenditures. The typical profit center segments shown in Table 13-3 are examples.

An analysis by region, district, customer, store, department, division, and so forth can be developed in a similar way to that presented in the table. Each of the profit centers would have its own budgeted revenues and expenses, and analysis could be made at least monthly and, in some cases, weekly. Each profit center would have a responsible individual whose job would be to make sure that agreed upon objectives are accomplished. The responsibility of both generating revenues and controlling costs would rest with this individual. In some instances, a business may decide to eliminate or consolidate profit centers when activity is too low or when the business changes in such a way that separate centers are no longer needed.

Cost Centers

Cost centers represent segments of the business that incur costs but that do not generate revenue. Without the generation of revenues, individuals with

TABLE 13-3	Operating Income by Product Line Format			
		Product		
	A	*B*	*C*	*Total*
Net sales				
Cost of sales				
Gross profit				
Operating expenses				
Selling expenses (list)				
Administrative expenses (list)				
Allocated expenses (list)				
Other expenses (list)				
Total				
Operating income				

responsibility for profits cannot be held accountable. However, it must be recognized that within profit centers there can be many cost centers. These centers are controlled by establishing cost budgets and are monitored by a total monthly review. Such cost centers include the accounting departments, financial departments, administrative departments, shipping departments, and any other support department not directly involved in generating revenue.

CHECKLIST OF TYPES OF COSTS

There are many different types of costs and definitions of costs, and each is influenced by a different segment of the business. Some costs are influenced by the nature of the activity, some are traceable by segment of a business, some are associated with products, and still others are based on the passage of time. One can see that understanding costs takes some basic knowledge of the various concepts. The types of costs are as follows:

Period costs are costs that are incurred as a function of time as opposed to level of activity. An example would be executive salaries paid over periods of time, advertising, and interest.

Variable costs are costs that change in direct proportion to levels of activity. Examples are direct labor, direct materials, and utilities that are based on usage.

Fixed costs are costs that do not fluctuate as levels of activity vary. Examples are fixed interest payments, insurance, and property taxes.

Controllable costs are costs influenced by management during a specific period of time.

Indirect costs are costs not directly traceable to a specific unit of production.

Programmed costs, or *discretionary costs,* are costs that result from specific decisions, without any consideration given to volume activity or passage of time. Examples would be the costs of research and development projects and replacing carpeting in an administrative office.

Product costs are production costs that relate to the product's unit output and are charged to the product's cost when it is sold. Examples are the materials and labor used in manufacturing the product.

Assignable costs are all costs incurred by a specific project, such as an advertising campaign for a specific product or segment of the business.

Unassignable costs are those that cannot be directly traced to a specific product and/or segment of the business without arbitrarily allocating the cost. For example, certain administrative expenses must be allocated based on acceptable guidelines.

Opportunity costs represent benefits that are foregone as a result of not using other alternatives. An example is the return on investment on other possible project alternatives.

Out-of-pocket costs are those that require cash outlays either currently or in the future. An example would be taking a client out for lunch. The amount paid for lunch is an out-of-pocket cost.

Sunk costs are costs incurred in prior periods. An example is the purchase of an asset such as an automobile.

Book costs are those in which accounting allocations of prior expenditures were made to the current period.

Standard costs are anticipated or predetermined costs of producing a unit of output under given conditions. For example, standards are established for material and labor costs.

Job order costing is a method of organizing costs that accumulates costs of an identifiable product, known as a job, and follows the product through the production stages.

Process costing is a method of organizing costs that accumulates costs by a process or operation as it flows through production.

For further discussions on full and direct costing, see chapter 14.

It is evident that many different terms are applied to costs, and each is used to define a different controllable segment of the business. Let us review some of the costing applications by first looking at standard costing.

STANDARD COSTING VARIANCES

As was previously explained, standard costing uses anticipated or predetermined costs of producing a unit of output. Given certain standards, it is necessary to compute the favorable or unfavorable variances that affect the cost of manufacturing the product. Let us look at two of the major items, namely, material and labor.

How to Compute Material Variances

Assume that the standard cost of material is $10 per unit, based on estimated costs from suppliers. Remember that these standards will have been prepared in advance of the actual purchase date. At the time of purchase, the company bought 10,000 units of materials at a unit price of $11 because of an increase in the price of raw materials. Given these facts, it is clear that there was an unfavorable variance to the standard of $10,000, computed as follows:

$$
\begin{array}{ll}
\text{Purchase price} - 10{,}000 \text{ units} \times \$11 = & \$110{,}000 \\
\text{Standard} - 10{,}000 \text{ units} \times \$10 = & \underline{\$100{,}000} \\
\text{Unfavorable material variance} & \$10{,}000
\end{array}
$$

The material variance of $10,000 is unfavorable because it cost $1 more per unit of material as compared to the predetermined standard of $10.

Now that we have computed the material variance, we need to reflect on the material quantity variance, which is computed at the time the raw materials are used. Assume that 8,000 units were estimated as a standard quantity for production. Actual units used were 9,000. What is the quantity variance?

$$
\begin{array}{ll}
\text{Actual usage} - 9{,}000 \text{ units} \times \$10 = & \$90{,}000 \\
\text{Standard} - 8{,}000 \text{ units} \times \$10 = & \$80{,}000 \\
\text{Unfavorable quantity variance} & \$10{,}000
\end{array}
$$

You can see that 1,000 more units of material were used, and at the standard cost rate of $10 per unit, an unfavorable quantity variance of $10,000 materialized.

Taking both variances into account, the total material variance of $20,000 resulted because of higher raw material unit prices and more material used in the manufacturing of the product. In both cases, this comparison was made to a predetermined amount, or a standard cost.

How to Compute Labor Variances

The labor variances comprise two factors: rate and efficiency. Together they form the labor variance from the standard previously assigned. To illustrate, let us use the following data for both calculations:

	Standards	*Actuals*
Number of hours	5,000	5,200
Wage rate per hour	$6.00	$5.50

Let us compute the labor rate variance first.

$$
\begin{array}{ll}
\text{5,200 hours at \$6.00} & = \ \$31,200 \\
\text{5,200 hours at \$5.50} & = \ \underline{\$28,600} \\
\text{Favorable labor rate} & \\
\quad \text{variance} & \quad \ \$\ 2,600
\end{array}
$$

The variance is favorable because of the lower wage rate of $5.50. If you multiply $0.50 (the difference) times 5,200 hours, you will arrive at the same favorable variance of $2,600.

The labor efficiency deals with the efficiency of labor hours actually used versus estimated labor hours. By keeping the labor rate at standard, the variance is calculated as follows:

$$
\begin{array}{ll}
\text{5,200 hours at \$6} & = \ \$31,200 \\
\text{5,000 hours at \$6} & = \ \underline{\$30,000} \\
\text{Unfavorable labor} & \\
\quad \text{efficiency variance} & \ \$\ 1,200
\end{array}
$$

The unfavorable variance of $1,200 is due to 200 more hours having been worked. At a rate of $6 per hour, a $1,200 unfavorable labor efficiency rate resulted.

By combining both labor rate and labor efficiency variances, the total labor variances are favorable by $1,400 ($2,600 − $1,200).

TABLE 13-4	Data for Analyzing Gross Profit		
	19X1	*19X2*	*Variance*
Units sold	75,000	100,000	25,000
Net sales	$500,000	$700,000	$200,000
Per unit	$6.67	$7.00	$0.33
Cost of sales	$390,000	$525,000	($135,000)
Per unit	$5.20	$5.25	($0.05)
Gross profit	$110,000	$175,000	$ 65,000
Percentage of net sales	22.0%	25.0%	3.0%

GROSS PROFIT VARIANCES

Now that two of the major elements of manufacturing a product, namely, material and labor, have been reviewed, it is fitting to explore the variances and affect gross profit. As explained previously, gross profit, or net sales less cost of sales, provides the dollars from which all other expenses are to be paid, still generating an adequate return to the owners. It is extremely important to understand what factors affect gross profit and what one can do about improving the gross profit results. This is perhaps one of the most important figures in the statement of income. Remember that it is this amount that will pay for the distribution costs, general and administrative costs, other operating costs, and taxes, yet still provide a company with that adequate return it desires.

Let us use Table 13-4 to illustrate how to analyze gross profit. One of the key factors is the gross profit percentage. The table shows that this percentage for year 19X1 was 22% and for year 19X2, 25%. This means that $0.22 and $0.25, respectively, are available for paying the other operating costs of the business and for providing an adequate return.

Also note that net sales increased $200,000 as a result of the higher volume of 25,000 units and the slightly higher average selling price of $0.33. Because both sales volume and sales price are affected, we need to calculate a sales volume variance and a sales price variance.

Sales Volume Variance

Part of the change in net sales from one period to another is caused by changes in the number of units sold. To reflect the impact of units sold on dollar net sales, the 19X1 selling price must be kept constant, with units sold being variable. The calculation is as follows:

19X2 units sold at		
19X1 unit prices		
100,000 times $6.67	=	$667,000
19X1 units sold at		
19X1 unit prices		
75,000 times $6.67	=	$500,250
Favorable sales volume variance		$166,750

Sales Price Variance

The other factor affecting net sales is price. By keeping 19X2 unit sales constant and calculating changes in unit selling price, the following calculation results:

19X2 units sold at		
19X2 unit selling price		
100,000 times $7.00	=	$700,000
19X2 units sold at		
19X1 unit selling price		
100,000 times $6.67	=	$667,000
Favorable sales price variance		$33,000

Note that, combining both variances, the total change is $200,000, the same amount of variance as shown on the original data.

Change in net sales	$200,000
Sales volume variance	$166,750
Sales price variance	$33,000
Rounding difference	$250

Cost of sales increased $135,000 because of higher unit costs of $.05 and will be referred to as the "cost price variance." In addition, unit volume increased 25,000 units and will be referred to as a "cost volume variance." Because both volume and cost affects cost of sales, let us calculate both variances.

Cost Volume Variance

By keeping the 19X1 unit cost of sales constant and reflecting changes in unit volume, the cost volume variance is calculated as follows:

19X2 units sold at		
19X1 unit cost of sales		
100,000 times $5.20	=	$520,000
19X1 units sold at		
19X1 unit cost of sales		
75,000 times $5.20	=	$390,000
Unfavorable cost volume variance		($130,000)

Cost Price Variance

This variance is used to measure changes in the cost of the product. It is calculated as follows:

19X2 units sold at		
19X2 unit cost of sales		
100,000 times $5.25	=	$525,000
19X2 units sold at		
19X1 unit cost of sales		
100,000 times $5.20	=	$520,000
Unfavorable cost price variance		($5,000)

Combining both cost variances results in the total cost of sales variance of $135,000, as follows:

Change in cost of sales	($135,000)
Cost volume variance	($130,000)
Cost price variance	($5,000)

Summary of Gross Profit Analysis

An explanation of the $65,000 gross profit variance from period 19X1 to 19X2 is summarized in Table 13-5. Note how each variance previously calculated has an impact upon the gross margin.

TABLE 13-5	Summary of Gross Margin Analysis	
	Variance Calculations	*Variances from Original Data*
Net sales		$200,000
Sales volume variance	$166,750	
Sales price variance	33,000	
Rounding difference	250	
Cost of sales		(135,000)
Cost volume variance	(130,000)	
Cost price variance	(5,000)	
Gross profit		$ 65,000

It is clear that an understanding of costs in a business will provide the awareness of, and in many cases the answers to, decisions that must be made in order that the business remain healthy and profitable. It is not suggested that you become familiar with all the skills of a cost accountant, but rather that you develop a clear understanding of how your costs affect your financial outcome. Such an understanding is a necessary tool not only for controlling your business in the present but also for planning for the future. Ultimately, the business will reflect higher return on investment rates.

DECISION-MAKING STRATEGIES

- Develop a checklist for identifying cost control problems.
- Establish standards for controlling individual expenses.
- Classify all costs into different types (e.g., period, variable, indirect) for use in decision making and impact on return on investment results.
- Determine how volume, price, and cost variances affect profitability.
- Improve human resource productivity.
- Develop a formal cost control program.

14

THE IMPACT OF DIRECT VERSUS FULL-ABSORPTION COSTING ON ROI DECISIONS

In Chapter 13, costs were defined in many ways. Two terms were briefly defined that relate to methods of costing. They were direct costing and full-absorption costing. It is important to understand the two costing methods, since they are commonly used in business as alternatives in the recording of product income and product costs for management decision making. The basic difference between the two methods is how the fixed manufacturing overhead is recorded in the evaluation of inventory. Under full-absorption costing, the fixed manufacturing overhead is part of the inventory cost. Under direct costing, it is not part of the inventory value. Let us explore the two concepts in further detail and see their influence on the profitability rate, or operating profit as a percentage of net sales.

USING THE FULL-ABSORPTION COSTING METHOD

The full-absorption costing method is the more traditional method and is more widely used, since it is required for external reporting and for tax purposes. Therefore, data are easily available using the existing traditional accounting records. It includes all manufacturing costs, both variable and fixed, for all units that are produced on a functional basis. As can be seen in Table 14-1, no mention is made of fixed and variable costs by product directly. They are, however, included in the functional areas of components of cost of sales and in the other operating expenses, such as selling and

| TABLE 14-1 | Illustration of the Full-Absorption Costing Method |
| The Great Company, Inc. |
| Statement of Income 19X2 |

| | Product | | | |
	A	B	C	Total
Net sales	$130,000	$400,000	$170,000	$700,000
Cost of sales	100,000	290,000	135,000	525,000
Gross profit	$ 30,000	$110,000	$ 35,000	$175,000
Percentage of net sales	23.1%	27.5%	20.6%	25.0%
Other operating expenses				
Depreciation	$ 900	$ 2,700	$ 1,400	$ 5,000
Selling expenses	5,700	17,000	7,300	30,000
Administrative expenses	4,700	14,000	6,300	25,000
General expenses	2,800	8,500	3,700	15,000
Total	$ 14,100	$ 42,200	$ 18,700	$ 75,000
Operating income	$ 15,900	$ 67,800	$ 16,300	$100,000
Percentage of net sales	12.2%	17.0%	9.6%	14.3%

administrative and general expenses. It is therefore difficult to apply any volume, cost, or profit analysis of various alternatives since variable and fixed expenses are not clearly identified. The other disadvantages result from not being able to measure profit performance for segments of the company and the lack of motivation to control costs that may be transferred to other segments of the company.

Note that no contribution margin is shown in the table. Such a margin is important as a management tool for two reasons. First, it will assist a company in analyzing product performance and will indicate which products require more effort and which may be candidates for elimination. Second, it gives a company the ability to see the effects of alternative decisions on different product lines and on the total company. For example, such decisions include those relating to sales mix, changes in advertising expenditures, alternative methods of acquiring inventory, pricing, and others that relate to product performance.

Also note that fixed and variable costs are not identified by product in all of the major account classifications shown in the table. The costs are not period costs but are considered as part of the product. Also note that the manufacturing overhead costs are not reflected in the statement of income until the product is sold because the costs are still part of the cost of inventory. This costing method does present some problems in understanding the behavior of costs because it does not enable managers to simulate "what if's" on the impact of profit using various alternative decisions.

USING THE DIRECT COSTING METHOD

Direct costing is sometimes referred to as variable costing because it applies only the variable portion of production costs to the product costs. This costing method will give an executive a better understanding of how costs behave by segmenting costs into both variable and fixed and by providing a product contribution for each product. As previously explained, this product contribution is a valuable tool in operating the business.

Taking the same set of data used in Table 14-1 for full-absorption costing, the statement of income in Table 14-2 reflects a direct costing approach. This statement is to be used for internal purposes only and is not acceptable as an external statement for reporting financial results.

Note that the costs are identified by product and are charged in the period in which the costs were incurred. Therefore, profits are more directly related to sales. Under this method, a product contribution is established for each product, thus giving information as to each product's contribution. Decisions can then be reached as to expanding, continuing, or eliminating a product or product line. This same analysis can be used to measure sales segments such as branches, districts, and regions, as well as individual performance for salespersons and sales executives.

Profit Differences

With direct costing, profits by product will vary because of the timing of the charging of fixed factory overhead to the statement of income. As pointed out previously, in using full-absorption costing, this expense is charged to inventory and is not reflected on the statement of income until such time as the inventory is sold. Therefore, it becomes part of the cost of sales. On the other hand, with direct costing, fixed factory overhead is included as an expense immediately, and only the variable cost is included in the cost of inventory.

The two methods will show differences in reported profits as to levels of sales volume and production. For example, when production is higher than sales, higher profits are reported using full-absorption costing. When sales are

TABLE 14-2   Illustration of Using Direct Costing
                   The Great Company, Inc.
                   Statement of Income 19X2

	Product			
	A	*B*	*C*	*Total*
Net sales	$130,000	$400,000	$170,000	$700,000
Variable cost of sales				
Manufacturing	$ 90,000	$276,000	$ 98,000	$464,000
Selling	3,200	8,300	4,500	16,000
Total	$ 93,200	$284,300	$102,500	$480,000
Variable contribution	$ 36,800	$115,700	$ 67,500	$220,000
Percentage of net sales	28.3%	28.9%	39.7%	31.4%
Direct fixed expenses	3,300	6,500	4,200	14,000
Product contribution	$ 33,500	$109,200	$ 63,300	$206,000
Percentage of net sales	25.8%	27.3%	37.2%	29.4%
Indirect fixed expenses				
Manufacturing				$ 66,000
Selling				—
Administrative				25,000
General				15,000
Total				106,000
Operating income				$100,000
Percentage of net sales				14.3%

higher than production, higher profits are reported using direct costing. Other conditions exist that will also change reported profits under the different costing methods. In cases where sales and production are equal, both costing methods will generally reflect the same profits. Also, over long periods, differences in reported profits will level off or will become less significant.

Using Direct Costing for Decision Making

You may begin to see the many advantages to using direct costing for many important decisions in operating a business. Using this method for internal

TABLE 14-3   Comparison of Gross Profits Using Different Costing Methods

	Absorption Costing	Direct Costing	Difference
Projected unit sales	10,000	10,000	—
Projected unit price	$7.00	$7.00	—
Projected sales dollars	$70,000	$70,000	—
Manufacturing cost	$52,500	$47,000	$5,500
Gross profit	$17,500	$23,000	$5,500
Percentage of sales dollars	25.0%	32.9%	7.9%

reporting will assist a company in knowing more about the product costs and in the following:

- Marketing decisions to be made relative to sales mix, since this method is a function of sales volume.
- Distinguishing differences between fixed and variable costs in manufacturing, selling, general, and administrative costs.
- Avoiding the need to establish any basis for allocating fixed expenses and thereby eliminating the tedious allocation of expenses and sometimes the inequities of these allocated expenses.
- Establishing a method of responsibility reporting based on controllable cost data.

Exercise caution when using this method for pricing decisions. Since not all costs are charged to the product, it is important to keep in mind that other costs are involved and must be recognized in the costing structure when applying it to a pricing decision. You may create an underpricing condition because direct costing takes into consideration only direct costs and may understate the product's cost and inflate product margins. You cannot change costing methods to calculate prices because different costing methods will give the reviewer different conclusions. Let us use the illustration in Table 14-3 to make this point.

The two methods result in differing gross profits and percentages. This differential in gross profit can mean the difference between a profit and loss when other expenses are applied to the gross profit in the short term.

HOW DIFFERENT ASSUMPTIONS CAN
IMPACT OPERATING DECISIONS

As indicated, direct costing represents an excellent tool for showing how certain decisions will affect the overall profitability of a company and return on investment. By separating fixed and variable costs, an executive can see how costs behave by identifying product costs. Therefore, it is possible to simulate business decisions by changing various segments for different products to see how these decisions affect the profitability of the company. This planning mechanism will show how best to utilize the resources that make up the product mix of the company.

In order to show the effects, certain simulated decisions will be presented and increases or decreases to product contribution will result using the data from Table 14-2. Additions to operating income will be accepted, and subtractions to operating income will be rejected. The data will reflect the statement of income previously developed using the direct costing method. Let us look at a sampling of selected operating decisions and observe the impact on operating income.

Assumption 1. You would like to increase indirect administrative expenses by 10%. To offset this additional cost, you will increase the sales revenues of product B, your best-selling product, by 5% and maintain the same product contribution percentage of 27.3%.

Increase indirect administrative expenses	
($25,000 × .10)	($2,500)
Increase product B sales revenues	
($400,000 × .05 × .273)	$5,460
Increase in product contribution	$2,960

Assumption 2. To increase sales revenues by 10% on product A, you must decrease your selling by 5%.

Lower selling price for product A	($6,500)
Increase product A sales revenues	
($130,000 - $6,500 of sales at 10%	
increase in sales [$12,350] at a product	
contribution rate of 21.9%, which was	
recalculated using the new net sales figure)	$2,705
Decrease in product contribution	($3,795)

Assumption 3. You would like to increase sales revenues of product C by 20% and decrease sales revenues of product A by 8% using the same product contribution percentage.

Increase product C sales revenues by 20%	
($34,000 × .372)	$12,648
Decrease product A sales revenues by 8%	
($10,400 × .258)	($2,683)
Increase in product contribution	$9,965

Assumption 4. You would like to shift the sales revenues of products A and B to product C, which is more profitable. You estimate that you can shift 15% of the sales revenues of products A and B, without any customer problems, to product C, which has an expanding marketplace, and still maintain the same product contribution percentage.

Lower product A sales revenues	
($19,500 × .258)	($5,031)
Lower product B sales revenues	
($60,000 × .273)	($16,380)
Increase product C sales revenues	
($79,500 × .372)	$29,574
Increase in product contribution	$ 8,163

Summary of Impact on Operating Income

The preceding simulated assumptions and their impact on product contribution are summarized in Table 14-4. It is recognized that, from a practical point of view, all these assumptions would not occur at the same time. Nevertheless, they do illustrate the advantages of calculating the impact on product contribution of "what if" assumptions using data from a direct costing statement.

The only assumption that should be rejected is assumption 2, because it will have a negative effect on product contribution. The other three assumptions will contribute $21,088 to product contribution. If we were to add this additional product contribution to the original operating income as shown on page 186, a substantial return on net sales would materialize:

	See Table 14.2	Revised	Change
Net sales	$700,000	$749,450	$49,450
Operating income	100,000	121,088	21,088
Percentage of net sales	14.3%	16.2%	1.9%

Additional net sales ($49,450) due to the previous assumptions are shown in Table 14-5. The return on net sales has increased 1.9 percentage points, which reflects the four simulated assumptions.

TABLE 14-4   Summary of Impact on Operating Income

Assumptions	Impact on Product Contribution	Accepted or Rejected
1	$ 2,960	Accepted
2	(3,795)	Rejected
3	9,965	Accepted
4	8,163	Accepted
Total	$17,293	

TABLE 14-5   Summary of Additional Sales Based on Assumptions

	Product			
Assumptions	A	B	C	Total
1		$20,000		$20,000
2	$ 5,850			5,850
3	(10,400)		$ 34,000	23,600
4	(19,500)	(60,000)	79,500	—
Total	($24,050)	($40,000)	$113,500	$49,450

What has been demonstrated is the value of using direct costing as a method of simulating the impact of certain operating decisions. An understanding of the differences between fixed and variable costs is a much needed tool for any company. It will assist in making many managerial decisions needed to operate the business.

DECISION-MAKING STRATEGIES

- Utilize direct costing method for establishing profitability rate objectives.
- Use different assumptions to project the impact on product contribution.
- Determine policy for allocating of company overhead to operating divisions.

15

HOW TO APPLY ACTIVITY-BASED COSTING FOR IMPROVING ROI

Activity-based costing (ABC) approaches a strategy based on a customer's needs and the competition between various services of a company. The link between activity-based costing and return on investment is based on providing a more effective way of measuring and allocating resources to effectively increase earnings and, thus, return on investment performance.

We saw in the previous chapter how direct and absorption costing differs from conventional accounting principles. For example, under absorption costing, more overhead expenses are allocated as production increases. This is in spite of those products produced that may need a greater proportion of overhead expenses from service departments such as engineering and purchasing. To overcome this inequity, activity-based costing associates costs with specific activities used to create these costs. It is based on the idea that any good or service needs organizational structures to perform the necessary activities, which in turn incur costs. This costing system recognizes costs that are not directly attributed to the flow of a product/service into a required activity. The cost of each activity eventually flows into the product cost.

AN EXAMPLE OF ALLOCATING INDIRECT COSTS USING ACTIVITY-BASED COSTING

ABC costing uses a different method of allocating indirect costs. It assigns direct costs to specific production units, and indirect costs based only on direct labor hours or the volume of production.

Illustration

For example, let's assume the following facts for an engineering department:

Engineering Department

Monthly direct labor - Product X	$30,000
Monthly direct labor - Product Y	$30,000
Engineering department overhead	$ 6,000
Engineering department effort - Product X	70%
Engineering department effort - Product Y	30%

Note: The total direct labor of both product X and Y is $60,000, and the cost of operating the engineering department is $6,000. Also note that the amount of effort needed to service product X is 70% of the total cost of operating the department, or $4,200 ($6,000 times .70), and the cost needed to service product Y is $1,800 ($6,000 times .30).

Under traditional cost accounting systems, the allocation of the overhead for the engineering department would be calculated by dividing the department overhead ($6,000) by the total direct labor ($60,000), resulting in an overhead rate of 10%. This 10% overhead rate would be applied to each product's direct labor of $30,000, thus resulting in a $3,000 allocation of indirect overhead costs to each product.

As stated above, using the ABC method, $4,200 would be allocated to product X, and $1,800 to product Y. The following summarizes the allocation of the indirect overhead for the engineering department using the traditional cost accounting method versus the activity-based costing method.

	Traditional Costing	ABC Method	Difference
Product X	$3,000	$4,200	$ 1,200
Product Y	3,000	1,800	(1,200)
	$6,000	$6,000	0

You can see that both methods allocate the total indirect overhead costs, but are different between products. This could easily change the decisions determining the price of a product and the expected contribution rate for each product.[1]

DEFINING ACTIVITY-BASED COSTING

To fully understand activity-based costing, it is important to define the terms used. They include:

The Five Categories of Activities

These categories represent a series of related processes or procedures that work together toward a common need of the organization that is needed by a particular work unit. This work unit, in order to accomplish its objective, has many activity centers that work together and create work. For example, in reviewing an accounts receivable department, activities may include establishing over credit policies and procedures, establishing credit limits on customers, invoicing the customer, filing and collecting the invoices, depositing and reconciling cash receipts, follow-up letters on past-due accounts, entering credit data into the computer, coding and recording the necessary accounting journal entries, and auditing these invoices. While all these activities may appear minute to a large organization, they may represent significant activities in small organizations. The activities of an accounts receivable department form the basis of what is referred to as an activity center.

There are five different categories of activities. They include:[2]

Service activities provide services for other activities within the business or outside the business as needed. For example, referring to the prior example of an engineering department, this department may support other operating units, such as research and development cost structures for new products, and perform outside services to customers on a billable basis. Regardless of where the support is given, they can be billed out on a project or hourly basis.

Operation support activities provide service activities in support of other activities. They differ from service activities in that they are not identifiable and are not charged directly to products or services. It is not practical to charge these costs, since they benefit an overall activity. An activity such as production scheduling is an excellent example. This activity manages and monitors production scheduling to optimize productivity. It does not manage and monitor specific projects. Therefore, it would be impractical to bill the cost of the activity to a specific product.

Administrative support activities provide support for the overall managing and administering of an organization. Such activities include accounting, finance, sales, human resources, payroll, and overall administrative costs.

Product/customer support activities are identified with specific products, product lines, and customers. For example, let's assume a company has 100 customers. Each customer accounted for approximately 1% of its sales. The company had a group that administered support to the sales effort. Assuming 80% of the activity's time was spent on 20 customers, then two activity groups would be needed, one to accumulate and distribute costs to the 20 customers and one to accumulate and distribute costs to the 80 customers.

Operating and process activities are insignificant cost activities that are part of producing a product/service. They are usually behind-the-scene activities such as in a warehouse, where receiving, put-away, picking orders, packaging, and shipping take place.

In classifying activity categories, it is important to review how each activity becomes part of the overall organization when developing a cost system.

Cost Objectives and Their Four Categories

Cost objectives can be classified as final cost or interim cost objectives.[3] In both cases, they represent an accumulation of costs to meet an end objective. For example, final cost objectives are products/services that are provided to customers such as a finished product or engineering service that eventually transfers ownership outside the organization with accumulated costs being matched to revenues generated.

Interim cost objectives are accumulated costs charged elsewhere within the company, such as tooling costs used to manufacture products, and are accumulated and later capitalized and amortized.

Costs can be grouped in four categories. They include:[4]

Throughput related costs These represent nonpayroll costs and are traceable to a specific product/service. They can be treated either as direct or indirect costs. Examples of direct costs include fees paid for witness fees in legal proceedings, as well as title search fees paid to an outside company for processing a real estate loan. An indirect cost would include temporary materials applied to a product that does not become part of the finished product. Such a cost would include coating materials applied to a part before it is extruded or forged.

Salaries and wages include all gross payroll costs such as salaries, bonuses, overtime, and paid benefits such as vacations and sick leave.

Purchased fringe benefits These are other payroll costs not included above, such as employee insurance, payroll taxes, and pension contributions.

Specific assignment costs All other costs not included above, such as depreciation, leases, insurance premiums, and utilities.

Six Common Cost Drivers

A cost driver is the "factor used to measure how a cost is incurred and/or how best to charge the cost to activities or products."[5] It determines where and how to charge costs. Some commonly used cost drivers are grouped as follows:

Labor group Determines the primary cause of some element of labor that creates an activity cost. Includes such costs as labor dollars, labor hours, and head count.

Operating time group Represents the elements of time, such as the time spent on an operating line, machine time, and the amount of time within an operating cycle.

Throughput group Represents a measurement of units as a primary cause of an activity's cost. Such unit measurements as pieces, tons, truck-loads, tankerloads, and the like are examples.

Occupancy group Based on distributing fixed costs on physical location of activities or assets. Examples include building and equipment depreciation, real property taxes, and so on, where costs are based on square footage, location, and evaluation of equipment.

Demand Based on the demand for an activity's service. The most common example is maintenance where these costs are distributed to those activities that demand them.

Surrogate cost drivers Represents cost activities that are difficult to collect or maintain. Therefore, these cost drivers are not easy to measure, or the activity is not large enough to justify a separate cost driver, such as material handling, accounting, marketing, and general management costs.

TEN STEPS FOR ESTABLISHING AN ACTIVITY-BASED COST SYSTEM

To establish an activity-based cost system, ten steps are necessary.[6] As with the development of any cost system, continuous review must be given throughout its development. Where necessary, changes in decisions, and sometimes philosophies, must be considered. A review of the ten steps are as follows:

Step 1. Establishing Relevant Activities

This step requires the identification and definition of relevant activities within the organization. This is accomplished by reviewing organizational charts and other facilities to determine what each function does. Once this is done, activities can be identified as discussed previously under the heading "Activities."

Step 2. Develop Cost Centers

Upon completion of Step 1, cost centers can be organized. Such factors as materiality and activity application (where activities can be confirmed) must be considered. For example, cost accounting, general accounting, and data entry and processing are activities that can be classified as a cost center under the heading "Accounting and Information Systems."

Step 3. Identifying the Major Cost Elements

These cost elements relate closely to budget line items, or as contained in a company's chart of accounts. These were discussed previously under the heading "Cost Categories."

Step 4. Determining Activity and Cost Relationships

This step merely determines which costs pertain to which cost centers. For example, electricity costs can pertain to many different cost centers.

Step 5. Assigning Costs to Activities and Products through Cost Drivers

By identifying cost drivers, costs can be assigned to activities and activities to products.

Step 6. Establishing the Cost Flow Pattern

This step allows the ability to develop a logical way for costs to flow down through the organization and eventually to the various products/services.[7]

Using the previous description of cost categories and activities, a cost flow-down diagram can be created. This is shown on Figure 15-1. Through-put-related costs have been separated because they are not subject to the cost flow-down analysis. This is due to the fact that these costs are already defined as traceable to a cost objective. The cost flow down, as shown in Figure 15-1, is further described in the cost flow-down diagram shown in Figure 15-2. The arrow and reference numbers will be used to describe the analysis further.

The number-1 arrow shows throughput-related costs being charged directly to the cost objective. Salaries and wages flow into purchased fringe benefits and into each of the activities (see arrow 2). Some of these costs may be charged directly to cost objectives, as also shown by arrow 2.

At this point, all throughput-related costs are distributed, salaries and wages and purchased fringe benefits are distributed, with other costs waiting to be distributed to a lower level.

Level II, purchased fringe benefits, now also includes "paid time off" benefits, which were distributed from level I. Therefore, arrows 2 and 3 are similar with the exception of salary and wages charges in level II. Different "fringe rates" are often established for different levels of employees (e.g., salaried versus hourly employees), and can be calculated as a percentage of labor dollars or as an hourly labor cost.

Arrow 4 shows specific assignment costs being charged to specific activities by using the appropriate cost driver.

At this stage of the diagram, all incurred costs have been distributed to either a cost objective or to an activity that will be distributed later. All costs beyond this point that were already incurred by the activity will be distributed to other activities and cost objectives that caused the cost.

For level IV, service activities, an analysis needs to be made for the demand for services on a project-by-project basis and other activities such as dealing with customers. Determining how much time is spent for these activities would determine what percentage of the accumulated costs to allocate, such as a predetermined hourly billing rate. This is represented by arrow 5. Notice that service activities can also charge cost objectives as well as other activities.

Level VI activities are distributed using predetermined percentages developed during employee interviews or some other measurable driver. These drivers are often associated with operations support activities such as machine hours, purchase requisitions, and the like and flow into levels VII and VIII activities as shown by arrow 6.

Administrative support activities cannot logically be distributed to other

FIGURE 15-1   Cost Flow-Down Elements—1

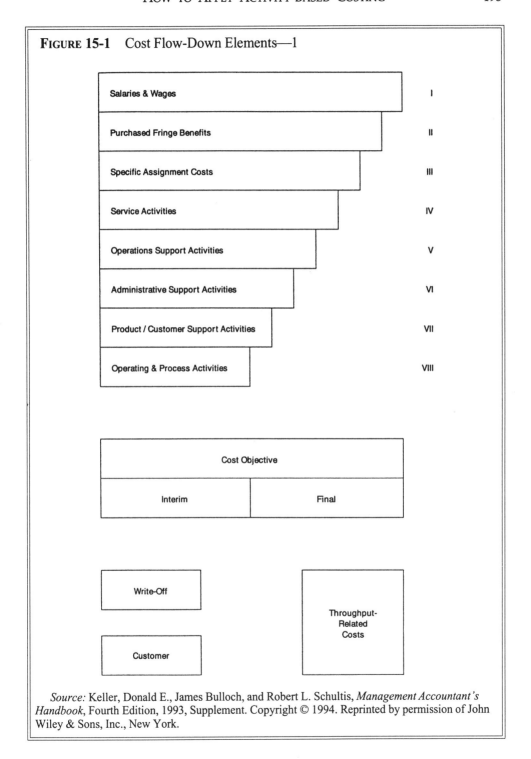

Source: Keller, Donald E., James Bulloch, and Robert L. Schultis, *Management Accountant's Handbook*, Fourth Edition, 1993, Supplement. Copyright © 1994. Reprinted by permission of John Wiley & Sons, Inc., New York.

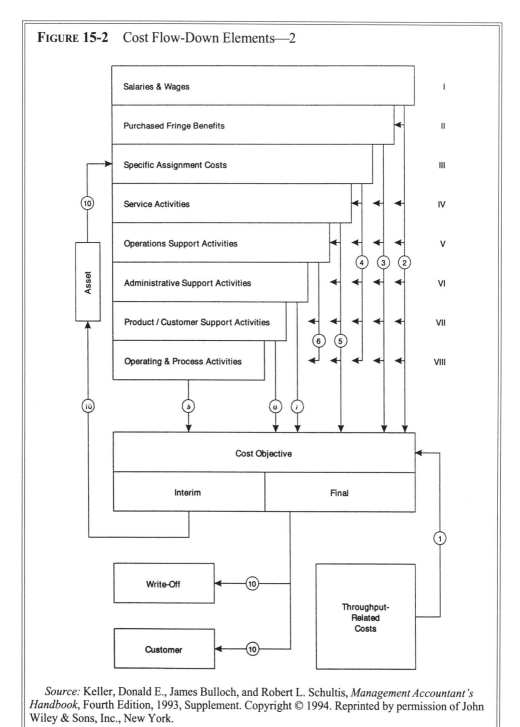

FIGURE 15-2   Cost Flow-Down Elements—2

Source: Keller, Donald E., James Bulloch, and Robert L. Schultis, *Management Accountant's Handbook*, Fourth Edition, 1993, Supplement. Copyright © 1994. Reprinted by permission of John Wiley & Sons, Inc., New York.

activities, but can be distributed to cost objectives using a percentage of the total cost input as a basis. Arrow 7 shows this flow of costs.

Product/customer support activities are also applied directly to those specific cost objectives and are distributed using such basis as unit cost and percentage of conversion cost. Most important to remember is that these activities should be charged to the products or customers they support. Arrow 8 shows this flow of costs.

Arrow 9 reflects the distribution of operating and process activities, which can use a variety of drivers such as machine hours, units produced, direct labor hours/dollars, and so on.

At this time, all costs have been distributed, some directly to a cost objective; others were distributed through one or more activities.

As discussed previously, there are two types of cost objectives: final and interim. As shown in Figure 15-2, the final cost objective does not get distributed internally. It is a resting place for costs to be accumulated for transfer outside of the organization. It is either charged against revenues generated by the cost objective or written off with no offsetting revenues.

The other type of cost objective is the interim cost objective. This type accumulates costs to be distributed within the organization. These costs are usually capitalized, such as maintenance and tooling costs, and are amortized over the life of the asset. Arrow 10 shows how these costs are charged either as a write-off to the customer or to the asset.

Step 7. Selecting the Appropriate Tools

Step 7 develops the tools necessary to build an activity-based cost system.[8] As discussed previously, one measure used to allocate costs to cost centers or cost objectives when it is not practical to collect and maintain data pertaining to a specific cost driver is referred to as a surrogate cost driver.

Conversion costs An important tool that is classified as a surrogate driver is conversion cost. This is defined as all direct labor and indirect costs charged to a cost center for which costs will be eventually distributed.

An example of how conversion costs are used is shown in Table 15-1. Assume three cost centers with Center 1 being a production support activity and Centers 2 and 3 operating activities. Each center incurred costs classified as indirect labor, fixed overhead, and variable overhead, with Centers 2 and 3 incurring direct labor costs. In addition, all three cost centers received charges from departments 1 and 3. Department 3 distribution will already have cost department 1 and 2 charges.

Note that Cost Center 1 is distributed to Cost Centers 2 and 3 and has no

TABLE 15-1	Example of a Conversion Cost		
	Cost Center 1	Cost Center 2	Cost Center 3
Direct labor		$20,000	$30,000
Indirect labor	$ 3,000	4,000	2,000
Fixed overhead	5,000	6,000	3,000
Variable overhead	4,000	5,000	3,000
Total specific assignment costs	12,000	15,000	8,000
Department 1 distribution	2,000	1,000	3,000
Department 2 distribution	3,000	2,000	1,000
Total conversion costs	17,000	38,000	42,000
Conversion cost percentage		47.5%	52.5%
Department 3 distribution	17,000	8,000	9,000
Total costs after distribution	0	$46,000	$51,000

cost after distributions were made to Cost Centers 2 and 3. While this method is not totally accurate, it does give a reasonable approximation of how costs are to be distributed.

Consumption units are variable costs that change automatically with a change in volume, or those variable costs that change when some action is taken by management. For example, production volume changes do not necessarily result in higher labor costs unless new people are hired. Certain costs, such as higher utilization and supplies, however, may result automatically when production volume increases. Therefore, consumption units such as kilowatt hours and poundage must be developed, which will turn units of production into measurable variable costs.

Labor-based cost distribution Used to accumulate and distribute costs using a labor-based approach. Costs such as fringe benefits can be distributed by the use of drivers such as headcount, labor dollars, and labor hours. Headcount drivers are preferable when distributing fringe benefit costs that are basically the same for each employee, whereas labor hours are preferable for benefits that are based directly on hours worked, such as various types of pension plans. For example, headcount can be used to distribute health insurance and state and federal unemployment; labor dollars can be used to distribute workers' compensation and employer FICA; and, as discussed previously, pension costs are best distributed using the labor hour driver.

Demand-based cost distribution Whereby businesses within the business (service centers) that charge their costs to those who utilize these activities on a time-and-materials basis. The goal is to develop an hourly rate so that services can be charged back as if they were customers.

Illustration

Let's assume the following facts in illustrating how costs are distributed using demand-based cost distribution.

Billable employees	3
Available employee hours	750
Total available hours	2,250
% of available billable hours	80%
Billable hours	1,800
Departmental costs	$110,000
Hourly billing rate	$61.11
Activities	
Accounting	320
Purchasing	180
Engineering	410
General administration	500
Production scheduling	390
Total hours	1,800

Applying the hourly rate of $61.11 to the various activities by hours, the following cost charges are calculated:

	Costs Charged
Accounting	$ 19,555
Purchasing	11,000
Engineering	25,055
General administration	30,555
Production scheduling	$110,000

Piece-rate cost distribution - This tool distributes high-dollar indirect costs directly to those products that consume them. Costs such as coating materials and perishable tools are examples.

TABLE 15-2   Illustration of Calculating Machine/Cycle Rate Per Hour

Pieces of equipment	3
Annual hours per machine shift	500
Annual shift hours	1,500
Operation shifts	2
Total annual hours	3,000
Nonproduction hours*	800
Annual production hours	2,200
Cost center costs	$40,500
Machine/cycle rate per hour	$18.41

  * Hours used for setup and maintenance, etc.

Machine hours/cycle time cost distribution - Charges costs to cost objectives that are based on the amount of time the objective is processed on a particular piece of equipment. Table 15-2 illustrates how the machine/cycle rate per hour is calculated.

Under this tool, it is important to note that each piece of equipment is charged to each cost objective and each product is charged from each piece of equipment that uses it.

Line/cell time distribution - This tool is used when more than one piece of equipment is used on a group of similar products. It uses a cell/line concept for developing an hourly rate instead of for each piece of equipment on that line. The rate is then applied to each product produced by that line based on the product's hourly rate of production.

Production manpower pool - This tool makes use of a manpower pool to distribute costs. This occurs when various cost centers are serviced by a pool of workers.

Step 8. Planning the Cost Accumulation Model

At this stage, all of the techniques and tools can be selected for implementation ideally to generate how cost will flow within the organization. Such decisions as a cost-flow diagram, distribution bases, and a series of worksheets and schedules must be developed for the organization.

Step 9. Gathering the Necessary Data

At this point, the gathering of historical data and employee interviews needs to take place.[9] The ultimate goal is to develop a process that is accurate but not necessarily precise. The contents of the prior steps need to be put into effect and developed specifically for each organization's operations.

Step 10. Establishing the Cost Accumulation Model

The final step is to build the model based on the prior nine steps. This could be aided by simple computer models of cost flows using the cost flow-down analysis previously discussed.

In summary, caution needs to be given when using activity-based costing to the use of irrelevant cost information and the inappropriate use of cost information as a decision-making tool. If not understood, profitability and return and investment rates may lead to erroneous management decisions. Using this method requires a greater understanding of the meaning of costs and how it is used to make effective management decisions.

DECISION-MAKING STRATEGIES

- Determine workloads by department to project true costs accurately.
- Reduce the capital base by making assets more flexible.
- Recognize internal and external customers and suppliers.
- Change the culture of the organization from individual departmental concerns to one of coordination between internal departments.
- Establish targets for levels of performance.

NOTES

1. Krallinger, Joseph C., and Karsten G. Hellebust, *Strategic Planning Workbook,* Second Edition, p. 142. Copyright © 1993. Reprinted by permission of John Wiley & Sons, Inc., New York.

2. Keller, Donald W., James Bulloch, and Robert L. Schultis, *Management Accountant's Handbook,* Fourth Edition, 1993, Supplement, pp. 4A9–4A.11. Copyright © 1994. Reprinted by permission of John Wiley & Sons, Inc., New York.

3. Hicks, Douglas, T., *Activity-Based Costing for Small and Mid-Sized Businesses,* pp. 35–36. Copyright © 1992. Reprinted by permission of John Wiley & Sons, Inc., New York.

4. Keller, Donald E., James Bulloch, and Robert L. Schultis, *Management Accountant's Handbook,* Fourth Edition, 1993, Supplement, pp. 4A.8–9. Copyright © 1994. Reprinted by permission of John Wiley & Sons, Inc., New York.

5. Hicks, Douglas T., *Activity-Based Costing for Small and Mid-Sized Businesses,* pp. 36–39. Copyright © 1992. Reprinted by permission of John Wiley & Sons, Inc., New York.

6. Ibid., ch. 6.

7. Keller, Donald E., James Bulloch, and Robert L. Schultis, *Management Accountant's Handbook,* Fourth Edition, 1993, Supplement, p. 4A.12–17. Copyright © 1994. Reprinted by permission of John Wiley & Sons, Inc., New York.

8. Hicks, Douglas T., *Activity-Based Costing for Small and Mid-Sized Businesses,* ch. 8 and 9. Copyright © 1992. Reprinted by permission of John Wiley & Sons, Inc., New York.

9. Ibid., ch. 10

16

HOW TO USE BREAK-EVEN TECHNIQUES FOR ROI DECISION MAKING

A business must know what volume of activity is needed to cover all expenses over and above the cost directly associated with the product and/or company activity. To put it another way, how many dollars of sales are needed to cover the company's fixed costs? At this point, revenues generated and costs incurred are equal, and neither a profit nor a loss will materialize. When this occurs, the results are said to be at the break-even point, that is, the point where variable costs and fixed costs equal net sales dollars.

This concept can be expressed in numerical terms by the use of formulas or graphically by the use of a break-even chart. In any case, the shifts or changes in revenues and costs are ultimately reflected in the operations of the business, as well as in the return on investment objectives. Thus break-even analysis can be an important tool in managing the business by providing the necessary information for effective decision making. It can aid in making decisions in pricing, financing, capital investments, setting ROI objectives, and other decisions where volume, cost, price, and profits are factors.

Nevertheless, certain conditions have to be assumed when using this technique. Because various volume levels will be used to show the influence on the break-even point, it is assumed that changing sales volume will not have any effect on the per unit selling price. It is also assumed that both types of expenses, variable and fixed, will react differently. For example, those expenses categorized as variable will change in direct proportion to sales volume, whereas fixed expenses will remain constant regardless of the volume level.

DEFINING TYPES OF COSTS

In computing the break-even point, it is necessary to take a conventional statement of income (Table 2-1) and to divide the costs into variable costs and fixed costs.

Variable costs, as previously explained, are those that will vary in direct proportion to levels of activity and that are directly related to the product. Costs that are typically classified as variable include costs of materials (raw and packaging), labor (including fringe benefits), shipping materials, and sales commissions.

Fixed costs are those that do not vary with the level of activity, remaining constant within a given range of activity. They include such costs as rent, property taxes, depreciation, insurance premiums, salaries (not hourly), administrative costs, and general overhead.

Considering both types of costs, let us examine the following table illustrating how these costs are affected by changes in production on a total cost and per unit basis:

	Total Costs	
	Variable Costs	Fixed Costs
Production increase	Increase	No change
Production decrease	Decrease	No change

Production changes clearly have no impact on fixed costs, but they affect variable costs in the same direction. If we looked at an example of the effect on per unit costs, however, a different answer would result:

	Per Unit Costs	
	Variable Costs	Fixed Costs
Production increase	No change	Decrease
Production decrease	No change	Increase

Note that, on a per unit basis, variable costs do not change because these costs vary with production levels. The more units produced, however, the lower the fixed costs per unit, because these costs are spread over more units. Conversely, the fewer units produced, the higher the

TABLE 16-1 The Great Company, Inc.
Statement of Income, 19X2

	Variable	Fixed	Total
Unit sales			100,000
Net sales			$700,000
Operating expenses			
Cost of sales	$447,000	$ 78,000	$525,000
Depreciation		5,000	5,000
Selling expenses	23,000	7,000	30,000
Administrative expenses		25,000	25,000
General expenses		15,000	15,000
Total	$470,000	$130,000	$600,000
Per unit	$4.70	$1.30	$6.00
Operating income			100,000
Other (income) expense			2,000
Income before income taxes			98,000
Income taxes			48,000
Net income			$ 50,000
Percentage of net sales	67.1%		7.1%

fixed costs per unit, because fewer units must absorb more of the fixed costs.

The hypothetical statement of income shown in Table 16-1 has been arbitrarily classified into variable and fixed costs. Breaking it down on a per unit basis, the variable costs per unit are $4.70 and the fixed costs per unit $1.30, for a total per unit cost of $6.00. With a selling price of $7.00 per unit ($700,000 ÷ 100,000 units), the operating income per unit is $1.00 ($100,000 ÷ 100,000 units). In addition, 67.1%, or $0.671, of every dollar pays for variable costs for every unit produced. Because fixed costs do not vary with volume activity, however, the total must be stated in terms of whole dollars. The difference of 32.9%, or $0.329 ($1.00–0.671) represents the amount needed for every sales dollar to cover fixed costs. This is referred to as the marginal income ratio. We discuss this approach later in the chapter.

BREAK-EVEN CALCULATIONS

The basic calculation for determining the break-even point is:

Basic
Break-even   Net sales = Variable costs + Fixed costs
Equation

The break-even point is reached when net sales equal variable costs plus fixed costs. It is at this point, that is, when both revenues and expenses are equal and neither a profit nor a loss results, that the company is said to be at break-even. The solution can be calculated either in units or in sales dollars.

Break-Even in Units

Let us review the break-even point in units first by using the following formula and the data previously presented:

Sales price per unit (SP)	$7.00
Unit sales (US)	100,000 units
Fixed costs (FC)	$130,000
Unit variable costs (VC)	$4.70

$$SP \times US = FC + VC$$
$$(SP \times US) - (VC \times US) = FC \times SP$$
$$US (SP - VC) = FC$$

$$US = \frac{FC}{(SP - VC)}$$

or

$$US = \frac{\$130,000}{\$7.00 - \$4.70}$$
$$US = 56,521.7 \text{ units}$$

The break-even in units sold is 56,521.7 units. To prove that these many units are needed to break even, multiply the units (56,521.7) by the selling price of $7.00 and by the variable unit cost of $4.70. Subtract the variable cost from the total sales dollars, as well as the fixed costs of $130,000. The result should equal zero.

Net sales (56,521.7 × $7.00)	$395,652
Variable costs (56,521.7 × $4.70)	265,652
	130,000
Less fixed costs	130,000
Total	0

If a specific profit were desired, the formula would be changed to include the desired profit, shown as follows:

Break-even + Desired Profit Equation

Net sales = Variable cost + Fixed costs + Desired profit

This is discussed later in the chapter.

Break-Even in Sales Dollars

This solution solves how many sales dollars are necessary to equal the fixed costs. It is used where there are multiple products and/or lines and the convenience of using sales dollars is greater than using units of output. In addition, where specific unit data is not available, such as competitive data, this method will assist in estimating the break-even in sales dollars. The formula of break-even is as follows using the previous data:

Break-even sales dollars (BE)	
Fixed cost (FC)	$130,000
Total variable costs (TVC)	$470,000
Net sales (NS)	$700,000

$$BE = \frac{FC}{1 - (TVC/NS)}$$

or

$$BE = \frac{\$130,000}{1 - (\$470,000/\$700,000)}$$

$$BE = \frac{\$130,000}{0.3286}$$

$$BE = \$395,617.77$$

The results show that $395,617.77 is needed to equal the fixed costs without showing any profit or loss. This is proved as follows:

Net sales	$395,617.77
Variable costs at 67.14%	265,617.77
Variable margin	$130,000.00
Less fixed costs	130,000.00
Total	0

Contribution Margin

This solves for how many units are necessary both to recover fixed costs and to generate a desired profit. The contribution margin is calculated as follows:

$$\text{Net sales} - \text{Variable costs} = \text{Fixed costs} + \text{Desired profit}$$

When this equation is applied to the previous data, the contribution margin is $230,000, assuming a desired profit of $100,000.

$$\$700,000 - 470,000 = \$130,000 + 100,000$$

$$\$230,000 = \$230,000$$

Using the $230,000 contribution margin, or $2.30 per unit ($230,000 ÷ 100,000 units), the following number of units is needed to generate a profit of $100,000:

$$\frac{\text{Fixed expenses} + \text{Desired profit}}{\text{Unit contribution margin}}$$

or

$$\frac{\$130,000 + \$100,000}{\$2.30} = 100,000 \text{ units}$$

Returning to the statement of income presented in Table 16-1 you will recognize the similar data presented in the following prove that 100,000 units are the correct answer:

Net sales (100,000 units at $7.00)	$700,000
Variable costs (100,000 units at $4.70)	470,000
Contribution margin	230,000
Less fixed costs	130,000
Desired profit	$100,000
Percentage of net sales	14.3%

In this case, the desired profit represented the operating profit and results in a profitability rate of 14.3%. Any change in volume, selling price, cost, and desired profit will change this percentage.

A significant advantage of using the contribution margin approach allows a manager to develop optimum levels of sales using different pricing structures. Given that volume varies inversely with the selling price, whereas higher than the market price generally reduces volume; lower than market prices will generally increase volume. Table 16-2 illustrates a "what if" scenario using alternative pricing levels and the impact it has on contribution margin.

TABLE 16-2   Impact of Alternative Pricing on Contribution Margin

| | | Price Increase | |
	Current Price	5%	10%
Sales price per unit	$7.00	$7.35	$7.70
Expected volume	100,000	95,000	90,000
Net sales	$700,000	$698,250	$693,000
Unit variable cost	4.70	4.70	4.70
Variable cost	470,000	446,500	423,000
Contribution margin	$230,000	$251,750	$270,000

| | | Price Decrease | |
	Current Price	5%	8%
Sales price per unit	$7.00	$6.65	$6.44
Expected volume	100,000	105,000	120,000
Net sales	$700,000	$698,250	$772,800
Unit variable cost	4.70	4.70	4.70
Variable cost	470,000	493,500	564,000
Contribution margin	$230,000	$204,750	$208,800

The above analysis shows that price increases of 5% and 10% respectively will increase contribution margin and thus net income, assuming the fixed cost remains unchanged. Price decreases of 5% and 8% respectively, however, will not increase contribution margin or net income. Therefore, based on this scenario, management will be wise not to decrease the price below the $7.00 level.

Profit Contribution Ratio

This ratio is computed by dividing the contribution margin ($230,000) by net sales ($700,000):

$$\frac{\$230,000}{\$700,000} = 32.86\%$$

Note that this is the reciprocal of the relationship of variable costs to net sales (67.14%).

Margin of Safety

This calculation reflects how much sales can decrease before losses can be expected. It is calculated by subtracting sales at the break-even point ($395,618) from actual sales ($700,000) and by dividing this sum by the actual sales ($700,000). The following results:

$$\frac{\$700,000 - \$395,618}{\$700,000} = 43.48\%$$

Thus 43.48% of the actual sales can decrease before losses will occur. This is shown as follows:

Actual sales	$700,000
Less margin of safety (.4348 × $700,000)	304,360
	395,640
Less sales dollars at break-even	395,618
Plus rounding difference	22
Total	$ 0

USING BREAK-EVEN CHARTS

Break-even can also be explained graphically using a chart. It is sometimes easier to visualize and demonstrate the relationships between volume, price, costs, and profits by such means. Knowing what these relationships are can be valuable in analyzing business performance as well as in preparing projections for budgeting and planning purposes. Of particular interest is knowing the effects of volume changes, cost changes, price changes, and tax changes on the break-even point of the company. This is explored later in the chapter. In addition, specific product data are necessary as measures of performance when planning for changes in any of the preceding elements that affect a product's financial performance.

Using the data previously presented, Figure 16-1 illustrates a break-even chart. The first step is to establish along the horizontal scale, volume in units, sales dollars, capacity percent, or any other measurement relating to volume. In this case, we use dollar sales volume.

The vertical scale of the chart represents total costs and profits. A horizontal line, which represents total fixed expenses, is drawn parallel to the horizontal axis. In this case, fixed expenses were $130,000.

In our previous illustration, each unit of sales had variable expenses of $4.70

FIGURE 16-1   Break-Even Point Illustrated

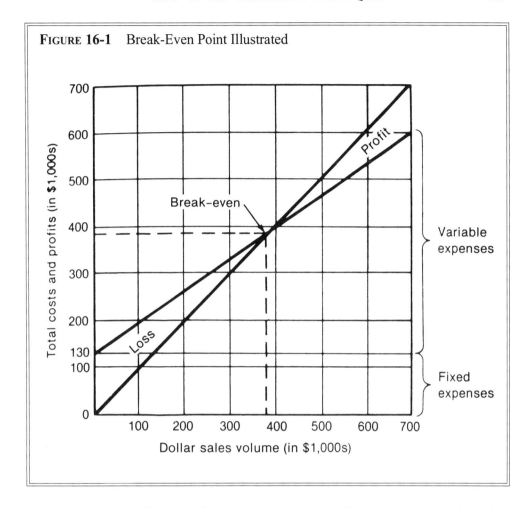

per unit. Therefore, for each level of volume a line is plotted upward starting from the beginning of the fixed expense line to a point that represents total expenses of $600,000 ($470,000 variable plus $130,000 fixed).

A diagonal line is then drawn through the chart, representing total sales dollars, as in Figure 16-1. This is done from the left-hand corner to the right-hand corner, because the same scale is used on both axes. The point at which both lines intersect in Figure 16-1 is the break-even point. In this case it is $395,617.77.

HOW CHANGES AFFECT THE BREAK-EVEN POINT

As previously discussed, break-even can be affected by changes in volume, cost, price, and desired profit. Changes in any one or in combinations of these will affect the break-even. One of the advantages of the break-even concept is that it allows a business to simulate future business conditions and results and to show how many units are needed to break even. Once this is established, decisions can be made as to the most profitable course of action.

Let us use the same data as were previously used in this chapter to see how the various changes occur. These data are:

	Total	Per Unit Data
Unit volume	100,000	—
Net sales	$700,000	$7.00
Variable costs	470,000	4.70
Variable contribution	230,000	2.30
Less fixed costs	130,000	1.30
Operating income	$100,000	$1.00
Percentage of net sales	14.3%	

These data will now be used to simulate the effects of changes in volume, cost, price, and profit, respectively, with hypothetical situations used as illustrations.

Changes in Volume

What would happen to operating income if unit volume increased to 150,000 units from 100,000 units?

$$\$7.00 \times 150{,}000 = (\$4.70 \times 150{,}000) + (\$130{,}000 \times X)$$

$$\$1{,}050{,}000 = \$705{,}000 + \$130{,}000X$$

$$\$1{,}050{,}000 = \$835{,}000X$$

$$X = \$215{,}000$$

The operating income would increase $115,000, to $215,000. The revised data would be shown as follows:

Unit volume	150,000 units
Net sales	$1,050,000
Variable costs	705,000
Variable contribution	345,000
Less fixed costs	130,000
Operating income	$ 215,000
Percentage of net sales	20.5%

The results show that a 50% increase in unit volume increased operating income by 115%. In addition, the profitability rate (operating income ÷ net sales) increased from 14.3% to 20.5%.

Changes in Cost

Assuming that the same data are used, what would an increase of $20,000 in fixed costs ($150,000) mean in terms of additional units needed to avoid a reduction in the original operating income of $100,000?

$$\$7.00X - \$4.70X = \$150,000 + \$100,000$$
$$\$2.30X = \$250,000$$
$$X = 108,695.7 \text{ units}$$

An additional 8,695.7 units (108,695.7 – 100,000) are needed to absorb an additional $20,000 of fixed costs and still maintain the same $100,000 of operating income. The original data would now look like this:

Unit volume	108,695.7 units
Net sales	$760,870
Variable costs	510,870
Variable contribution	250,000
Less fixed costs	150,000
Operating income	$100,000
Percentage of net sales	13.1%

The profitability rate decreased from 14.3% to 13.1%.

Changes in Price

How many units would be needed to maintain the same operating income of $100,000 if the price were increased from $7.00 to $10.00?

$$\$10.00X - \$4.70X = \$130,000 + \$100,000$$
$$\$5.30X = \$230,000$$
$$X = 43,396.2$$

A 42.9% increase in price reduced the number of units to be sold by 56,603.8 (100,000 – 43,396.2), or 56.6%. The revised operating income statement would appear as follows:

Unit volume	43,396.2 units
Net sales	$433,962
Variable costs	203,962
Variable contribution	230,000
Less fixed costs	130,000
Operating income	$100,000
Percentage of net sales	23%

The profitability rate increased from 14.3% to 23.0%.

Changes in Profit

What would be the number of units needed to increase operating income to $150,000?

$$\frac{\$130,000 + \$150,000}{\$2.30} = 121,739.1 \text{ units}$$

To increase operating income $50,000, an additional 21,739.1 units are needed. The following now reflects the increase in operating income:

Unit volume	121,739.1 units
Net sales	$852,174
Variable costs	572,174
Variable contribution	280,000
Less fixed costs	130,000
Operating income	$150,000
Percentage of net sales	17.6%

Table 16-3 summarizes how changes in the volume, price, costs, and profit operating decisions affect the financial results of a company. The break-even concept allows a business to simulate the effects of these changes.

TABLE 16-3	Impact of Operating Decisions on Financial Results				
Decisions	Unit Volume	Net Sales	Total Costs	Operating Income	Profitability Rate
Changes in volume	50,000.0	$350,000	($235,000)	$115,000	6.2%
Changes in cost	8,695.7	60,870	(60,870)	—	(1.2)
Changes in price	56,603.8	(266,038)	(266,038)	—	8.7
Changes in profit	21,739.1	152,174	(102,174)	50,000	3.3

Caution: The preceding analysis points out the flexibility that break-even provides in projecting revenues and expenses under different assumed conditions. By reviewing these data, a company can see how certain actions integrate with the overall managerial decision-making process. However, caution should be taken in regard to such problems in computing break-even as the accuracy of the revenue and expense projections and the extent to which competition will react in an ever-changing market environment. Classifying expenses as variable and fixed can also be difficult, and some reasonable rationale is sometimes called for. Although break-even analysis is a valuable tool, it can be oversimplified to the point where it does not conform to reality. The relationships between volume, cost, and price must be studied carefully and in relation to the marketplace in which the business operates.

DECISION-MAKING STRATEGIES

- Develop break-even strategies to determine levels of volume and sales dollars needed to cover fixed costs.
- Concentrate on sales margins before sales volume.
- Determine the most feasible levels of production to reduce unit costs.

17

HOW THE MARGIN RATE IS USED TO PROJECT PROFITS

As we have seen in chapter 16 (on break-even analysis), it is important to establish simulations in order to estimate the amount of volume necessary to absorb fixed expenses. At the least, total revenues should equal total expenses (both fixed and variable). In order to ensure that revenues far exceed expenses, and to ensure the survival of the business, it is necessary to establish some method of financial control. The margin rate will assist in meeting that objective. For companies with limited product lines, or for companies that can computerize these data, this method provides an excellent tool for use in controlling the business. It also provides a tool for maximizing return on investment rates, since the profitability rate will greatly affect the overall return on investment equation.

HOW TO DETERMINE BREAK-EVEN— A DIFFERENT APPROACH

To say that your business is successful because it breaks even is erroneous because breaking even does not provide any monies for growth and expansion. It is certainly not sufficient for the survival of the business. In the previous chapter, we saw that using a sales price per unit of $7.00, unit variable costs of $4.70 per unit, fixed costs of $130,000, and unit sales of 100,000 units, the break-even in units was 56,521.7 units.

An easier way to calculate the break-even would be to calculate the margin rate, which is $2.30, or the selling price of $7.00 less the variable cost of $4.70. The margin rate of $2.30 is used to recover the fixed costs of $130,000. The fixed costs are recovered at the rate of $2.30 per unit and by 56,521.7 units as follows:

Margin Rate
Equation

$$\frac{\text{Fixed costs}}{\text{Margin rate}} = \text{Recovery units}$$

or

$$\frac{\$130,000}{\$2.30} = 56,521.7 \text{ units}$$

The break-even can now be found by using this formula, without any knowledge as to what total sales dollars are or what total variable expenses are. Note that the only data required are the margin rate and fixed expenses. For example, if the variable cost per unit increased $0.30 to $5.00 and this cost was passed on to the customer, the selling price would be $7.30. The margin rate does not change, remaining at $2.30 per unit.

COMPUTING ESTIMATED PROFITS

Using this method would make the break-even chart unnecessary. Those units that are beyond the break-even point, or in the profit sector of the chart, would generate a profit at the margin rate of $2.30 per unit. Conversely, those units below the break-even point would result in losses at the rate of $2.30 per unit. Let us illustrate this point by using the break-even of 56,521.7 units.

What would be the result if an additional 4,000 units were sold, or 60,521.7 (56,521.7 + 4,000.0) units?

$$4,000 \text{ units} \times \$2.30 = \$9,200$$

An additional $9,200 of operating income would be generated as follows:

Unit volume	60,521.7 units
Net sales	$423,652
Variable cost	284,452
Variable contribution	139,200
Less fixed costs	130,000
Operating income	$9,200
Percentage of net sales	2.2%

What would be the impact if 4,000 fewer units were sold?

$$(4,000 \text{ units}) \times \$2.30 = (\$9,200)$$

A loss of $9,200 would result as follows:

Unit volume	52,521.7 units
Net sales	$367,652
Variable costs	246,852
Variable contribution	120,800
Less fixed costs	130,000
Operating loss	($9,200)
Percentage of net sales	(2.5%)

Unlike the original break-even analysis, which needed data such as total sales dollars, total fixed expenses, total variable expenses, and the selling price, this method has already taken all these factors into consideration by the calculation of the margin rate. We have been dealing here with only one product, so let us explore the use of this method using more than one product.

MULTIPLE-PRODUCT ANALYSIS

In a typical business environment, it is more likely that a company will produce more than one product or sell more than one product. To illustrate break-even in such cases, the following product data will be used:

	Product		
	R	S	T
Selling price	$7.00	$6.00	$8.00
Variable cost	4.70	4.00	5.50
Margin rate	$2.30	$2.00	$2.50

If fixed costs were $130,000, what would be the break-even in number of units and sales dollars for each product?

		Product		
		R	S	T
Line No.				
1	Fixed costs	$130,000	$130,000	$130,000
2	Margin rate	$2.30	$2.00	$2.50
3	Break-even in units (line 1 ÷ by line 3)	56,522	65,000	52,000
4	Selling price	$7.00	$6.00	$8.00
5	Break-even in sales dollars (line 3 × line 4)	$395,654	$390,000	$416,000

TABLE 17-1   Using Product R as an Equivalence

	Product			
	R	S	T	Total
Sales volume	60,522	67,050	55,600	183,172
Margin rate factor	1.00	0.8696	1.087	
Equivalent sales volume	60,522	58,307	60,437	179,266
Break-even—product R				56,522
Excess over equivalent				122,744
Margin rate—product R				$2.30
Operating income				$282,311

Let us see how margin rates and sales dollars can be combined.

Combining Margin Rates

It is possible to combine margin rates and to determine estimated operating income at different levels of sales volume. Let us assume the following levels for the preceding products in a given month:

	Unit Sales
Product R	60,522
Product S	67,050
Product T	55,600

Using product R as a base, the margin rate factor is computed by dividing $2.30 into $2.00 and into $2.50. The results are as follows:

Margin Rate Factor	
Product R	1.0000
Product S	.8696
Product T	1.0870

Each of the products has the ability to recover the fixed costs at the given rates. By doing this, all the product lines are put on an equal basis and can now be combined as if only one product were being sold. Each relates to product R as an equivalence, and all are added together to arrive at a total operating income as shown in Table 17-1.

TABLE 17-2   Calculation Using Conventional Statement

| | Product | | | |
	R	S	T	Total
Unit volume	60,522	67,050	55,600	183,172
Net sales	$423,654	$402,300	$444,800	$1,270,754
Variable costs	284,454	268,200	305,800	858,454
Variable contribution	$139,200	$134,100	$139,000	$ 412,300
Less fixed costs				130,000
Rounding difference				11
Operating income				$ 282,311

TABLE 17-3   Illustration of Combining Margin Rates

| | Product | | | |
	R	S	T	Total
Unit volume	60,522	67,050	55,600	183,172
Margin rate	$2.30	$2.00	$2.50	
Variable contribution	$139,200	$134,100	$139,000	$412,300
Less fixed costs				130,000
Rounding difference				11
Operating income				$282,311

Let us prove that $282,311 is the correct combined operating income by the conventional statement shown in Table 17-2. Note in the table that the same $282,311 was calculated using the preceding conventional method. This same calculation can be applied to many products but can involve lots of time when many products are used. A simpler method is to combine margin dollars.

Combining Margin Dollars

When combining margin rates, as previously discussed, we used the margin rate and the break-even point. In this method, we will concentrate on the elements of margin rates and fixed costs. Using the same set of data, we can calculate the same estimated $282,311 operating income, as shown in Table 17-3.

One can see how easy this method is and why it is preferred over the previous method when break-even data are not necessary.

DECISION-MAKING STRATEGIES

- Apply break-even techniques for multiple products.
- Review operations of the company with marginal results and develop a strategy, that is, eliminate or reduce resources, or maintain level of current activity.
- Eliminate geographic areas and/or product lines that fall below a minimum profit margin and turnover rate.

18

AN ROI APPROACH TO EVALUATING INVESTMENTS IN HUMAN RESOURCES

As will be seen in chapter 19, companies invest substantial amounts of money for capital investments, or fixed assets. These fixed investments appear on the balance sheet, while the expected earnings appear on the statement of income as profits materialize. The profits may be reflected in the short run or, as in most cases, may continue to be generated for many years to follow. These concepts and applications have been used successfully for many years by companies that require investments in capital assets. In more recent times, the need has arisen for evaluating the impact of investments in human resources on the return on investment rate.

Many companies are currently using sophisticated techniques to measure the value of their employees. The idea of return on human resources is to make the measurement as accurate and inclusive as possible, and it is being distorted when costs of training programs are put in as an expense in one year while the return comes back in future years. On the other hand, critical decisions should be made on relative return on investments rather than absolute ones. Given a situation where two companies in an industry have similar employee programs, the present measurements should give an accurate comparison between them. This is the narrow view, and no doubt there are great differences between programs costing the same. The main value of this concept would be in the larger view, which measures actual present values of people. I suggest the methods detailed in this chapter be refined over several years before they are accepted in a company's internal financial reporting. If the right program of measurement is installed, it could more than offset its cost of implementation in the value accruing from the fact that both the individual and management would know what the results were. An ineffective plan could cause employee unrest and easily cost more than the value of the benefits of more accurate return on investment indexes. Determining a ROI rate on human resources can be of extreme value in managing a company, since it puts a cost value on personnel decisions, which previously were largely subjective in nature.

EVALUATING THE IMPACT OF
HUMAN RESOURCES ON ROI

The method of evaluating human resources in terms of their effect on ROI is a nontraditional technique. By that I mean it does not fit the traditional way in which human resources have been evaluated. In addition, it is not consistent with such traditional accounting procedures as are used for fixed assets.

As explained in chapter 1, on using the concept of defining ROI by the investment base, or denominator of the ROI equation, the term can be referred to as "return on human capital," "return on human resources," or "return on human assets." While the original concept of return on investment does not change, the definitions of the components and the inputs will have to be redefined. Keep in mind that most companies do not employ any measure of efficiency in human resources using the ROI concept in any calculations in their financial statements. Remember, employees are probably the most important asset of a company. This method will provide the conceptual framework to evaluate the true costs and the anticipated benefits of a company's human resources on ROI results. Therefore, one can say that this is a new way of thinking in looking at an organization's human resources.

In general, it appears that it is not possible to calculate any meaningful return on investment rate for people, even though they are one of the key resources of any organization. One of the reasons for this is that people represent a somewhat unmeasurable asset as applied to ROI results. In any event, the measurement of employee capabilities, such as basic aptitudes, skills, and experience, and an individual's organizational capabilities, such as leadership skills, team skills, and cooperativeness, tends to be highly judgmental and not subject to quantification. Despite these difficulties, there has been a great deal of time and effort expended in the study of this largely unexplored area. Most studies concentrate either on cost savings or improved employee morale, however, such as job enrichment. While many of

tively by such techniques as management by objectives or cost reduction opportunities, it appears that there may be some basis for determining at least a return on some marginal contribution basis.

For example, assuming no change in sales, cost reduction results occur through increases in income, and any reduction in cost can be treated as marginal income for purposes of a return on investment, as will be discussed for the capital budgeting process. Some approaches to the investment value include capitalizing the cost of hiring and training employees, and amortizing these costs over an estimated useful life of the employee's position/function based on the assumption that a lower employee turnover would contribute to a higher return on a company's investment in people. This is explored later in the chapter.

THE MECHANICS OF HUMAN RESOURCE ACCOUNTING

Evaluating investments in human resources centers on the technique of human resource accounting. What is it? This concept is concerned with capitalizing costs incurred in the training and future development of employees rather than expensing. The use of return on investment for human resource evaluation will not deal entirely with the human resource accounting mechanism, but also with the basic concept as it would apply in this case. Under this concept, a portion of the expenses incurred in training and development can be spread and expensed as an employee becomes productive within the organization. If an employee leaves the company, the unamortized or remaining expenses would be written off to expense and recognized as a loss to the company. This is very similar to depreciating a capital asset, where portions of the capital investment are written off over the life of the asset in the form of depreciation.

If we look at the mechanics of human resource, or HR, accounting, we see three bases by which human resources can be evaluated. They are acquisition, replacement, and economic values to a company. Acquisition costs relate to historical transactions necessary to acquire a resource. Replacement costs are estimated costs necessary today to replace a resource. Economic values represent the present value of an individual in relation to the person's contribution to the future earnings of the organization. These bases provide us with the ability to measure the potential earnings ability as to (1) what the resource cost is, and (2) what its value is. Conceptually, any human resources used during a period in which benefits are derived are classified as expenses. On the other hand, any resources used and derived

classified as expenses. On the other hand, any resources used and derived in future periods are considered assets in the consideration of investments in employees.

The capitalization of costs for human resources can provide a useful tool for managing and developing policies in the hiring practices of an organization. While this concept appears to have more value as an internal management tool, it can be an informative device for reporting the investment of human resources to stockholders and the effect it might have on future earnings of the company. Nevertheless, there is still some doubt as to the acceptance and/or validity that this type of reporting would have among the outside community. Many questions can be raised to argue the pros and cons of capitalizing employee costs and determining a return on investment rate. Just a few examples are such questions as these: Can an employee be owned as an asset is? Can the work life of an employee be defined in such a way as to determine amortizable costs for a specific functional position? Do expenses match revenue during the training and development stage? And what personal and social impact will this have on employees?

ADVANTAGES AND DISADVANTAGES OF USING THE ROI CONCEPT FOR HR EVALUATION

There are many advantages in using the return on investment concept for human resource evaluation. While they are mostly internal reporting advantages, the ultimate rewards will be reflected to the outside community at a later date through higher earnings and ultimately a higher return on investment. There are, of course, also some disadvantages to the use of this concept, and a list of these follows the more optimistic list.

Advantages
- Determines how to allocate human resources in a competitive environment.
- Provides a mechanism to use ROI concepts to reflect a financial or quantitative return for measuring human resources.
- Helps in evaluating investment opportunities, that is, human resource versus capital projects.
- Assists in determining the costs of human resource turnover.
- Aids in planning the monetary needs for human resources in the future.

- Develops a skill for organization planning, such as promotions and transfers, based on quantitative values.
- Highlights human resource costs of plant relocations and plant closings.
- Determines the cost of human resources for starting up a new plan or other form of operation.
- Assists in evaluating an employee's performance in the light of such factors as promotion, remaining on the job, or dismissal.
- Helps to develop costs attributable to permanent or part-time hires.
- In merger situations, provides a system for evaluating the management of the company to be acquired.

Disadvantages
- The so-called human resource assets are highly mobile and not owned and as such are not in keeping with the traditional definition of assets.
- The possibility of reported earnings manipulation.
- The possible inability to amortize the asset balance on a rational basis once it has been established.
- Employees will possibly resent being treated as assets.

HUMAN ASSETS VERSUS CAPITAL ASSETS

The basic difference between human and capital assets is that human assets are considered incapable of being sold. Probably the most important contribution that management can make to an organization is providing the right people for the right job. On the other hand, capital assets are capable of being sold or transferred to other owners. In addition, accounting practices have allowed companies to write off the investment in capital assets through depreciation. In human resources, investments can be amortized over the useful life of the employee under this suggested concept. If an employee leaves before the end of his/her estimated useful life in that position, a write-off would occur. It is anticipated that when an employer invests in a new employee, those returns or benefits will exceed the costs of employment. An employee's worth can be measured by two interrelated variables, that is, the expected life or tenure with the company and the contributions over that expected period measured in some predetermined monetary value.

The expected life of an employee can be varied, unlike that of a capital project, which is more definitely fixed. Employees can voluntarily or involuntarily leave the organization. Therefore, it is recommended that management initiate shorter evaluations, such as two- and five-year evaluations, than it applies to capital projects. It is also important to reassess an employee after five years to evaluate past performance and to project performance for a defined future period.

METHODS FOR MEASURING THE VALUE OF HUMAN RESOURCES

There are six suggested methods for measuring the value of human resources. The order in which they are listed does not imply one is preferred over the other. Each method must be evaluated on its own merit and its value as a measurement tool.

Return on Effort Employed

A point value is given to the job title (i.e., 1 point for a clerk up to 10 for the president or chairman of the board), and this is multiplied by a personal assessment factor and multiplied again by a factor based on length of employment (i.e., 1–2 years, 1.1; up to 4 years, 1.2; etc.). The overall figure would be divided by total profits to determine a defined return rate.

Cost Approach

The cost approach measures an investment in human resources similar to the capital expenditures investment concept. Such costs as hiring, recruiting, transportation costs, training, and development can be totaled and amortization schedules compiled and expensed to the statement of income as utilized. An additional approach reflects current replacement costs and considers the human resource investment beyond the historical costs of obtaining employees. This method assumes a current value of replacing employees of equal qualifications and tends to reflect economic trends by providing an up-to-date cost estimate for both turnover costs and long-range human resource planning.

Value Approach

The value approach relates the value of the human resources as a function of the wages or earnings of the company. For example, the part of future earnings that differs from industry averages could provide the basis for establishing the value of human resources in terms of investment return on human resources. A more sophisticated approach establishes the estimated costs of present and future wage payments and develops a current return on human resources ratio to forecasted future profits. The result is then compared to the industry rate, and the difference represents the value of the human part of the organization.

Economic Approach

The economic approach suggests that the value of an employee is based on the marketplace, that is, on the supply and demand factors in which competitive bidding takes place, whereby the employer bidding the highest price usually hires the services of the employee. Therefore, the value of the employee is the price needed to obtain the services of the employee.

Goodwill Method

In this method, earnings in excess of an industry average would be calculated and then a proportion of this would be attributed to human factors.

Behavioral Variables Method

This method would involve statistical analyses of variations in leadership ability correlated with increases in earnings, productivity, and other income factors. This would seem to depend on subjective evaluations despite the mathematics.

COSTS OF HUMAN RESOURCES

The investments made for human resources take many different forms, which are reflected in the earnings of the company, for example, out-of-pocket expenditures for activities such as recruiting and acquisition, training and development, and allocating salaries during training and development periods. We can suggest that expenses that can be capitalized as assets be included on the balance sheet and those expenses not capitalized be included on the statement of income. Keep in mind that these categories may not meet

---

TABLE 18-1   Typical Costs of Human Resources

Salaries & Wages	*Benefits*
Salaries	Group life insurance
Commissions	Accident and health plans
Overrides	Dental plans
Bonuses	Disability insurance
Overtime	Pension plan contributions
Payroll Taxes	Profit-sharing plans
Social Security	Stock plans
State and local taxes	Travel insurance
Federal taxes	*Supplies*

---

the standards as presented by the accounting profession, but nevertheless can be a valuable tool for internal evaluation. Table 18-1 illustrates an example of some of the expenses used to calculate total costs of human resources.

Table 18-2 illustrates typical asset classifications that would become part of the investment in human resources as shown on the balance sheet. These costs would be capitalized, and periodic write-offs would occur during the estimated life of a particular position.

TECHNIQUES FOR DETERMINING A RETURN ON INVESTMENT RATE FOR EMPLOYEE MEASUREMENT

Since this concept remains relatively new in its application, different methods can be employed in reaching its objectives, with no one method having an advantage over another. Nevertheless, each company must evaluate its needs and objectives and choose the one feasible method, or adaptation of several, for measuring human resources.

Measuring Staff Personnel

The original formula of return on investment, that is, the profitability rate times the turnover rate, can be adapted to measure staff personnel as follows:

Employee Measurement Equation

$$\frac{\text{Job earning}}{\text{Net sales}} \times \frac{\text{MBO job value}}{\text{Insurance value}}$$

TABLE 18-2 Illustration of Typical Asset Classifications of Human Resources

Professional Development
Costs used to increase an employee's
capabilities in skills training and
organizational development beyond what
is needed in the current position.
  Seminar fees
  Continuing education both outside and
    inside the company
Professional dues and fees
Professional meeting and travel expenses

Training
Costs incurred immediately after
employment.
  On-the-job training
  Orientation
  Costs of other employee(s) including
    salary allocations
  Costs of integrating new employees such
    as philosophy, history, policies,
    reporting relationships, etc.

Recruiting Costs
Costs involved in locating and selecting
new personnel.
  Employment advertising
  Interviewing expenses, both internal
    and external
  Testing and evaluation
  Search fees

Acquisition Costs
Costs used to acquire and indoctrinate a
new employee to a point where the
employee becomes operational.
  Fees to employment agencies and
    search firms
  Medical examination fees
  Moving and relocation costs
  Time spent in administering paper work
    to hire employees
  Cost of initial supplies needed to perform
    job

Three new terms are introduced, namely, "job earnings," "MBO job value," and "insurance value." These terms are defined as follows:

Job earnings is the calculation of MBO job value less the discounted cash flow (DCF) of salary, training, and related employee benefits. To such items as actual salary, bonuses, and monetized benefits, cash flows are added to return such items as hiring costs and training over a specific period of time at a specific opportunity cost. The opportunity cost represents a desired rate of return. The discounted cash flow calculation is the total payment to keep an employee in his/her job.

MBO job value is the value of a job measured through a management by objectives (MBO) process. The staff employee and his/her immediate superior agree to certain objectives to be reached over the next year. These objectives are then measured as to the employee's worth to the company. Thus, the calculation of job earnings ÷ MBO job value indicates the productivity of the employee. If the employee is earning more than the worth of the calculated objective, then the equation of MBO job value less DCF will be equal to, or less than, zero. With a zero or negative numerator, the productivity ratio will be zero or negative.

Insurance value The total value or assets of the employee can be defined as to what amount a company is willing to insure an employee. Thus, the calculation could be the aggregate of an employee's salary, benefits, training and development, hiring costs, cost of replacement, and corporate property value. The value of the staff employee to the company is the total value, not just the yearly or MBO job value. If the employee increases productivity by setting and reaching higher MBO objectives, then achievement of a greater and shorter turnover of assets results. At this point, the insurance value should probably be increased to bring the ratio back into line. For example, a ratio of over 50% suggests that the employee should be scheduled for further training to enhance the job. If the ratio falls below 10%, then training of a remedial nature may be suggested. These ratio levels are for illustration purposes only, and a company should develop its own standards. It is well to note that no attempt is made here to minimize the problems of measuring the worth or MBO job value of an employee, since many other subjective items must be considered, such as keeping family control of the business and special forms of compensation.

Measuring Professional Service Firms

One type of organization that seems to be more adaptable than others to the use of return on investment is the professional service firm. These would include law firms, CPA firms, consulting firms, and other firms operating for profit. The assumption is that the firms can reasonably forecast the demand for their services, and, based on this, the firm can calculate a return on investment rate of a new employee. The calculation will be based on the previously mentioned calculation of return on controllable human assets:

Professional Service Measurement Equation

$$\frac{\text{Marginal contribution}}{\text{Net billings}} \times \frac{\text{Net billings}}{\text{Controllable human resource assets}}$$

or

$$\frac{\text{Marginal contribution}}{\text{Controllable human resource assets}}$$

The terms "marginal contribution" and "controllable human resource assets" require further explanation.

Marginal contribution Both marginal contribution and net billings will be illustrated by the following sets of facts.

Estimate of chargeable hours	2,000 hours
Times	
Billing rate of new hire	$50/hour
Equals	
Gross billings	$100,000
Less: Allowance for doubtful accounts	5,000
Net billings	95,000
Less: Salary, employee benefits,	
and other variable training costs	35,000
Marginal contribution	$ 60,000

Controllable human resource assets. For a professional firm, this represents accounts receivable and work-in-process (that is, time charged to a particular client or clients, but not yet billed). The following illustrates the calculation of controllable human resource assets.

Accounts receivable	$40,000
Work-in-process	35,000
Controllable human resource assets	$75,000

Using the above facts and the following formula, a calculation can be made for what is referred to as return on controllable human resource assets.

$$\frac{\text{Marginal contribution}}{\text{Net billings}} \times \frac{\text{Net billings}}{\text{Controllable human resource assets}}$$

Substituting the factual data in the formula results in the following equation:

$$\frac{\$60,000}{\$95,000} \times \frac{\$95,000}{\$75,000}$$

or

$$63.2\% \times 1.267$$

equals

Return on controllable human resource assets = 80%

TABLE 18-3 The Great Company, Inc.
Statement of Income
Comparison of Financial versus Financial
and Human Resources

19X2	Financial and Human Resources	Financial
Net sales	$700,000	$700,000
Cost of sales	525,000	525,000
Gross profit	175,000	175,000
Other operating expenses		
Depreciation	5,000	5,000
Selling expenses	30,000	30,000
Administrative expenses	25,000	25,000
General expenses	15,000	15,000
Operating income	100,000	100,000
Other (income) expense	2,000	2,000
Income before income taxes	98,000	98,000
Net increase (decrease) in human resources investment	(3,000)	—
Adjusted income before taxes	95,000	98,000
Income taxes	46,500	48,000
Net income	$ 48,500	$ 50,000
% to net sales	6.93%	7.14%

$$\frac{\$60,000}{\$95,000} \times \frac{\$95,000}{\$75,000}$$

or

$$63.2\% \times 1.267$$

equals

Return on controllable human resource assets = 80%

THE OVERALL IMPACT OF HR EXPENDITURES ON THE FINANCIAL STATEMENT

Return on investment performance relates to a combination of volume performance, cost control, and asset utilization, all of which are related to people to the degree to which they do or do not perform their task and to amount for human resource investment. In addition, the balance sheet (Table 18-4) reflects not only the asset investment in human resources but an apportionment of retained earnings for human resource appropriations. Unlike the traditional financial statement, both financial statements reflect the organization's investment in human resources.

USING RATIO COMPARISONS

Many comparisons can be made that will act as an indicator for measuring performance. Like all ratios, they are merely management tools and should be used with other acceptable tools of management as outlined in previous chapters.

Net Investments in Human Resources to Total Assets

The human asset investment ratio is a useful indicator of future profit performance. A correlation exists between the profitability of a company and the training and development costs associated with human resources. A higher ratio suggests potentially higher profits; conversely, a lower ratio suggests potentially lower profits. The calculation is:

$$\frac{\text{Net investments in human resources}}{\text{Total assets}} = \frac{\$15,000}{\$275,000} = 5.5\%$$

Computing Return on Total Assets

Applying the return on total asset concept, the impact of investments in human resource assets is clearly reflected. In previous illustrations, the return on total assets was 19.2%, computed as follows:

$$\frac{\text{Net income}}{\text{Net sales}} \times \frac{\text{Net sales}}{\text{Total assets}}$$

or

$$\text{Profitability rate} \times \text{Turnover rate}$$

They are calculated as:

$$\frac{\$50,000}{\$700,000} \times \frac{\$700,000}{\$260,000} = 19.2\%$$

TABLE 18-4 The Great Company, Inc.
Balance Sheet—Comparison of Financial versus Financial and Human Resources

19X2	Financial and Human Resources	Financial
Asset		
Current assets		
Cash in banks	$ 5,000	$ 5,000
Marketable securities, at cost that approximates market	7,000	7,000
Accounts receivable—net of allowance for doubtful accounts	80,000	80,000
Inventories	40,000	40,000
Prepaid expenses	5,500	5,500
Total current assets	137,500	137,500
Fixed assets—net of accumulated depreciation	118,000	118,000
Net investments in human resources	15,000	—
Other assets	4,500	4,500
Total assets	$275,000	$260,000
Liabilities		
Current liabilities		
Accounts payable	$ 38,000	$ 38,000
Debt due within one year	4,500	4,500
Accrued expenses	10,000	10,000
Income taxes payable	12,500	12,500
Total current liabilities	65,000	65,000
Long-term debt	24,000	24,000
Deferred federal income taxes as a result of appropriation for human resources	7,500	—
Total liabilities	$ 96,500	$ 89,000
Shareholders' equity		
Common stock	$ 40,000	$ 40,000
Capital in excess of par value	10,000	10,000
Earnings retained in business	121,000	121,000
Appropriation for human resources	7,500	—
Total shareholders' equity	$178,500	$171,000
Total liabilities and shareholders' equity	$275,000	$260,000

or

$$.0714 \times 2.69 = 19.2\%$$

With human resource investments added, the return on total assets is 17.6%, or

$$\frac{\$48,500}{\$700,000} \times \frac{\$700,000}{\$275,000} = 17.6\%$$

Viewed this way, the impact of human resources exhibits a lower return on investment rate, both in the profitability rate and the turnover rate. The evidence points to the conclusion that when human resources are reflected in the financial statements, they will result in lower return on investment returns, particularly when a company is operating at a low productivity rate and has a high human resource turnover rate.

DECISION-MAKING STRATEGIES

- Apply return on investment techniques to human resource evaluation for determining how human resources affect return on investment rates.
- For analysis purposes, treat human resources in the same way as capital assets.
- Develop return on investment standards for investments in human resources.
- Promote a program that rewards employees for contributions to the company (e.g., cost reduction ideas, high productivity, ideas for new products).
- Develop a training and development program for increasing skills with specific career objectives as the central theme.

19

CAPITAL INVESTMENTS—THE KEY TO HIGHER PROFITS, CASH FLOWS, AND RETURN ON INVESTMENT

It is an accepted fact in business that capital investments are a key element of a company's long-term growth. Why are they so important? They provide a continuous flow of future profits and cash needed for operating and investment decisions.

It must be also recognized that all products and services have a life cycle, at the end of which they will no longer appeal to the marketplace and will be replaced by other forms of products or services. Although people generally associate life cycles with products, services have them also. Just look at bank services offered ten years ago and those being offered today. Therefore, in every business, new products and services must be provided to replace technology, to meet changing population trends, to meet obsolescence, to meet economic changes, and to meet changing end-user demands.

This chapter discusses the vital role top management plays in capital investment decisions, the classifications and process of capital investments, the methods of financing, and an example illustrating how debt can reduce the average weighted cost of capital. Chapter 20 provides the step-by-step methods for calculating and evaluating capital investments and concludes with examples of actual firms' capital investment policies and procedures.

WHY CAPITAL INVESTMENTS ARE IMPORTANT

Decisions on capital investments are extremely important to the continuous success of the company, and therefore top management usually assumes direct responsibility for the larger and more important expenditures. Because of the nature and substantial amounts of the expenditures, these capital investment decisions are important and deserve the attention of top management for the following reasons.

Substantial Amounts of Money

Most expenditures that are governed by the policies of the capital expenditures program involve substantial amounts of money. It is money invested not only in fixed assets but also in the working capital of the company. Since one of the main functions of top managers is to manage the assets and resources of the company, capital investment decisions are their responsibility.

Invested Over Long Periods of Time

Most capital investments are invested over long periods of time. They are investments for long-term benefits, made either in the short run or over long periods of time. In any case, the allocation of resources for capital investments involves long-term commitments and usually establishes many of the long-term objectives needed to maintain an adequate level of growth.

Commitments Are Hard to Reverse

Once the commitment is made, or more importantly, once the project becomes operational and is showing poor results, it is quite difficult to reverse the original decision to invest. Reversal of such decisions usually involves substantial losses or the loss of valuable cash funds.

Survival Dependence

The success or failure of a company is dependent upon the success of one or more investment decisions. Many companies have gone out of business or have suffered hard financial times because of poor investments or lack of investments.

Projecting the Future

Many capital investments tie in with the future plans of the company. These plans anticipate growth, recovery of resources, and directions that a company must take to succeed in a given economic environment. Sometimes, a shift of emphasis is placed on the direction through certain investment opportunities. The ability to project the future becomes more and more difficult.

In addition to the support of top management, other key elements go into the success or failure of a capital investment. They center on the ability of top management to time the capital investment in such a way that maximizes the benefits expected for the project. Timing is a vital ingredient to the success or failure of most capital investments. Not only is it important for the acquisition of machinery and equipment but also for investments in working capital. Knowing when to tighten up on accounts receivable and add inventory and what cash balances to maintain are all important questions that revolve around timing.

Top management must also give clearly defined directions and make sure that the entire capital process is adequately coordinated throughout the company.

The capital investment process involves investing in many different areas of the company. It may require investments in a functional activity of a company, such as to support the sales effort, production requirements, distribution, or administrative needs. There are usually no guidelines as to how much is spent on functional activities of the company. As long as funds can be made available, and justification can be supported, investments in these areas are usually made.

TYPES OF ASSET INVESTMENTS

There are many different types of investments in assets. But such investments can be categorized into three major areas: physical assets, working capital, and research projects.

Physical assets, or *fixed assets,* are investments that are fixed in nature, including such items as land, land improvements, factories, office buildings, warehouses, machinery, and equipment.

Working assets are investments in the current working assets of the business that are used in operating the firm. Although it is recognized that current liabilities are part of working capital, only current assets will be used. Because current liabilities are a result of investing in current assets, one may consider them as another form of financing. Investments in working assets include cash, marketable securities, accounts receivable, materials and supplies, in-process inventories, and finished-goods inventories.

Research projects are investments made for research in support of the operating functions of the company. These investments can be made prior to a major expenditure, such as a feasibility study for building a new plant, or expenditures can be made on an ongoing basis, such as for marketing research, production efficiencies, financial studies, and economic analysis.

TYPES OF CAPITAL EXPENDITURE CLASSIFICATIONS

Within a capital expenditures program, there are classifications that encompass all capital investment projects. This is to allow grouping types of projects according to spending priorities, which in turn results in establishing return on investment objectives for each major classification. This method allows a company to allocate resources in a positive effort to maximize return on investment not only for each classification but also for the investment objectives of the entire company.

For example, during different stages of a company's economic life, there will be periods when emphasis will be placed on capital expenditures that reduce costs; other times there will be a need to modernize, meet environmental standards, upgrade technology, increase capacity, develop new products, expand, or contract. The resources would be allocated between these classifications to ultimately maximize return on investment.

The following is a typical list of capital expenditure classifications. It must be noted that many companies use their own classifications depending upon the industry in which they operate.

- Maintenance and replacement projects
- Profit improvement projects
- Quality improvement projects
- Cost savings projects
- Expansion projects
- New product introduction projects
- Other projects

Maintenance and replacement projects are projects needed for the continuance of existing machinery and equipment. For example, this classification would include repairs and general maintenance functions.

Profit improvement projects are those anticipated to add additional profit to existing earnings. Such projects clearly state how much is expected and in what time periods and are important in maintaining adequate profit margins and, more important, cash flows.

Quality improvement projects are those that bring about a general improvement of the quality of a product(s) in keeping with the quality standards of the company.

Cost savings projects are projects that anticipate sufficient economic value over and above existing costs. Such savings could occur in labor, productivity, or material.

Expansion projects deal with the purpose of expanding production, sales in existing markets, and sales in new markets.

New product introduction projects are projects whose primary objective is providing facilities for the introduction of new products. New products in this context are those products not currently manufactured and/or marketed by the company.

Other projects include projects that do no fall under any of the preceding classifications. Examples are contaminant control, developments, meeting legal requirements, public image, employee morale, noise abatement, and cafeteria improvement.

Where projects provide for more than one benefit, it is necessary to determine which benefit is the primary objective of the project. This is done by reviewing the end results of the project and the major phase of the project creating the benefit.

Projects may also be classified into major versus minor projects. These projects are usually dependent upon the dollar limits and the objective to which the major benefit is being directed. For example, a project requiring a small sum of funds to replace a part may be considered a minor project, whereas a project requesting substantial funds for a major expansion would therefore be considered a major project.

It is important to recognize that companies within different industries use different classifications. For example, the pharmaceutical industry has a classification called community responsibility; the food and beverage industry uses a classification called risk hedging; replacement required by law or community relations is found in the soap and cosmetic industry; venture projects in the petroleum refining industry; strategic investments in the office machine industry; and defensive projects in industries dealing with products from stone, concrete, clay, and glass.

You can see that any standardization of classification does not exist. Nevertheless, it is quite clear that most companies use project classifications that deal with profit improvement or cost savings, expansion, replacement and maintenance, new products, and non-income-producing projects.

FACTORS INVOLVED IN THE INVESTMENT DECISION

In any investment decision many questions must be considered. These are questions that go into making up the final decision regarding "go" or "no go." Although the answers to different questions will have varying weights, all of these questions must be considered in the thought process preceding every project. Some of these questions may not apply to some projects, but a checklist should be made so as not to overlook any crucial decisions that may have an impact.

To help a company understand each of the complex variables, a brief explanation will be given for each variable, which will be phrased in the form of a question. Each investment will have its own characteristics and should be considered as a separate entity when evaluating the merits of the expenditure. Remember that each capital investment must be evaluated as if nothing else existed. In other words, the capital investment must be supported on its own merits.

What are the alternatives? Consideration must be given to reviewing alternatives to the proposed investment. Each proposal should have an alternative, although the alternative may very well be to do nothing. If this is the case, one must ask the following question: What are the consequences over the short run and over the long run? Management should be presented with alternative options whenever possible.

How important is the investment? Each investment opportunity must be classified as to its importance in terms of both size and survival to the company. Investments that are very important receive a more critical review by more individuals and at higher levels within the organization. Investments of lesser importance usually require fewer reviews and approval at a lower organizational level.

How risky is the investment? Every investment has some inherent risks. These should be noted by reviewing the potential consequences of not achieving desired results. It is the old "all your eggs in one basket" theory. The degree of risk will also determine the level of return on investment that a company should expect. The higher the risk, the higher the expected return; the lower the risk, the lower the expected return.

What is the effect on the financial structure of the company? Many investments will change the financial structure of a company's balance sheet. This may be favorable or unfavorable in both the short and the long run. The impact on the balance sheet may create a negative situation for future financing negotiations.

Is this the right time for this investment? Throughout the history of business, timing of capital investments has played a major role in the success or failure of a product and, in some cases, of the company. Before approving any investment—such as plant expansion, new products, expanding markets, new markets, increasing raw material, inventory stockpiling, and so forth—a company must determine whether the timing is right.

How will competitors react? Most companies will not enjoy the competitive edge for long periods. As soon as a company begins to flourish and to have a competitive advantage, competitors will react by offering a similar product and/or services. Therefore, when investment decisions give your company the competitive edge, be sure that the company is not led to expect continued upward movement, particularly at the same rate of growth. One major factor to consider is how long it will take a competitor to enter the market. A longer entry period will not hurt a company's competitive edge in the short run.

Does the investment have a desirable return on investment? Does the investment assist in meeting the overall company return on investment objectives? Will it enhance the rate of return in future years? Is it necessary to maintaining the existence of the business? Is the rate of return in keeping with the riskiness of the investment? How does it relate to competitive investment rates? Is it in keeping with industry averages? Does it exceed the company's cost of capital? These are some of the questions that must be answered to determine whether the return on investment is desirable.

How will the investment affect the financial results both in the short and the long run? Because profits are derived from investments that have been made in the past and from those that will be made in the future, this question is critical. Many companies fail because poor investments were made, which did not produce sufficient profits to meet rising costs. Cash flow analysis will assist in validating estimated future profits and amounts of cash that will be generated. Remember, its validity is only as good as the soundness of the projections. Knowing the impact of these investments in both the short and the long run will assist managers in planning future growth and future financial needs.

How reliable are the projections of the contents of the investment? The reliability of the investment data will depend upon such analysis as experience with other similar investments internally, engineering studies, feasibility studies, competitor experience with similar projects, and industry studies. Every effort should be made to validate the contents of each major investment, since the risk with larger investments is greater.

Does the investment deviate from the image and philosophy of the company? Every company projects some image to its customers and certainly has a basic philosophy in operating the business. It is important that investments, particularly the introduction of new products, reflect that image and philosophy to ensure recognition by the marketplace.

Does the investment meet the approval of all concerned? The investment should be approved by all responsible individuals involved in the business. Because each individual will have a different perspective, that is, a different background and different area of expertise, universal consensus should be strived for. This is even more important on major investments.

Are there any legal problems as a result of this investment? Most investments should be cleared by legal counsel. Because many new laws affect many aspects of operating a business, it is important that significant investments be reviewed by legal counsel.

Are there any unique political situations involved? This is a hard question to answer, since many of these observations are difficult to access. In certain circumstances, however, local political situations may have more meaning. Major investments may be tied more closely with national policy, such as changes in the tax laws, conservation policies, or foreign policy.

WHAT THE CAPITAL INVESTMENT PROCESS SHOULD ACCOMPLISH

The capital program is important because it provides the necessary recovery of funds to overcome the replacement of assets and, more important, provides the necessary funds in future years and excess funds for growth. Through planning for growth, a sound and adequate capital program will ensure that the strategies, plans, objectives, and goals of the company are met in an orderly fashion.

Therefore, in understanding the capital investment process, it is necessary to review the reasons for operating a controlled and administered capital program.

Coordinates short-term programs with long-term goals. The accomplishment of short-term programs are often tied in with long-term goals. This is particularly true when new plants and equipment are needed to support new product introductions and anticipated growth in sales volume. In addition, it is a vital part of the funds generation to support future growth.

Utilizes the tax advantages of tax legislation. Depreciation, special tax incentives by both local and federal agencies, leasing, and special bond issues provide the company with certain tax advantages.

Determines what capital investments offer the highest return. Through the process of evaluating capital investments, a selection process is made on which capital projects offer the highest return and benefits to the company. In many cases, the projects with the highest return on investment rates and shortest payback period will be chosen. However, projects may also be selected for nonfinancial factors.

Determines financial capabilities. It is a recognized fact that most companies do not have all the funds necessary to fulfill all of the requests for capital expenditures that are presented. Therefore, it is a matter of determining how capable a company is in the financing of capital expenditure needs.

Identifies the most suitable asset. Through the preparation of a capital expenditure request, careful attention is given to what type of equipment or plant is necessary to meet the specific needs of the company.

Determines the best method of financing. There are many ways in which to finance an acquisition of an asset, which are discussed later in the chapter. Internally they include cost reductions, selling marketable securities, managing assets more effectively, selling parts of the business, retaining sufficient earnings in the business, selling certain assets of the business, and expanding short-term liabilities. Externally they include debt financing, equity financing, and leasing.

Establishes authorization levels. Authorization levels are needed to assign responsibilities for the approval of capital projects. These authorization levels can increase from year to year and should be reviewed every year for updating.

Determines accountability. Since each project is usually requested by an accountability center, the acquisition of an asset is assigned to a specific accountability center for managing. This accountability becomes part of the normal operational review process when the asset becomes functional.

Highlights timing. Capital projects will require certain investment dollars and generate certain cash flows over the life of the asset. These cash flows must be adjusted to reflect economic changes throughout the life of the asset. In addition, it is important to know when both the cash outflows and the cash inflows are to materialize. The capital investment process will highlight both of these elements.

Assists in redeploying investment dollars to maximize return on investment. The capital investment process will assist a company to determine how to allocate the funds for capital investments in order to maximize return on investment. Table 19-1 illustrates a proposed capital budget by listing the estimated investment dollars by type of project, the estimated earnings and expected return by type of project, and overall return on investment to the company. For example, the company is planning to spend $1,500,000 for cost savings projects with an estimated earnings throughout the life of the project of $550,000. The projects result in a return on investment rate of 36.7%. The overall capital investment program is estimated to be $5,000,000 with an expected return of $1,500,000, or a return on investment of 30%.

Now let us assume that the company redistributes some of the funds to different types of projects that generate higher returns and see what the impact is on the return on investment rate. The individual project returns

TABLE 19-1   Proposed Capital Budget Program

Types of Projects	Investment	Estimated Earnings	Return
Maintenance and replacement	$ 500,000	$ 125,000	25.0%
Profit improvement	1,000,000	400,000	40.0%
Cost savings	1,500,000	550,000	36.7
Expansion	1,000,000	125,000	12.5
New product introduction	700,000	300,000	42.9
Others	300,000	—	—
Total	$5,000,000	$1,500,000	30.0%

TABLE 19-2   Proposed Capital Budget Redistributed

Types of Projects	Investment	Estimated Earnings	Return
Maintenance and replacement	$ 400,000	$ 100,000	25.0%
Profit improvement	1,300,000	520,000	40.0
Cost savings	1,700,000	624,000	36.7
Expansion	500,000	62,500	12.5
New product introduction	900,000	386,000	42.9
Others	200,000	—	—
Total	$5,000,000	$1,692,500	33.9%

will not change but will be used to recalculate the earnings and overall return on investment rate, as shown in Table 19-2.

You will note by redistributing the investment dollars by type of project, the earnings increase $192,500 ($1,692,500 − $1,500,000) and the return on investment rate increases from 30% to 33.9%.

A CHECKLIST OF STEPS IN THE CAPITAL INVESTMENT PROCESS

The process of generating capital investments within a company involves many steps and usually follows a logical sequence of events. The actual mechanics of execution may vary, but the basic steps still apply in most company situations. The sequence starts with an idea and ends with a decision. This decision is then reviewed to compare the expected results against what actually happened. In itself, the simplicity is logical. If you have a problem, find out what it is and what actions are necessary to remedy it, and act accordingly. In essence, it is a problem-solving exercise, one that encompasses the definition of a problem or opportunity and the implementation and completion of a project. The following is a brief summary of how the total process operates.

Determine the need for an investment. This is the initial stage that establishes the existence of a problem or an opportunity. This need is generated at all levels of the company, in all parts of the organization, and at all location sites. It may be in the form of adopting new technology, doing things better and in a less costly way, entering the marketplace with new ideas through new products, or merely making an investment for employee safety and morale. Prior discussion highlighted the types of typical investments.

Determine what alternatives are available. In conjunction with the above, determine alternative solutions and present these alternatives as part of the overall capital expenditure project. The alternatives should be measured and weighted against each other as to the economic benefits that will materialize to the company. A decision is reached as to the recommended alternative and stated in the initial presentation.

Consider the applicability to the future plans of the company. Once the decision is reached as to what alternative should be approved, it must then be evaluated in keeping with the long-term plans and objectives of the company. This is considered so as to assure continuing future development in terms of markets, product lines, philosophy, and projected size of the company. The long-range plans, including capital investment requirements, will highlight these factors.

Determine the availability of funds. Total investments should be consolidated and coordinated with the total availability of funds for the company. This will be determined in the next step by the completion of a capital expenditures budget. If future funds are required, additional financing may be necessary. Be sure that capital investments are in keeping with the long-range plans of the company.

Prepare a capital expenditures budget. Based on the proposed capital investments, a capital expenditures budget is prepared. The budget would include such information as the nature of the investment, the type of investment, the urgency, the impact upon the total company or the accountability center, the amount of funds required for the investment (including working capital, expenses, and investments in fixed assets), economic justification (such as payback or discounted cash flow), estimated starting date, schedule of estimated cash payments, project number and control identification, necessary authorizations, and any other pertinent data necessary to evaluate fully the capital expenditure proposal. Supporting documentation for each proposal would be included in keeping with the company's policy and procedure.

Develop measurement tools. As part of the capital investment process, evaluation techniques must be established to measure and weigh the consequences of each alternative investment. These measurement tools are found in such techniques as payback, net present value, internal rate of return, risk analysis, and sensitivity analysis. These concepts are discussed in chapter 17. Most companies use the payback period method with some form of discounting techniques, such as the internal rate of return.

Develop cash flow estimates. Each capital investment proposal should have an estimate of cash flows that are generated by the proposed investment. These cash flows represent all the estimates of the project making up the anticipated net earnings, plus noncash charges (principally depreciation), additions to working capital, and fixed asset investment dollars. These projections are estimated for each period (usually in one-year increments) over the life of the capital investment. "Life" in this case can represent either the physical life, the technological life, or the economic life. Whichever technique is used, it will determine how many years' estimates of cash flow are necessary. A more detailed discussion is given in chapter 20.

Establish approval limits. Many companies establish approval limits for approving capital expenditures, licensing agreements, and computer software. These approval limits are determined by different levels of the organization. For example, the board of directors may want approval for expenditures exceeding $10 million, whereas approvals below $10 million would be broken down at different levels and/or units of the organization. This amount would vary depending upon the size of the company and the number of projects being presented yearly at each approval level. For example, a company may not want more than 10% of all capital expenditure requests to be presented to the board of directors for approval. Under this scenario, the cut-off dollar amount would be reached by approximating where 10% of the estimated expenditures (projects) fall. At this level (10%), whatever the dollar amounts are at that level, the projects would be sent to the board of directors for approval. Using the above guidelines, an approval process might be developed as follows:

Approval Required By	Expenditure Levels	%of Total Projects
Board of directors	Over $10 million	Not more than 10%
Executive committee	$5–$10 million	50%
Business segments	$1–$4.9 million	30%
Operating units	Under $1 million	10%

It is important to review the above guidelines each year since the number of projects would change and project costs would increase due to inflation. Remember, larger companies may have very different guidelines than small-to medium-size companies. Therefore, a careful review and experimentation is needed periodically (preferably yearly).

Establish expenditure controls. Once the investment has been approved, expenditure controls should be established to ensure that actual spending is in keeping with authorized expenditures. A mechanism for doing this is to resubmit a summary of the approved projects with a request to issue funds for segments of the proposal against the authorized amounts. This represents the authorization to spend the money. Amounts, vendors, purpose, and timing of the expenditures should be included. In addition, a total of how much has been spent for the project and any expected underruns or overruns should be included.

Identify disposal candidates. When a proposal is submitted for approval, it should contain any candidates of fixed assets that can be disposed of during the life of the investment. Sometimes trade-ins as well as disposals are involved that would help in offsetting the initial investment costs. This helps in increasing cash flow, speeds up the payback period, and ultimately increases the return on investment rate.

Develop forms and procedures. This step will vary by company and by industry, but should include all the data necessary to make a valid and intelligent decision on the capital investment. The key is to standardize the forms and procedures so that all investments have an equal opportunity for approval. Standardization means using the same methods for calculating depreciation, cash flows, payback, and return on investment and for presenting the data. Once this discipline is cohesive, a company can fairly and more accurately measure the validity of what is presented. It also establishes a self-discipline in making sure that all aspects of the proposal are considered.

Prepare postcompletion audits. Much has been written about post-completion audits. This process of evaluating actual performance of a project as compared to its estimate is a long-discussed issue. It is important to monitor a capital project when comparing estimated cost of acquiring a fixed asset to actual costs. Review of the project after completion is also well advised, particularly to see if the project is still anticipated to generate the cash flows originally estimated.

Nevertheless, reviewing projects over a long period of time against what was originally estimated may defeat the purpose. This is so because, in many cases, accountability for the project may have changed, and the originators and approvers may have other functions within the company or may have left the company. At that point, where should the blame for not meeting estimates be directed? To individuals possibly no longer having that specific responsibility? More important, it is recognized that when projects are completed and become operational, they become part of the normal process of evaluating operations. Caution should be taken before deciding at what stage, how long, and with what intensity projects will be postaudited.

CAPITAL INVESTMENT PROPOSAL— A PRACTICAL EXAMPLE

A typical capital investment proposal would contain the basic fundamental data needed to make an accurate decision. Remember, these approved capital expenditures create future cash flows for future capital projects, profits, higher equity values, and, ultimately, higher stock prices for publicly traded companies. For nonpublicly traded companies, the value of the company would be enhanced and supply the necessary capital for growth and expansion.

Justifying the Project Proposal

Every capital project must be justified. Not only is there a financial justification, but other criteria such as the competitive impact, long-term implications, legal ramifications, environmental issues, and the impact on human resources must also be justified. This justification is contained in a written commentary that accompanies supporting schedules outlined later. This commentary must contain at least the following explanations.

General Background

A brief description of the present situation and why this project is needed is a basic element of any capital project proposal. Examples might include the replacing of obsolete machinery and equipment due to technology, to meet growth demands, to comply with environmental issues, and to maintain current levels of activity. Basically, what is being asked is why do you want to spend the money and how will it help the company.

Project Details

Once the brief description is given, a more detailed project description is needed as to what is the possible competitive reaction and what are the commercial and/or economic considerations. The type of machinery and equipment and related data is contained in a later section of this proposal.

Estimated Benefits

This section addresses the issue of measurable benefits of the investment proposal. They include estimated cost savings (savings from human resources, an analysis of profit contribution from incremental volume, and other measurable benefits).

Estimated Costs

This section summarizes the amount of capital costs and where they are going to be spent; why this particular machinery and equipment was chosen (include copies of manufacturers specifications and a picture if possible), if the project requires an outside contractor, (a background including the financial strength and capabilities are necessary), and if the project is not part of the current capital program (unbudgeted), how will the project be funded or self-financed from the project's cash flow.

Alternatives

Like all investment proposals, there should be one or more alternatives to the request. This would include financing alternatives such as leasing, outsourcing, and the consequences of not committing the funds.

Financial Results

This section should highlight the estimated after-tax payback period and the estimated return on investment using a discounted cash flow technique such as the internal rate of return (IRR).

Recommendation

This final section should include your recommendations as to which alternative is preferred, the timing of the project, and any other comments as to why this capital project is needed. Often, categories of urgency are required, such as very urgent, urgent, somewhat urgent, and low priority. Caution should be given to making sure that every project is not labeled very urgent. Guidelines for each of these categories should be given to eliminate this occurrence happening.

Key Forms

A typical set of key forms is generally used by most companies. These forms capture the pertinent data needed to make a decision as to the viability of the proposed capital investment. In addition to these key forms, supporting documents, such as marketing data, economic issues, human resource issues, and other pertinent data, which would support the decision to approve the project are necessary.

Capital Investment Proposal—Summary (Exhibit 19-1)

This form summarizes all the necessary information pertinent to this capital investment request. Remember, that only all data pertinent to this specific project should be included. While different companies may request more or less data, this form is typical of most companies. The form is usually accompanied by a set of instructions explaining how each item is to be calculated or what the items mean. For example, under the heading "Category of Expenditure," guidelines would be explained as to what parameters are to be used in categorizing the project, such as what distinguishes a cost savings project from a replacement project. Since not all projects create revenues/profits/cash flows, such as projects dealing with legal/safety/social issues, it is important to put into perspective how much moneys are being spent for each category. Obviously, profit-making projects should constitute most of the spending since they provide funds for future growth.

Capital Investment Proposal—Summary of Incremental Sales, Costs, Profits, and Market Data (Exhibit 19-2)

This form allows the preparer to estimate profit and loss projections and key marketing data over a specific period of time. This company requires that all capital investment proposals be projected over a ten-year period. It allows the reviewers to see the long-range potential of the project and when this project may reach its peak on the life cycle curve.

Capital Investment Proposal Cash Flow Projections (Exhibit 19-3)

As the title implies, this form is used to calculate the cash flows, payback period, and internal rate of return projected from this project over the required ten-year period. This calculation will weigh heavily on the decision to accept or not to accept the capital investment proposal. This is due to the fact that all projects must meet different requirements as to a maximum payback period and a minimum internal rate of return (IRR). For other forms with appropriate policies and procedures, refer to Exhibits 20-1–20-3.

CONSIDERATIONS IN FINANCING CAPITAL INVESTMENTS

There are many vehicles through which a company can finance a capital investment. Each method falls into an internal source, an external source, or both. The external sources available to a company include issuing company securities, bank borrowings, leasing, or combinations thereof. Internally, a company can sell selected assets, expand short-term liabilities, sell its marketable securities, sell parts of the business, or generate funds through operations (retained earnings). In each situation, many factors must be considered in evaluating which financial source should be used.

The cost of financing. A prime consideration is the effect on the earnings of the company or how much is available to the company. A minor investment would not be as significant to the overall earnings as would a major investment with high-interest-bearing debt. Each capital source will impact differently and must be evaluated separately to determine the effect on the overall earnings and the balance sheet. For example, bank borrowings would have a tendency to reduce earnings through higher interest costs, whereas selling equity may dilute the earnings participation to existing shareholders. In addition, selling assets may decrease operating revenues and increase operating costs. Tax laws must be reviewed for further influences on the company.

The risk involved. As with the cost of financing, the risk will depend upon the type of financing methods used. The ultimate objective is not to expose the company to any undue risk. For example, in equity financing, the investor, rather than the company, assumes most of the risk. In debt

EXHIBIT 19-1   Capital Investment Proposal—Summary

CAPITAL INVESTMENT PROPOSAL - SUMMARY

Project Title	Division/Location:	Project No.:
		_____
		Date:

Description:

Purpose:

Cost
- Total Cost of Project per this Proposal $ _____
- Total Cost of Project per Budget $ _____

Operational Date:

Life Of This Investment:	Total Cost	Accounting Life (Years)	Operational Life (Years)
(1) Land			
(2) Buildings			
(3) Plant and Equipment			
(4) Computer Equipment			
(5) Other (specify)			
(6) Total Gross Cost			

Category of Expenditure:

(1) Cost Saving..............	(4) New Product Develoment...............
(2) Expansion................	(5) Legal/Safety/SocialRequirement.....
(3) Replacement............	(6) Diversification/Other......................

Annual Cash Flows   Annual
Cumulative

- Year 0 (19   )..
- Year 1 (19   )..
- Year 2 (19   )..
- Year 3 (20   )..
- Year 4 (20   )..
- Year 5 (20   )..
- Year 6 (20   )..
- Year 7 (20   )..
- Year 8 (20   )..
- Year 9 (20   )..
- Year 10 (20   )..

Continued............

EXHIBIT 19-1 *(continued)*

CAPITAL INVESTMENT PROPOSAL - SUMMARY
(Continued)

(L) RETURN ON INVESTMENT
    (1) Payback After-Tax   :_____Years

    (2) Internal Rate Return

(M) RETURN ON INVESTMENT SENSITIVITY ANALYSIS   Internal Rate of
    Assuming that :   Return afterTax

    (1) Capital Expenditure is over-spent by 12%
    (2) Sales are under-achieved by 12% per annum
    (3) Cost Savings are under-achievedby 12% per annum

(N) OTHER RELEVANT INFORMATION:

(O) PROJECT APPROVED

BOARD OF DIRECTORS:	FULL SIGNATURE	DATE
EXECUTIVE COMMITTEE:		
BUSINESS SEGMENTS:		
OPERATING UNITS:		
Date approved		

EXHIBIT 19-2 Capital Investment Proposal—Summary of Incremental Sales, Costs, Profits, and Market Data

CAPITAL INVESTMENT PROPOSAL
SUMMARY OF INCREMENTAL SALES, COSTS, PROFITS AND MARKET DATA

Division:

Location:

Project No.

Project Title / Profit and Loss Projections	Year 0	Year 1	Year 2	Year 3	Year 4	Year 5	Year 6	Year 7	Year 8	Year 9	Year 10
Year	19	19	19	20	20	20	20	20	20	20	20
Net Sales											
Gross Profit											
Advertising											
Selling											
Promotion											
Other Marketing											
Medical											
Administration											
R&D											
Other Income/Expenses											
Total Operating Expenses											
Profit Before Taxes											
Taxes-Federal and State Income											
Net Profit											

Market Data

Total Market Data:
- Volume (units)
- % growth

Market Data:

Volumes:
- Existing Volume (units)
- Incremental Volume (units)
- Total Volume (Units)
- Total Volume Growth (%)

Market Share (%)

EXHIBIT 19-3 Capital Investment Proposal—Cash Flow Projections

CAPITAL INVESTMENT PROPOSAL

CASH FLOW PROJECTIONS

Project Title

Location: _____

Project No. _____

Year	Year 0	Year 1	Year 2	Year 3	Year 4	Year 5	Year 6	Year 7	Year 8	Year 9	Year 10
	19	19	19	20	20	20	20	20	20	20	20
Incremental Profit:											
-Profit on Incremental Sales Volumes											
-Cost Savings											
-Other (details)											
-Total Incremental Profit											
Capital Expenditure											
Gross Expenditure											
-Land											
-Buildings											
-Plant and Equipment											
-Computer Equipment											
-Sales Proceeds of Assets Disposals											
-Net Capital Expenditure											
Incremental Working Capital:											
-Cash											
-Receivables											
-Inventory											
-Prepaid and Deferred Expenses											
-Current Liabilities											
-Total Incremental Working Capital											
Taxation											
-Federal and State											
-Other											
-Total Taxes											
Net Cash Inflows/(Outflows):											
-Annual											
-Cumulative											

Return on Investment:	
Payback (after tax)	Years
Internal Rate of Return (after tax):	%

financing, the company assumes risk, since it imposes certain repayment obligations that must be met.

The impact of capital sources upon other financing sources. Certain capital sources will place restrictions upon other potential capital sources. For example, some loan agreements prevent a company from using such assets as accounts receivable and inventories as collateral for other borrowings.

Dilution of control. Under certain loan arrangements, relinquishing some control may be required. Such control as giving up voting rights, representation on the board of directors, and the like will result in giving up some control. Caution should be taken not to give up too much control when entering into a financing arrangement.

Availability of funds. All available funds must be explored to seek out the best possible source of financing. In certain cases, funds may not be available because of reaching the company's credit limits and exhausting internal sources.

Once these factors are determined as to what sources are available at what cost and risk, and the extent of the control that must be released, the decision must be made as to how to finance a proposed capital investment and the extent of the financing.

HOW FUNDS CAN BE GENERATED INTERNALLY

Sources of capital are usually available internally but are often overlooked. These sources of capital can be used to finance part, if not all, of capital investment proposals. These sources can be found throughout the company in the form of cost reductions and more effective managing of assets and through retaining more earnings in the business.

Cost reductions. Management should always be trying to seek areas within the company where costs can be reduced. These reductions can be made in the costs of manufacturing, labor costs, utilities, administrative costs, purchasing costs, and so on. By closely monitoring costs and establishing tight controls, funds are made available to help meet the demand for much-needed capital.

Managing assets. Effective asset management can be a major source of capital to the company. Periodically reviewing your assets for excessive and nonproductive assets is necessary to maintain the proper balance of assets. Such assets as accounts receivable, inventories, and fixed assets are usually the most obvious. These assets can generate substantial funds for capital investments.

Retaining more earnings in the business. In many cases, businesses can meet rising capital needs by retaining more of the earnings in the business. This is accomplished by either eliminating or reducing dividend and/or earnings distributions to owners/stockholders. This retention will be a major source of cash and a major factor in reducing external capital requirements. In addition, lenders will look favorably on a business that can generate funds internally before seeking external funds, particularly in meeting capital investment needs.

HOW FUNDS CAN BE GENERATED EXTERNALLY

Debt Financing Considerations

Debt financing and equity financing are vehicles to generate funds for capital investments. While both are considered external sources of funds, they affect the financial structure of the company in different ways. Let us explore the unique features and sources of both debt and equity financing.

Debt financing may take many different forms, such as from banks in the form of commercial loans, lines of credit, inventory financing, accounts receivable financing, unsecured term loans, financing of real estate and equipment, and even leasing. Other forms of financing include loans from commercial finance companies, savings and loan associations, life insurance companies, factors, consumer finance companies, the Small Business Administration, and governmental agencies such as state and local industrial development commissions.

Debt financing is usually accompanied by a formal document in which the borrower agrees to repay the borrowed principal plus interest in specified amounts on specified dates. These payments become part of the fixed obligations of the company and are included in the computation of cash flows for capital expenditure evaluation.

In certain instances and specific periods of times in a company's history, debt financing may not be available because of lenders' doubts about the nature of the business or about its future in terms of its financial capability, the industry, the product, the markets, the capital project, and so forth or, in some cases, about the ability of the management to operate the business effectively. In addition, the supply of money may be such that only preferred customers of lending institutions would have access to their funds. For example, when the money market is low, such financial institutions as banks are limited as to how much they will lend to their customers regardless of the prime rate and tend to select only borrowers with whom they have had

Table 19-3	Weighted Average Cost of Capital			
Financing Method	*Dollar Amount*	*Percentage Proportion*	*After-Tax Cost*	*Weighted Average Cost*
Debt	$100,000	33.3%	9%*	3.00%
Equity	200,000	67.7	15%	10.16
Total	$300,000	100.0%		13.16%

* 18% debt cost @ 50% tax rate

a continuous and profitable relationship with very little risk. In addition, other factors such as the financial condition, stability, and liquidity of the company will also play a major role in whether or not the institution will lend it the needed funds.

Determining How Much Debt a Company Should Acquire

With debt financing constantly changing, it is important to determine whether a company should acquire debt and, if so, how much debt it should acquire. In most companies, debt will play an important role in the financing of capital investments. In many companies, it is the prime source of capital. The question often arises as to how much debt should a company have in relation to equity. The answer is not a simple one and is not always reduced to a mathematical formula. Rather, there are many decisions to make in determining the level of debt within a company. Since debt may provide proportionately more funds as a percentage of equity, these decisions are extremely important and must be evaluated from company to company.

Evaluating the cost of average capital. Since the cost of debt is tax deductible, it is generally cheaper to acquire debt than equity funds. Let us look at a simple example of how debt can reduce the average weighted cost of capital. Assume a company has a capital structure with a weighted average cost of 13.16%, as shown in Table 19-3.

Let us assume that this company borrows $80,000 at 20% interest to finance a capital project. Even though more debt is acquired at a higher rate (20%), the weighted average cost for the company is now 12.63%, assuming no change in the total equity, as illustrated in Table 19-4.

You can see that financing a capital project with additional debt reduced

TABLE 19-4	Weighted Average Cost Assuming $80,000 Additional Debt @ 20%			
Financing Method	Dollar Amount	Percentage Proportion	After-Tax Cost	Weighted Average Cost
Debt	$180,000	47.4%	10%*	4.74%
Equity	200,000	52.6	15%	7.89
Total	$380,000	100.0%		12.63%

* 20% debt cost @ 50% tax rate

the weighted average cost of the company's total capital from 13.16% to 12.63%. Under this situation, it would be advisable to add more debt to finance not only capital investments but other areas of the company, such as working capital.

Determining the impact of additional debt on return rates. The adding of more debt can produce more earnings even when that additional debt has a higher cost. Let us use data presented in Table 19-3 and Table 19-4 as an example by assuming that the after-tax return on capital on the original capital is 15%. The debt of $80,000, which was used to finance a capital project, generated a return rate of 20%. Using both of these return rates, you will see that the overall earnings increased $16,000, or a total of $61,000 ($45,000 + $16,000). The new return on capital rate increased 1.05 percentage points, to 16.05%, compared to the original return on capital rate of 15%. Table 19-5 illustrates these results.

Under this situation, it might be suggested that more debt be added as long as overall return rates can be increased, even though the interest rate may seem high. Remember, interest payments on debt are tax deductible and therefore reduce the overall cost of acquiring funds.

Other considerations. It is also important to determine how certain you are of your cash flows in the future. Remember, debt implies contractual agreements to repay certain amounts at specified times, and cash flows must be available to repay these commitments. Where this situation exists, that is, uncertainty of cash flows in the future, it is suggested that debt be either avoided or limited to smaller amounts.

Another consideration is how liquid a company is in relation to historical patterns, as well as current conditions. When declining liquidity occurs, it may be a sign that a company cannot handle additional debt.

TABLE 19-5   Impact of Incremental Investment
               on Return on Capital Rate

	Amount of Capital	After-Tax Return on Capital Rate	Net Income
Original capital	$300,000	15%	$45,000
Incremental investment of $80,000 debt	80,000	20%	16,000
	$380,000		$61,000
Weighted return			16.05%

However, companies with adequate or flourishing liquidity can usually handle more debt.

Equity Financing Considerations

The concept of equity capital is different from that of debt financing. Although both are sources of capital, debt financing requires repayment of both principal and interest. Under equity financing, capital permanently invested by the investors entitles them to share in some form of earnings distribution and therefore to be considered part owners in the business. Equity may in fact create higher weighted average cost of capital, as well as result in the loss of some control over the company. Since shareholders arc part owners in the business, they do have some control or voice in the business through the stock owned. Obviously, the greater the percentage of ownership, the greater the control.

One other consideration to remember is that equity financing involves very little risk to the company. The investor usually absorbs all the risks and shares in the rewards. When a company prospers, so does the investor. Conversely, when the company does not produce sufficient earnings, neither does the investor share in the rewards. On the other hand, debt financing, unlike equity financing, involves substantial risk because both principal and interest payments are obligatory. Default of these payments could lead to serious financial difficulties for a company.

One other consideration in financing certain types of investments is the use of venture capital. Venture capitalists can be used to create investment opportunities by taking high risks in entrepreneurs. They will individualize and negotiate financial structures and maintain direct and continuing involvement of the investors. Further consideration and analysis should be done to evaluate whether venture capital is a viable alternative for capital and other types of investments.

DECISION-MAKING STRATEGIES

- Establish an effective capital investment program.
- Tie the capital investment program to the long-range plans of the company.
- Classify capital investments into categories to allow for establishing return on investment objectives by classification.
- Determine how much funds will be allocated by project classification.
- Always require capital investment proposals to have alternatives—with full comparative analysis.
- Assign risk analysis to each capital investment proposal.
- Measure the impact of each type of capital project on the anticipated overall return on investment to the company.
- Develop a checklist for submitting a capital investment proposal.
- Make sure the capital investment program has a policy and procedure manual outlining all the details of submitting a capital investment proposal.
- Estimate the cost of financing capital investment proposals and compare it to the overall return objective.
- Focus on long-term projects that contribute to increased productivity, cost reduction, and energy efficiency.

20

HOW TO USE CAPITAL INVESTMENT EVALUATION TECHNIQUES TO INCREASE ROI

The success of most companies depends upon the success of capital investments. Profits and cash flows are generated through capital investments in future periods. Most companies will continue to plow back earnings into investment opportunities as well as borrow funds to finance profitable opportunities.

This chapter will deal with the concepts involved in evaluating capital investments and show actual examples of how companies evaluate capital investments. Each of the many concepts has its advantages and disadvantages. Ultimately, the method that fits a company's needs is the one that should be used. The key is to establish consistency both in technique and in computation, so that each investment is evaluated fairly against another.

THE PREREQUISITES OF AN ACCEPTABLE
METHOD OF CALCULATION

Certain prerequisites are important for the overall effective evaluation of capital investments. Each is part of the overall process, and its importance cannot be overemphasized. The prerequisites are:

Universal application. The method of evaluation must be capable of being applied throughout the entire organization. Its universal application must be understood and workable for all parts of the organization.

Time value of money. Because money has a cost and is related to time, it is important that a method of calculation include the time value of money. This is found when computing discounted cash flow, which will be discussed later in the chapter.

Consideration of the life of the project. The method must consider the life of the project, whether it be the economic, technological, or physical life. The total life must be considered in order to evaluate fully the effectiveness of the capital project.

Consideration of the payback period. This is accomplished by using the payback period method of evaluation. As will be discussed later in the chapter, the payback period method measures recoverability and not the rate of return. Therefore, it is one of the calculations used in conjunction with other methods for evaluating capital investments.

Ease of calculation. Because of the preparers of capital investment proposals will represent different disciplines throughout the company, and because the expertise of these individuals may not be uniformly sophisticated, the calculation should be reasonably easy to carry to its conclusion.

Consideration of the risk. The method must be capable of high-lighting certain elements of risk. Whether it be cash risk, financial risk, or obsolescence, it is important that it be reflected in a good method of calculation. Evaluating risk will be discussed later in the chapter.

HOW TO CALCULATE A PROJECT'S CASH FLOW

Once all of the facts surrounding a capital investment project are gathered, a calculation of cash flow must be made. This calculation anticipates future financial results that are to be generated from the project. These projections are made over the life of the project and provide the basis for calculating future cash flows and ultimately the return on investment rate. The following data are necessary for calculating cash flow projections and are found in the capital expenditure request form.

1. Life of the asset
2. Amount of investment and expense
3. Types of investments (machinery, equipment, etc.)
4. Classification of investment (expansion, cost reduction, etc.)
5. Working capital requirements
6. Human resource requirements
7. Salvage and disposal values

8. Earnings projections (include sales revenues, cost of sales, sales and administrative expenses, interest, taxes, etc.)

Illustration

Using the above criteria, let us put together a hypothetical capital investment project. To simplify the calculations of the data to follow, we will use a four-year life and straight-line depreciation.

Determining the Life of the Asset

While this project is estimated to have a four-year life, the estimate is not always simple. It requires a careful analysis of the options that are available and must be measured using the most realistic period of time. The various options are economic life, technological life, physical life, obsolescence, and the life as determined by the marketplace. Let us briefly outline the nature of each life and some guidelines as to its use.

Economic life represents a period of time whereby economic conditions might shorten or limit the continuation of operating a specific asset. This determination is the hardest of all the methods of calculating the life of an asset, and therefore it is recommended that one of the other methods be used.

Technological life. With rapidly advancing technology, certain assets will have shorter lives. Certain investments do not change technologically, whereas others have a rapid rate of technological change. The computer sciences provide an excellent example of the latter.

Physical life. As the name implies, this method uses the estimated time it takes for an asset to wear out and cease to function without any form of replacement.

Obsolescence. Refers to the asset and/or the product produced having no value due to conditions that make it obsolete.

Marketplace. This is a condition whereby the process, method of production, trends, and other conditions dictated by the marketplace create a loss of value to the existing asset.

Use the method that offers the most realistic life. where several options are available, use the shortest life to avoid excessive risk caused by passage of time. Remember, these methods are to be used for internal purposes only, since tax laws will govern the type and amounts of depreciation that can be taken for tax purposes.

Year	Cost of Machinery	Yearly Depreciation	Remaining Balance
0	$80,000	—	$80,000
1		$20,000	60,000
2		20,000	40,000
3		20,000	20,000
4		20,000	—

Calculating straight-line depreciation. This proposed project will use the straight-line depreciation method using a cost of machinery of $80,000 and a life of four years. The result of each year's depreciation is $20,000, as shown above.

Amount and Type of Investment

The investment for the piece of machinery is $80,000.

Classification of Investment

Given the type of investment, it is classified as a cost reduction project.

Working Capital Requirements

It is estimated that the initial working capital requirement for this project is $40,000. This estimate is calculated by using certain key ratios such as inventory turnover, average collection period, average cash balances, etc. Based on historical patterns of the company and/or product lines, the total working capital components can be calculated.

Estimated Salvage and Disposal Values

The project does not have any estimates for salvage or disposal values.

Earnings Projections

This project is estimated to have the following revenues and expenses during the four-year life.

Year	Net Sales	Cost of Sales	Depreciation Expense	Selling, General, and Administrative Expenses	Taxes	Net Income
1	$120,000	$50,000	$20,000	$10,000	$20,000	$20,000
2	120,000	50,000	20,000	10,000	20,000	20,000
3	120,000	50,000	20,000	10,000	20,000	20,000
4	$120,000	$50,000	$20,000	$10,000	$20,000	$20,000

The above projections are based on estimates from various departments of the company such as sales, manufacturing, distribution, administration, etc. Only those revenues and expenses directly related to this project proposal are to be included. For simplicity, each year's projections are forecasted evenly. A more realistic forecast would generally have different estimates for each year.

HOW TO DEVELOP A CAPITAL EXPENDITURE CASH FLOW STATEMENT

Based on the above facts, a capital expenditure cash flow statement can be developed as shown in Table 20-1. The data in Table 20-1 will be used in calculating the payback period and return on investment.

To further explain why depreciation is added back to net income and is used to calculate cash flow, let us look at the Table 20-1 data for all four years of cash flow. Assume also that example A in Table 20-2 has no charge for depreciation and that example B is as given.

The increase of $40,000 in cash flow represents the after-tax savings of depreciation. In this case, a 50% tax rate was used, resulting in the tax rate times depreciation (.50 × $80,000). Although depreciation is not a source of cash, it provides higher cash flows by reducing income taxes paid.

THE PAYBACK PERIOD METHOD FOR EVALUATING A CAPITAL EXPENDITURE

The payback period method has long been used in capital expenditure evaluations. As will be seen, it is a method that is used in conjunction with

TABLE 20-1 Illustration of a Cash Flow Statement for a Capital Investment Project

(in $1,000s)	0	1	2	3	4	Total
			Year			
Machinery and equipment	$ 80					
Working capital	40					
Total gross investment	$120					
Net sales		$120	$120	$120	$120	$480
Costs		60	60	60	60	240
Depreciation		20	20	20	20	80
Income before income taxes		40	40	40	40	160
Taxes		20	20	20	20	80
Net income		$ 20	$ 20	$ 20	$ 20	$ 80
Cash Flow						
Net income		$ 20	$ 20	$ 20	$ 20	$ 80
Depreciation		20	20	20	20	80
Cash Flow		$ 40	$ 40	$ 40	$ 40	$160

TABLE 20-2 Impact of Depreciation on Cash Flows

	A	B	Difference
Net sales	$480,000	$480,000	—
Total costs	240,000	240,000	—
Depreciation	—	80,000	$80,000
Income before income tax	240,000	160,000	(80,000)
Taxes @ 50%	120,000	80,000	(40,000)
Accounting net income	120,000	80,000	(40,000)
Plus depreciation	—	80,000	80,000
Cash flow	$120,000	$160,000	$40,000

other methods in determining the acceptability of an investment. The prime reason it is used with other methods of evaluation is that payback is not a true rate of return and does not measure profitability or return on investment. To understand payback, it is important to recognize its advantages and disadvantages.

Advantages of Payback

Easy to calculate and understand. Of all the evaluation methods, payback is the easiest to calculate and understand. It merely requires identifying the total of investment dollars of the project and dividing this amount by the annual cash flows.

Indicates cash risk. As compared to other methods of calculation, payback is an excellent indicator of the riskiness of a project. The longer the payback period, the higher the risk; the shorter the payback period, the lower the risk. When a company is in a tight cash position, payback will play a major role in the capital investment decision.

Measures recoverability. Payback measures the recovery period when the total in annual cash equals the total investment. At this point, the project is said to be at payback, meaning that your investment has been fully recovered. The importance of the calculation is given only up to the point of payback.

Gives greater weight to earlier cash flows. Because payback is measured only up to the recovery period, annual cash flows have greater weight in the earlier years. Annual cash flows beyond the payback period calculation are not significant for this calculation. Therefore, it is important that a project be structured whereby cash flows are generated more heavily in the earlier periods. Also, as will be discussed later in the text, it will have a favorable influence on other methods of calculating return on investment, such as discounted cash flow.

Disadvantages of Payback

Does not represent a true rate of return. As discussed previously, payback determines at what period the investment will be recovered from cash flows generated from the project. Therefore, it does not measure return on investment, since any method of return on investment would have to consider the total cash flows for the life of the project, which in this illustration is four years.

Difficult to compare between projects. Because the calculation of payback results in a time period, that is, years and months, it is difficult to measure projects on a comparable basis. For example, different types of projects can have the same payback period as well as different amounts of project investment. Therefore, the projects assume an equal status, but in reality they are quite different. The only similarity is that they have the same payback period.

Calculation of Payback

The calculation of payback is based on the cash flow projections previously discussed. Referring to the previous cash flow calculations (see Table 20-1), the annual cash flow is as follows:

		Year			
Investment	0	1	2	3	4
Machinery and equipment	$ 80,000				
Working capital	40,000				
Total investment	$120,000				
Annual cash flows		$40,000	$40,000	$40,000	$40,000

Applying the formula for determining the payback period, that is, investment divided by annual cash flows, the following number of years is required to recoup the initial investment:

*Payback
Equation*

$$\frac{\text{Investment}}{\text{Annual cash flows}} = \frac{\$120,000}{\$40,000} = 3 \text{ years}$$

The preceding calculation assumes that the annual cash flows are even each year. As explained earlier, in reality this will not be the case, because sales volume and costs will vary from year to year. Assuming that cash flows vary from year to year, the following annual cash flow data is presented as an illustration.

		Year			
Investment	0	1	2	3	4
Machinery and equipment	$ 80,000				
Working capital	40,000				
Total investment	$120,000				
Annual cash flows		$45,000	$50,000	$40,000	$35,000

The payback period has now changed from 3 years to 2.625 years, calculated as follows:

Total investment to be recovered	$120,000
First two years' cash flows	
($45,000 + $50,000)	95,000
Remainder to be recovered	
($120,000 – $95,000)	25,000

The partial year calculation is made by dividing the remaining balance to be recovered ($25,000) by the next year's cash flow ($40,000). The results are as follows:

$$\frac{\$25,000}{\$40,000} = 0.625$$

The payback period is now computed as follows:

Total full years to recover investment	2.0
Partial year to recover investment	0.625
Total payback period	2.625 years

Note how much shorter the payback period is when heavier cash flows are received in the earlier periods (3.0 years versus 2.625 years). It will be seen later in the chapter how favorable the return on investment rates will be on projects with heavier cash flows in earlier periods.

Payback Period—A Practical Example

A major international pharmaceutical company requires that the payback calculation be shown on an after-tax basis and in the number of years to the nearest decimal point, such as 2.5, 2.8, 3.2 years. Some companies may prefer a before-tax basis, which is acceptable. However, whichever method is used it is important to be consistent for all projects and that the acceptable payback time be reflected accordingly. For example, a before-tax basis would lower the payback period since cash flows would be higher and thus result in a speedier payback. Conversely, an after-tax basis would result in lower cash flows and a longer payback period. Other guidelines used by this company include a required ten-year cash flow projection and that the payback calculation must start from the date of any significant cash expenditure so that the time value of money can be considered and reflected in the return on investment rate (IRR).

For example, the following hypothetical cost saving project with the estimated cash flows results in a payback period of 3.125 years.

Year	Capital Expenditure	Cost Savings	Cumulative Cash Flows
0	($1,000)	0	($1,000)
1	($500)	$100	(1,400)
2		600	(800)
3		700	(100)
4		800	$ 700

Payback Calculation	
Three full years	3.00
Year 4 (cumulative Year 3 divided by Year 4)	.125
Total payback period	3.125 years

Discounted Payback

Applying the discounted cash flow concept (to be discussed later in the chapter), payback can now reflect the time value of money. Assuming the previous data, let us apply a 16% discount rate (see discount tables in Appendix A), with results as shown in Table 20-3. The discounted payback is approximately 16% over the four years, since after four years there is still a $900 balance to be recovered.

TABLE 20-3	Calculation of Discounted Payback			

Year	Investment	Annual Cash Flows	Present Value Factor—16%	Net Present Values
0	($120,000)		1.000	($120,000)
1		$45,000	0.862	38,790
2		50,000	0.743	37,150
3		40,000	0.641	25,640
4		35,000	0.552	19,320
Total				$ 900

Payback Reciprocal

One way of relating the payback period to the rate of return is to use the payback reciprocal. This represents a rough estimate of the rate of return where the project's life is at least twice the payback period. It is calculated as follows using the data previously presented:

Payback
Reciprocal
Equation

$$\frac{\text{Average annual cash flows}}{\text{Investment}} = \frac{\$40,000}{\$120,000} = 33.3\%$$

In this case, a three-year payback period is equivalent to a minimum rate of return of 33.3%. Note that when the payback period is multiplied by the rate of return (.333 × 3), the answer will always equal 1; therefore, they reciprocate each other. Minor differences may occur due to rounding.

THE DISCOUNTED CASH FLOW METHOD FOR EVALUATING A CAPITAL EXPENDITURE

The theory of discounted cash flow (DCF) has been one of the more difficult concepts to understand. The theory is, a dollar today is worth more than a dollar in the future. This relates to developing strategies that will generate more funds and less costs in the earlier years of a capital investment. This will result in a shorter payback period and a higher return on investment rate for the capital project—two major strategies for operating a successful company. By following a logical sequence of events, we will see that discounting is the reciprocal of compounding and that both methods relate to the interest rate.

The basic theory of DCF says that a dollar today is worth more than a dollar in the future. It is that rate, or percentage return, that indicates to an investor what he or she may expect to receive on those funds left to the company to invest over the life of the project. The common denominator for DCF calculations is the interest rate.

Discounted cash flows has many advantages. It provides a basic common ground for all types of projects, therefore providing an ideal method of ranking projects. To measure DCF, all cash flows must be included throughout the life of the project. Most important is the fact that DCF assumes the time value of money.

Some of its disadvantages include its lack of relationship to accounting records and the uncertainty of forecasted cash flows. This is extremely important because each year's cash flow will carry a different present value factor. In addition, the calculated cash flows are assumed to be reinvested at the assigned rate, or interest rate.

TABLE 20-4	Compounding Illustrated		
Year	*Principal*	*Interest—10%*	*Total*
0	$10,000	—	$10,000
1	10,000	$1,000	11,000
2	11,000	1,100	12,100
3	12,100	1,210	13,310
4	13,310	1,331	14,641
5	$14,641	$1,464	$16,105

Compounding

To understand the concept of discounting, it is important to understand compounding. Both methods have a common factor—the interest rate. Therefore, compounding uses a compound interest rate that computes a sum of money (principal) at the present to another sum of money at the end of X years. To illustrate, let us assume that you deposit $10,000 in a savings account at 10% interest. How much will you have after five years? From the results shown in Table 20-4, you can see that after five years, a $10,000 deposit is worth $16,105 at a 10% interest rate.

A more simple method is to refer to a compound interest table, Table 20-5, for the compound factor that equals five years at 10%, which is 1.611 and multiplying this compound factor by the principal. Rather than going through all of the previous calculations, you could have applied the compound factor to the initial deposit of $10,000 and arrived at the same answer, as follows:

$$\$10,000 \times 1.611 = \$16,110$$

The difference of $5 (1$16,110 - $16,105) between this result and the one obtained from the calculations is due to rounding caused by not carrying the compound factor out to additional decimal places.

Discounting

As explained previously, discounting is the reverse of compounding. Whereas compounding shifts the value of money from the present to the

TABLE 20-5   Compound Interest Table

Year	10%	12%	14%	15%	16%	18%	20%
1	1.100	1.120	1.140	1.150	1.160	1.180	1.200
2	1.210	1.254	1.300	1.322	1.346	1.392	1.440
3	1.331	1.405	1.482	1.521	1.561	1.643	1.728
4	1.464	1.574	1.689	1.749	1.811	1.939	2.074
5	1.611	1.762	1.925	2.011	2.100	2.288	2.488
6	1.772	1.974	2.195	2.313	2.436	2.700	2.986
7	1.949	2.211	2.502	2.660	2.826	3.185	3.583
8	2.144	2.476	2.853	3.059	3.278	3.759	4.300
9	2.358	2.773	3.252	3.518	3.803	4.435	5.160
10	2.594	3.106	3.707	4.046	4.411	5.234	6.192

TABLE 20-6   Discounting Illustrated

Year	Principal	Interest Factor	Total
0	$16,110	1.000	$16,110
1	16,110	0.909	14,644
2	16,110	0.826	13,307
3	16,110	0.751	12,099
4	16,110	0.683	11,003
5	16,110	0.621	$10,004*

* The additional $4 is due to the interest factors' not being carried out to more decimal places.

future, discounting shifts the value of money to be received in the future back to the present. To illustrate, let us take the same data used in compounding and apply it to discounting. If you need $10,000 in five years, how much must you deposit today at 10% annual interest? Or at what discount factor will X principal equal $10,000? Using the results of $16,110 previously computed, the amount of $10,004 results as shown in Table 20-6.

By applying each of the interest factors, or present values, the result is $10,004. Therefore, given a principal amount of $16,110 for five years at 10%, the value of that money today is $10,000. The interest factors in this case are referred to as the discounted cash flow factors (see Table 20-7 for

TABLE 20-7   Present Value Table

Year	10%	12%	14%	15%	16%	18%	20%
1	0.909	0.893	0.877	0.870	0.862	0.847	0.833
2	0.826	0.797	0.769	0.756	0.743	0.718	0.694
3	0.751	0.712	0.675	0.658	0.641	0.609	0.579
4	0.683	0.636	0.592	0.572	0.552	0.516	0.482
5	0.621	0.567	0.519	0.497	0.476	0.437	0.402
6	0.564	0.507	0.456	0.432	0.410	0.370	0.335
7	0.513	0.452	0.400	0.376	0.354	0.314	0.279
8	0.467	0.404	0.351	0.327	0.305	0.266	0.233
9	0.424	0.361	0.308	0.284	0.263	0.225	0.194
10	0.386	0.322	0.270	0.247	0.227	0.191	0.162

a sampling of the rates). A simple technique is to apply the discount factor of 0.621 to the principal of $16,110, giving the same answer, recognizing rounding differences.

Reciprocal

The compound interest rates and the present value factors are reciprocal to each other. For example, a summary of both the compound interest factors and present value factors are presented below at an interest rate of 10%.

Number of Period	Compound Factors	×	Present Value Factors	=	Reciprocal
1	1.100		0.909		1.000
2	1.210		0.826		1.000
3	1.331		0.751		1.000
4	1.464		0.683		1.000
5	1.611		0.621		1.000

Since, when the compound factors are multiplied by the present value factors and the results equal one, it is concluded that the reverse of compounding is discounting. Therefore, it is possible to find either the compound factor or the present value factor by knowing either of one factor.

HOW TO SELECT A DISCOUNT RATE

In selecting a DCF rate for any capital project, consideration must be given to selecting a rate that ties in with the company's objective. Because capital investments will provide future profits with today's cost of money, it is important that the DCF rate that is chosen coincide with the way the company establishes its corporate objective. This would include the cost of capital, the corporate rate of return, the risk potential, industry averages, and so forth. This rate then becomes the minimum acceptable rate for capital investment proposals.

ILLUSTRATION OF A LOAN REPAYMENT AND DETERMINING THE DCF RATE

As previously indicated, the DCF rate is equated with the interest rate. To illustrate this point, let us look at what happens when a company borrows $10,000 at 10% annual interest (see Table 20-8). The repayment schedule is $2,638 at the end of each year for a total of five years. The payment of $2,638 represents both principal and interest. You will note that the borrower pays an interest rate of 10% and the lender earns 10%.

TABLE 20-8 Illustration of a Loan Repayment at 10% Interest

Year	Outstanding Balance at Beginning of Year	Interest at End of Year	Annual Payments	Reduction of Principal
1	$10,000	$1,000	$ 2,638	$ 1,638
2	8,362	836	2,638	1,802
3	6,560	656	2,638	1,982
4	4,578	458	2,638	2,180
5	2,398	240	2,638	2,398
Total		$3,190	$13,190	$10,000

Applying this concept to discounted cash flow, we obtain the results shown in Table 20-9. The discounted cash flow rate is 10%, because when the cash flows are discounted at 10% as shown in the table, the outflows and inflows of cash equal zero. The figures in brackets represent outflows of cash, and the unbracketed figures are inflows of cash.

TABLE 20-9   Illustration of Discounted Cash Flow to a Loan Repayment

Year	Transaction	Cash Flows	Present Value Factors at 10%	Net Present Values
0	Borrow	$10,000	1.000	$10,000
1	Repayment	(2,638)	0.909	(2,398)
2	Repayment	(2,638)	0.826	(2,179)
3	Repayment	(2,638)	0.751	(1,982)
4	Repayment	(2,638)	0.683	(1,802)
5	Repayment	(2,638)	0.621	(1,639)
Total		($ 3,190)		—

ILLUSTRATION OF DISCOUNTED CASH FLOW METHODS

The calculation of DCF is relatively simple. There are basically two methods of computation—the net present value method and the internal rate of return method—both of which will be illustrated. There are other variations, but these two methods are the most commonly used.

Net Present Value Method

The net present value (NPV) method calculates the net present values of cash flows using a given discount rate. This discount rate is the rate used as the minimum requirement for all capital investments. If the net present values are positive, that is, higher than the investment, then the project is acceptable at that specific rate, in this case 10%. If the net present values are negative, then the project is unacceptable at that rate, since the cash flows, when discounted, are insufficient to cover the investment dollars. In addition, this method will indicate which projects should be selected when several projects are calculated. The projects with the higher net present values would have a higher priority. The example shown in Table 20-10 illustrates this point using the data as calculated in Table 20-1. Based on the results of $6,760 of net present values, the project illustrated would be an acceptable one since the project's net cash flows are positive at the acceptable minimum objective of 10%.

TABLE 20-10   Net Present Value Method Illustrated

Year	Cash Flows	Discount Factors at 10%	Net Present Values
0	($120,000)	1.000	($120,000)
1	40,000	.909	36,360
2	40,000	.826	33,040
3	40,000	.751	30,040
4	40,000	.683	27,320
Net cash flows	$ 40,000		$ 6,760

Internal Rate of Return Method

The internal rate of return (IRR) method solves for the discount rate (interest rate) that discounts the cash flows to equal the investment. Under this method one is solving for a discount rate, whereas under the net present value method a rate is assigned. The projects giving the highest internal rate of return are the ones accepted. Also, the calculated rate can be compared to the overall company objective to determine the acceptability of the investment.

The examples shown in Table 20-11 illustrates this method. Arbitrarily applying two discount factors that create a positive and negative net cash flow (10% and 15%), the actual internal rate of return can be calculated. For example, the residual at the 15% rate is a negative net cash flow of $5,760 and at the 10% rate, a positive net cash flow of $6,760. This means that the internal rate of return is between 10% and 15%. Therefore, an interpolation is required in order to arrive at the exact rate. It is calculated by taking the difference between the two rates, 15% - 10%, or 5%, and multiplying by the sum of the relationship of the total positive net cash flows of $6,760 divided by the sum of the positive net cash flows plus the negative net cash

TABLE 20-11   Internal Rate of Return Method Illustrated

Year	Cash Flows	Discount Factors @ 10%	Net Present Values	Discount Factors @ 15%	Net Present Values
0	($120,000)	1.000	($120,000)	1.000	($120,000)
1	40,000	.909	36,360	.870	34,800
2	40,000	.826	33,040	.756	30,240
3	40,000	.751	30,040	.658	26,320
4	40,000	.683	27,320	.572	22,880
	$ 40,000		$ 6,760		($ 5,760)

flows of $5,760. The result is as follows:

$$10\% + (\ 5\% \times \frac{\$6,760}{\$12,520}) = 12.7\%$$

The actual internal rate of return is 12.7%. If this rate were applied to the cash flows, the net cash flows would equal zero. A typical illustration of a cash flow statement using the internal rate of return is shown in Table 20.12. This illustration is from a major chemical company and is part of a project authorization policy and procedure. (See Exhibit 20.1 for the entire financial policy and procedure.)

The initial investment of this new mixing machine is $25,000 with an economic life of six years. The total cash flows are summarized in Table 20.13.

These cash flows are then discounted at the hurdle rate (minimum required rate of return usually based on the cost of capital rate) of 12%. Applying two arbitrary discount factors that create a positive and negative cash flow (in this case, 12% and 16%), the actual internal rate of return can be calculated through the use of interpolation as explained previously. Table 20.14 illustrates the discounted cash flows for both discount rates.

Using interpolation, the difference between 12% and 16%, or 4%, is multiplied by the total sum of the net present values for the positive cash flows of $2,844, and the sum of both the positive cash flows of $2,844 and the negative cash flows of $(782), or $3,626. The formula is as follows:

TABLE 20-12   Discounted Cash Flow Analysis and Value
                   Contribution—Example

Project Name - New Mixing Machine	(1) Initial Investment	(2) Year 1
Assumptions		
• **Cost - $25,000**		
• **Economic Life - 6 years**		
• **Hurdle Rate (Discount Rate of 12%)**		
• **Financials**		
Net Sales		$ 6,795
Cost of Goods Sold		3,500
Gross Margin		3,295
Margin %		48%
Depreciation/Amortization		2,500
Other/Operating Expenses		456
Pretax Profit		339
Cash Operating Taxes (a)		122
NOPAT		$ 217
Depreciation		2,500
Other Non-Cash Items		900
Decrease/(Increase) in W/C		(2,378)
Capital Expenditures	(20,000)	(5,000)
Proceeds From Sale/Terminal Value		-
Cash Flow	$(20,000)	$(3,761)
Present Value (at 12%)		
Capital Expenditures	$(20,000)	$ (4,464)
Forecast Period Cash Flow		1,106
Proceeds from Sale of Assets/Terminal Value		
NPV		
Present Value - Cash Flows From Ops.	$ 22,996	
Present Value - Proceeds From Sale	4,306	
Present Value of Investment	(24,464)	
Net Present Value of Project	$ 2,838	
Value Contribution		
Pretax Operating Income		$ 339
Taxes		(122)
Inc/(Dec) in Deferred Taxes		-
Depreciation/Amortization		2,500
NOPAT Cash Flow		2,717
Average Gross Assets		22,500
Average Net Working Capital		1,189
Capital Employed		23,689
Minimum $ Required Return @ 12%		2,843
Value Contribution (NOPAT CF - Min. Required Return)		$ (126)

(a) Income tax provision less increase in deferred taxes.

(3)	(4)	(5)	(6)	(7)
Year 2	Year 3	Year 4	Year 5	Year 6
$15,000	$20,500	$21,500	$24,000	$28,000
8,250	9,225	9,675	10,800	12,600
6,750	11,275	11,825	13,200	15,400
45%	55%	55%	55%	55%
5,000	5,000	5,000	5,000	2,500
502	552	607	668	734
1,248	5,723	6,218	7,532	12,166
449	2,060	2,238	2,712	4,380
$ 799	$ 3,663	$ 3,980	$ 4,820	$ 7,786
5,000	5,000	5,000	5,000	2,500
1,080	(72)	(763)	(763)	(382)
(2,872)	(1,925)	(350)	(875)	(1,400)
-	-	-	-	
				8,500
$ 4,007	$ 6,666	$ 7,867	$ 8,182	$17,004
$ 3,194	$ 4,745	$ 5,000	$ 4,643	$ 4,308
				4,306

Additional Information
IRR: 15.1%
Cost of Capital: 12%
Present Value Payback: 6.0 Yrs.
Profitability Index: 1.12

$ 1,248	$ 5,723	$ 6,218	$ 7,532	$12,166
(449)	(2,060)	(2,238)	(2,712)	(4,380)
-	-	-	-	-
5,000	5,000	5,000	5,000	2,500
5,799	8,663	8,980	9,820	10,286
25,000	25,000	25,000	25,000	
3,814	6,213	7,350	7,963	asset
28,814	31,213	32,350	32,963	sold
3,458	3,746	3,882	3,956	
$ 2,341	$ 4,917	$ 5,098	$ 5,864	

TABLE 20–13 Cash Flow Statement—Total Cash Flows

	Year 0	Year 1	Year 2	Year 3	Year 4	Year 5	Year 6
Capital expenditure	$(20,000)	$(5,000)					
Profit after taxes		217	$799	$3,663	$3,980	$4,820	$7,786
Plus depreciation and other noncash items		3,400	6,080	4,928	4,237	4,237	2,118
Less increase in working capital		(2,378)	(2,872)	(1,925)	(350)	(875)	(1,400)
Proceeds from sale of equipment							8,500
Cash flow	$(20,000)	$(3,761)	$4,007	$6,666	$7,867	$8,182	$17,004

$$12\% + \left(4\% \times \frac{\$2,844}{\$3,626}\right) = 15.1\%$$

Therefore, the actual internal rate of return is 15.1%.

TABLE 20-14 Discounted Cash Flow

	Year 0	Year 1	Year 2	Year 3	Year 4	Year 5	Year 6
Cash flow	$(20,000)	$(3,761)	$4,007	$6,666	$7,867	$8,182	$17,004
Discount factor @ 12%	1.000	0.893	0.797	0.712	0.636	0.567	0.507
Net present values	(20,000)	(3,359)	3,194	4,756	5,003	4,639	8,621
Total	(20,000)	(23,359)	(20,165)	(15,419)	(10,416)	(5,777)	2,844
Discount factors @ 16%	1.000	0.862	0.743	0.641	0.552	0.476	0.410
Net present values	(20,000)	(3,242)	2,977	4,273	4,343	3,895	6,972

USING RISK APPLICATIONS TO MEASURE CAPITAL INVESTMENT RETURN RATES

Risk applications play an important part in the decision-making process of accepting or rejecting capital investment proposals. It is a technique that takes projected cash flow data and estimates a series of possible results. These series of possible results are then adjusted by the use of probabilities, and an overall return objective is established within specified ranges of activity. The outcomes can then be evaluated when certain risk elements are considered. The important thing to remember is that risk analysis provides the approver(s) the opportunity to see "what if" situations and to see potential upside results, downside exposure, and likely results. These results may be seen as one series of results, or as three separate series of results. The difference between the spread of the downside risk to the upside potential will in many cases determine whether a project is accepted or rejected.

Definition of Risk

There are many definitions of risk. In the end result, they represent an estimate of thinking of the various disciplines in the company as to what can be expected to happen. Each project will have different values assigned to each of the risk definitions and therefore must be evaluated on an individual basis. In many instances, the projected cash flows would be adjusted to reflect the overall consensus and adjusted accordingly. Let us now explore the different definitions of risk

Achieving expected returns. It is important to establish probabilities of expected returns both in dollars and percentage rates. When capital projects are estimated to achieve very high returns, some estimate should be made to adjust the return rates to more realistic levels. This could be based on historical patterns and/or industry experience.

Adjusting expected cash flows. Since cash flows represent an overall estimate of what the capital project will generate in earnings, given a specific level of investment, an adjustment to cash flows is necessary. This adjustment will take the form of a range analysis (discussed later in the chapter) showing different levels of activity that will most likely occur, including the most optimistic situation and the most pessimistic situation. Such an analysis will show variations of expected cash flows and their impact on the overall return rate.

Payback period uncertainties. When uncertainties exist as to the payback period, a certain amount of risk is incurred. With economic uncertainties, the longer the project takes to return its investment, the greater the risk.

Market uncertainties. When changes occur at a more rapid pace, the uncertainty in the market takes on higher risk.

Operating a new venture in an inexperience area. Risk usually increases when capital projects result in a new venture in an inexperienced area, such as introducing a new product in a new market, or operating in a new geographic location.

Past relationship between success and failure. The amount of risk will sometimes be determined by the historical experience of the company, division, product, or other segments where risk patterns can be developed.

How to Cope with Risk

As risk increases, several criteria should be developed as a measure for coping with higher risks. They include the following:

- Require lower than usual payback periods. Be sure adjustments are made periodically as risk either increases or decreases.
- Adjust objective rates for the riskiness of the capital project and changes in economic conditions throughout the life of the project.
- Adjust the cash flows to more realistic levels based on the risk of the project.
- Develop a series of cash flow estimates based on the probabilities of achieving results.

Methods of Adjusting for Risk

Many methods can be used to adjust for risk. In many instances, risk will parallel swings in economic conditions such as recession, inflation, higher interest rates, and so forth. To assure that cash flows are protected to some degree against these economic conditions, different risk techniques are used. Some examples and applications will be shown as a means of providing direction in capital expenditure analysis.

Judgmental technique. Assessing how risky an investment is, depends

TABLE 20-15   Using the Present Value Technique in Sensitivity Analysis

Assumptions

Capital investment—$34,000   Current interest rate—20%

Cash flow estimates by year—$15,000; $15,000; $12,000; $8,000; and $5,000

Year	Cash Flows	20%	22%	24%	25%
1	$15,000	$12,495	$12,300	$12,090	$12,000
2	15,000	10,410	10,080	9,750	9,600
3	12,000	6,948	6,612	6,288	6,144
4	8,000	3,856	3,608	3,384	3,280
5	5,000	2,010	1,850	1,705	1,640
Cash inflows		$35,719	$34,450	$33,217	$32,664
Cash outflows		34,000	34,000	34,000	34,000
Net present value		$ 1,719	$ 450	$(783)	$(1,336)

upon the common knowledge of management. When applying this technique, caution should be taken against being too subjective and letting personal judgment enter into the assessment.

Adjustment of hurdle rates or objectives. Each capital investment project is assigned a different hurdle rate depending upon the riskiness of the investment, such as the cost of capital rate. Although this is easy to understand, too much is left to the arbitrary assigning of different rates.

Adjustment of cash flows. Under this method, cash flows are adjusted according to the probabilities of each of the cash flows at different expected interest rate levels. Table 20-15 illustrates this technique by answering the question of the economic worthiness should interest rates increase. Each percentage level—that is, 20%, 22%, 24%, and 25%—is calculated by applying the discount factors to the cash flows.

The conclusion states that if interest rates approach the 24% level, do not approve the capital investment since net present values will be negative, as shown by the parenthesized, or negative, $783 under the 24% column. To further enhance the decision-making process, one more step is required to apply probabilities to each of the levels of interest rates and to each of the discounted dollars. For example, year 1 is calculated by applying a 70% probability to $12,495 (discounted dollars using the 20% interest rate) and 30% probability $12,300 (discounted dollars using a 22% interest rate). The

TABLE 20-16   Expected Benefit Analysis

| | Probability by Interest Rate | | | | |
Year	20%	22%	24%	25%	Adjusted Net Present Value
1	70%	30%			$12,437
2	60	40			10,278
3		40	40%	20%	6,374
4		40	30	30	3,442
5		35	35	30	1,736
				Cash Inflows	34,267
				Cash Outflows	34,000
				Net Present Values	$ 267

results are $12,437 as shown in Table 20-16. Similar calculations are made for each year.

The conclusion results in an acceptance of the capital investment since if management's judgment about the probabilities of interest rates are correct, the capital project will generate positive net present values of $267.

Use of range analysis in capital investment decisions. As previously discussed, anticipated ranges can be established at different levels of activity. This approach identifies the range of return, from the pessimistic to the optimistic. In Table 20-17, you will see that given certain anticipated ranges, the spread between the worst situation and the most optimistic situation is 5.5% to 80.0%. The most likely series of events estimates a return on investment rate of 39.3%.

Use of probabilities. Another variation of the use of probabilities is the example shown in Table 20-18. The results indicate that even though the first project is estimated to generate $50,000 more cash flows, a different decision may be reached considering that the second project is now estimated to generate $5,000 less cash flow after probabilities have been applied.

Use of sensitivity analysis. A major international pharmaceutical company uses specific guidelines for sensitivity analysis to measure the effect on the internal rate of return (IRR). The company requires the following calculations be made to cash flows in its sensitivity analysis.

TABLE 20-17   Use of Range Analysis in Capital Investment Decisions

Formula

$$ROI = \frac{(\text{Unit price} \times \text{Unit sales}) - \text{Total costs}}{\text{Capital investment}}$$

Estimates	*Anticipated Ranges*
Unit price $12.50	$11.00 to $13.00
Total costs $3,000,000	$2,800,000 to $3,300,000
Unit sales 350,000	320,000 to 400,000
Capital investment $3,500,000	$3,000,000 to $4,000,000

Most likely: $\dfrac{\$12.50 \times 350,000 - \$3,000,000}{\$3,500,000} = 39.3\%$

Optimistic: $\dfrac{\$13.00 \times 400,000 - \$2,800,000}{\$3,000,000} = 80.0\%$

Pessimistic: $\dfrac{\$11.00 \times 320,000 - \$3,300,000}{\$4,000,000} = 5.5\%$

- Effect of overspending capital by 12%.
- Effect of underachieving sales forecasts by 12% per year.
- Effect of underachieving cost savings (where applicable) by 12% per year.

Use of decision tree analysis. It is a useful concept for the conceptualizing and structuring of management decisions. This type of analysis determines alternative decisions and indicates a sequence of uncertainties in a given capital investment proposal. The steps are as follows:

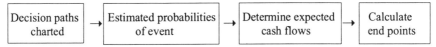

Now let us illustrate the use of the technique in the capital investment decision.

Assume a project is estimated to cost $200,000, with a two-year life. The

---

TABLE 20-18   Use of Probabilities

Two capital projects are presented, with an initial investment of $600,000 each. Capital project A has a total cash flow of $300,000, and capital project B has a total cash flow of $250,000. In both cases, it is estimated that alternative opportunities would not produce any cash flows.

Project A
Probability achieving success 60%
Alternative probability 40%
  Calculation
  .60 × $300,000 = $180,000
  .40 ×   0   =   0
  Total cash flow $180,000

Project B
Probability of achieving success 70%
Alternative probability 30%
  Calculation
  .70 × $250,000 = $175,000
  .40 ×   0   =   0
  Total cash flow $175,000

---

hurdle rate after tax is 20%. The alternative solution to this project is not estimated to produce any cash flows. However, the original project in question has the following cash flows and probability percents.

		Probability	
Year	Cash Flow	As Stated	No Cash Flow
1	$400,000	30%	70%
2	600,000	40	60

Given those facts, should the project be accepted or rejected? Table 20-19 shows the calculation. As you will see, the project's adjusted net present value is a positive $66,520 and, therefore, the capital project should be accepted.

Use of simulation. This method deals with computer models which use a trial and error approach. It gives management a fuller understanding of a project's possible outcomes by developing uncertainty profiles for key factors of a capital project. For example, results of such real-world profiles as market size, market growth, market share, selling price, manufacturing cost, etc., would be simulated for clearer meaning. This form of risk analysis simulation can be used to show changes in any of the uncertainties and to simulate its effect in actual practice.

Other methods of risk analysis. Other methods include scheduling techniques which are used to properly allocate resources so that a specific project will meet completion dates. Such techniques are PERT, CPM, GANTT charts, and Line of Balance (LOB).

Adding another dimension to the evaluation of capital projects will assist managers to accurately validate the approval of capital projects. While these techniques are not perfect, they do afford the opportunity to help in the decision to spend money for capital investments. In addition, they reveal to the company the amount of risk that would be undertaken should the project be approved. It is the risk that is anticipated at the time of the project's approval that is important to the decision-maker. In a changing economy, risk may change at a quicker pace in the later years of the project's life. This cannot always be avoided, but protection in the earlier years of the project's life is vital to the protection of the future cash flows, profits, and return on investment.

TABLE 20-19   Decision Tree Analysis in Capital Investment Decision Making

Year 0	Year 1	Year 2
		.4 $600,000
	.3 $400,000	
		.6 -0-
($200,000)		.4 $600,000
	.7 -0-	
		.6 -0-

*Calculation of net present values
Present values at 20% (hurdle rate): Year 1, .833; Year 2, .694

	Year 1	Year 2
$400,000 × .833	$333,200	
$600,000 × .694		$416,400
$400,000 × .833	$333,200	
$600,000 × .694		$416,400
Initial investment		

Present Values*	Probabilities	Adjusted NPV
$549,600	.12 (.3 × .4)	$65,952
133,200	.18 (.3 × .6)	23,976
216,400	.28 (.7 × .4)	60,592
		(84,000)
(200,000)	.42 (.7 × .6)	$66,520

Less Investment	Total Net Present Value
	$333,200
($200,000)	216,400
	$549,600
($200,000)	$133,200
($200,000)	$216,400
($200,000)	(200,000)

SAMPLE OF CAPITAL INVESTMENT POLICIES AND PROCEDURES

To illustrate the practical use of capital investments, exhibits of actual company policies and procedures are presented. What is interesting to note is that while all of these companies basically use the same techniques, their ability to arrive at the same conclusions varies. It varies as to the policies they establish and, to some degree, the methods they use vary. Nevertheless, as long as each company is consistent with the way it approaches capital investment evaluations, a similar conclusion will be reached.

EXHIBIT 20-1   Sample Policy—Authorization Process for Presenting Capital Investments and Measuring ROI Rates

MAJOR CHEMICAL COMPANY

This major chemical company has developed a project authorization process as part of their financial policies and procedures. This authorization process is used to assist managers in presenting capital investments, as well as measuring return on investment rates.

The process includes a two-page cover letter describing the nature of the project, how it will benefit the company, the estimated return on investment rate and the payback period, and any information that would justify the spending of monies.

The Project Authorization Document (PAD) is used as an authorization/approval document for all capital expenditures, lease commitments, cash/stock acquisitions and joint ventures. Note that such major discussions as the financial impact and calculations of the project and marketing information are included. The discounted cash flow analysis and value contribution (see example) highlights all the assumptions in numerical terms. The cash flow analysis is based on the incremental value of the project and its contribution to the corporation based on assumptions established by the company for all capital investment proposals.

The example shows that a capital investment of $25,000 will generate an internal rate of return of 15.1%, a present value payback period of six years, and a profitability index of 1.12. Since the hurdle rate (minimum acceptable rate of return) is 12%, which is based on the cost of capital rate, this project would be acceptable since the return rate (15.1%) exceeds the cost of capital (12%).

Financial Policies

SUBJECT: **PROJECT AUTHORIZATION PROCESS**	EFFECTIVE:	Policy No. 102
	SUPERSEDES:	Page 1 OF 33

TABLE OF CONTENTS

Reproduced by permission

Financial Policies

SUBJECT:	EFFECTIVE:	Policy No. 102
PROJECT AUTHORIZATION PROCESS	SUPERSEDES:	Page 2 OF 33

INTRODUCTION

These instructions describe the capital project authorization procedures to be used at all locations. These procedures supersede all local and regional procedures.

The project authorization process has been designed to focus on Product Line and Corporate management needs, as well as to minimize bureaucracy. Another objective of the process is to use all available technical resources (corporate as well as local and regional specialists) to maximize the potential for success, **beginning as early in project development as possible**.

It should be noted that project authorization documents produced in this approval process, including drafts, are **not necessarily confidential** and can be obtained by third parties (e.g., a party to a lawsuit or the government); in some cases, such documents **must** be delivered to the government as part of any Hart-Scott-Redino antitrust review. Accordingly, careful drafting should be used throughout the approval process. Any question concerning drafting or related matters should be directed to (___) Legal Services

1. **Overview of Capital Project Authorization Process**

   (a) Project Development Process Flow Chart
       In order to provide a visual understanding of the project development and authorization process the following flow chart was developed. It traces the Two Pager through the management and functional review process to final pad approval and status reporting.

   (Project Development Process Flow Chart follows)

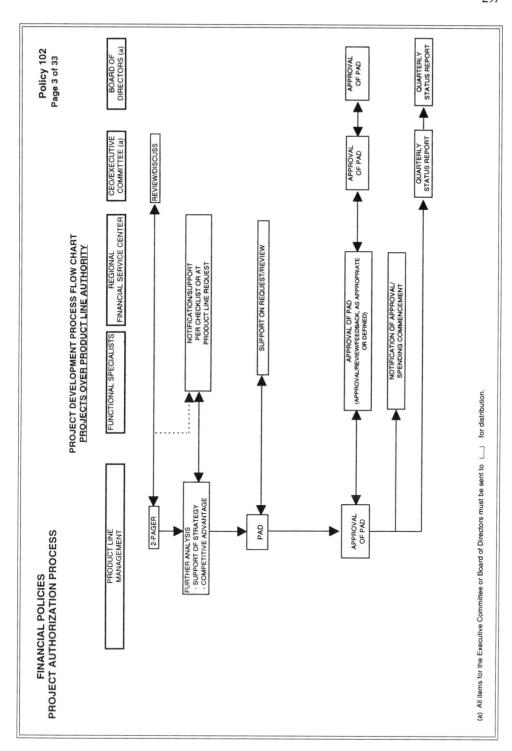

FINANCIAL POLICIES
PROJECT AUTHORIZATION PROCESS

PROJECT DEVELOPMENT PROCESS FLOW CHART
PROJECTS OVER PRODUCT LINE AUTHORITY

Policy 102
Page 3 of 33

PRODUCT LINE MANAGEMENT

FUNCTIONAL SPECIALISTS

REGIONAL FINANCIAL SERVICE CENTER

CEO/EXECUTIVE COMMITTEE (a)

BOARD OF DIRECTORS (a)

2-PAGER

REVIEW/DISCUSS

FURTHER ANALYSIS
- SUPPORT OF STRATEGY
- COMPETITIVE ADVANTAGE

NOTIFICATION/SUPPORT PER CHECKLIST OR AT PRODUCT LINE REQUEST

PAD

SUPPORT ON REQUEST/REVIEW

APPROVAL OF PAD

APPROVAL OF PAD
(APPROVAL/REVIEW/FEEDBACK, AS APPROPRIATE OR DEFINED)

APPROVAL OF PAD

APPROVAL OF PAD

NOTIFICATION OF APPROVAL/ SPENDING COMMENCEMENT

QUARTERLY STATUS REPORT

QUARTERLY STATUS REPORT

QUARTERLY STATUS REPORT

(a) All items for the Executive Committee or Board of Directors must be sent to ⸦_⸧ for distribution.

Financial Policies

SUBJECT:	EFFECTIVE:	Policy No. 102
PROJECT AUTHORIZATION PROCESS	SUPERSEDES:	Page 4 OF 33

INTRODUCTION (CONT.)

1. Overview of Capital Project Authorization Process (Cont.)

    (b)   Annual Strategic Plan: April To June (see Policy No. 104)

       - As part of the Business Planning Process, Product Line presents the big picture, 5 and 10 year long-term strategic plan to Corporate management.
       - Required resources, including estimated capital spending and significant capital projects, are highlighted.
       - Corporate management endorses strategic plan and required resources.

    (c)   Two-Pager Expenditure/Acquisition Notification: Quarterly And As Needed

       - Two-Pagers identify major projects scheduled for approval during the next quarter as well as major projects which arise during the quarter and require more immediate management attention (for example, acquisitions).
       - Corporate management and functional experts receive copies of Two-Pagers for review.
       - Two-Pagers provide preliminary justification and valuation for major projects, acquisitions and major strategic initiatives.
       - Two-Pagers for acquisitions, joint ventures, equity investments and long-term strategic initiatives are distributed to senior management prior to entering into substantive discussions or contractual agreements.

    (d)   Project Authorization Document (PAD)

       - Individual PADs are developed from Two-Pagers and approved by appropriate Product Line or Corporate authority levels.
       - Depending on the authorization requested, CEO and Board approval is sought.

    (e)   Post-Completion Review

       - At the request of the Executive Committee, a post-completion review of the project may be required. The Executive Committee will determine the date. The post-completion review will consist of an assessment of strategic objectives and opportunities cited in the original PAD and will not be strictly a number exercise

2. Scope

This policy applies to all project types as described under "Two-Pager" below, depending on magnitude and authority level. The Board has delegated the authority to approve certain projects to members of (___) senior management based on the magnitude of spending and other criteria such as lease term, contractual commitments, etc. In turn, selected authority levels are delegated to Product Line management. Policies 121-125 in the (___) Policy and Organization Guide detail Board and executive authorities.

Financial Policies

SUBJECT:	EFFECTIVE:	Policy No. 102
PROJECT AUTHORIZATION PROCESS	SUPERSEDES:	Page 5 OF 33

INTRODUCTION (CONT.)

3. Responsibilities

(a) <u>Product Line Management</u> - Responsible for the quality and integrity of the project and associated documents and projections. Seek input from functional specialists.

(b) <u>Regional Management Center</u> (includes North American dedicated Product Line administrative locations) - Provide analytical and document preparation services to the Product Lines, as agreed with the Product Line. Seek input and approval of regional and country management impacted by the proposed project and documentation of their approval in the Two-Pager/PAD.

(c) <u>Functional Specialists</u> - Provide input as appropriate for all projects. Each function has a responsibility to ensure their expertise is reflected in the project. Functional specialists include regional (including country managers) and corporate functions (tax, business development, business planning, treasury, engineering, legal, etc.).

These specialists should be brought into the loop as early in the project development as possible and should be viewed as complementary to the Product Line's staff. At the latest, they will be alerted to projects which may require their participation by the circulation of Two-Pagers, which will be distributed quarterly. (A list of functional specialists and the appropriate issues is provided in the section "Functional Specialists and Guidelines".)

While Two-Pagers have generally been prepared only for projects above the authority limit of the Product Line President, it is also recommended that early in the process functional specialists be involved in smaller projects, as appropriate. It is the responsibility of Product Line management, both locally and globally, to initiate the contact. It is the joint responsibility of both parties to ensure that a dialogue occurs and is kept informal (for example, via face-to-face discussions; avoid formal question and response memos). A bureaucracy will not be created to monitor or control such communications. It is simply expected that the best available talent will be brought to bear each time we plan to invest. All parties should operate as though there are no organizational boundaries separating them from the expertise/services they need or provide. This process should become a precedent for a "boundaryless procedure".

TWO-PAGERS

1. Introduction

Two-Pagers provide the link to the Product Line's strategic plan, current best estimate of a project's spending, financial justification and conceptual rationale. Two-Pagers are submitted quarterly and as needed for projects requiring the immediate attention of the Executive Committee.

Financial Policies

SUBJECT:	EFFECTIVE:	Policy No. 102
PROJECT AUTHORIZATION PROCESS	SUPERSEDES:	Page 6 OF 33

TWO-PAGERS (CONT.)

2. Scope

Two-Pagers are required for all significant projects scheduled for approval in the following quarter. These projects are defined as all projects over the Product Line President's approval limit (amount will vary among Product Line Presidents) as well as any other project which the Product Line believes might benefit from the involvement of functional specialists or to which Corporate management should be alerted. All investments and acquisitions, regardless of amount, are considered significant and require a Two-Pager. Two-Pagers are also required for Multi-product Line projects over the Regional President's approval limit.

Two-Pagers should be used for the following types of projects:

- Capital Expenditures   • Investments (b)   • Joint Ventures (JVs) (b)

- Lease Authorizations (a)   • Acquisitions (b)   • Long-Term Strategic Initiatives (b)

- Sale of major assets   • Divestment of businesses

    (a) Authorization includes rental expense and lease term. Also requested, as memo, is capitalized rent expense.

    (b) Authorization includes number of (___) shares and price per share, cash payments, debt assumed or repaid and lease payments assumed. Prior to entering definitive acquisition negotiations, a Two-Pager Pre-Acquisition Notification is required.

Authorizations not requiring a Two-Pager format are:

- Contracts (may be part of backup for Two-Pager)

- Purchases made in the normal course of business

- R&D grants or commitments

3. Purpose

(a) Provide information on specific projects to Corporate management.

(b) Provide the opportunity for the Executive Committee and the project sponsor to have early discussions on acquisitions, long-term strategic transactions, equity investments and joint ventures before substantive discussions have started with the other party.

(c) Trigger involvement of Corporate and regional functional expertise.

Financial Policies

SUBJECT:	EFFECTIVE:	Policy No. 102
PROJECT AUTHORIZATION PROCESS	SUPERSEDES:	Page 7 OF 33

TWO-PAGERS (CONT.)

4. Format

Two-Pagers should be brief; bullet-point format is encouraged. Content will vary as appropriate for each project. The format of the cover page should be as shown in the attached example. Acquisitions and joint ventures may require additional relevant cover page details such as number of shares, (___) share/100% basis, etc. For acquisitions and JVs valued over $100 million, the impact on total (___), including EPS, must be disclosed on the cover page. The following information should be included.

(a) Authorization Amount - Dollar and local currency amount and spending schedule by year. This should be the gross amount of the expenditure not offset by investment grants or proceeds from sale of assets, etc. Contingent payments which may potentially arise should not be included in the authorization amount, but should be clearly discussed in the Project Description. Also not included in the Authorization Amount but discussed in the Project Description and Cover Page are working capital, pre-operating and acquisition expenses.

(b) Planned Approval Date - Quarter and Year.

(c) Planned Completion Date - Quarter and Year.

(d) Average Exchange Rate - Show all Cover Page information in U. S. dollars and indicate the exchange rate(s) used for translation.

(e) Current Phase and Program Total Investment - Capital spending for the current phase should equal the Authorization Request. In order to provide a more complete financial impact, initial working capital requirements should be added. For Multi-phase Program projects capital spending and working capital requirements, by phase, is also required. Incorporate actual results from earlier phases, if appropriate.

(f) Financial Projections - Two bases are to be used for a project's financial projections - Economic and Fiscal.

    (1) Economic analysis forms the basis for the project's analysis: Cash Flows, NPV, Value Contribution, etc. The time frame begins with the project start date and continues for 12-month periods. For example, a project starting in July should show "economic " results for the periods July-June through the forecast horizon.

    (2) Fiscal (reporting) analysis, however, forms the basis for comparing the project's results with historical and forecasted results of the Product Line it supports which are on a fiscal year basis. For comparability, the economic analysis mentioned above must be restated to a calendar year basis for the relevant period, (i. e., from July-June to January to December).

Financial Policies

SUBJECT:	EFFECTIVE:	Policy No. 102
PROJECT AUTHORIZATION PROCESS	SUPERSEDES:	Page 8 OF 33

TWO-PAGERS (CONT.)

4. **Format (Cont.)**

(f)   Financial Projections (Cont.)

The cover page Summary and discussions in the text should be based upon the relevant product line financial reporting information (e. g., sales, pretax income, etc.) and marketing information, which should still be on a fiscal year basis.

(g)   Estimated Incremental Financial Impact - Net Sales, Pretax Income, Net Income, Value Contribution, NPV, IRR, Payout (years), Profit Index and Present Value Payback Period. The discounted cash flow schedule, as shown in the example format, should be attached.

(h)   Cost of Capital - The cost of capital is the rate of return "demanded" by capital providers. Each Product Line will be assigned a Cost of Capital rate for use in NPV calculations. These rates may change during the year, therefore, before starting a Two-Pager, request the latest cost of capital rates from   (_____)   (Treasury Dept.) for your project.

(i)   Linkage of Project to Strategy - Briefly discuss the linkage of the project to the specific strategy established and discussed with Corporate Management at the current year's Strategy meeting. Assess the impact of delay on achieving strategic objectives. If the proposal involves a shift towards a new strategy, this should be clearly addressed, including the impact on the "old" strategy.

(j)   Project Description - Brief description of project, risks, alternatives and discussion of assumptions on which incremental financial impact was based. Include any early input from regional and functional specialists (engineering, finance, legal, etc.).

(k)   Potential acquisitions will normally be strategic or financial in terms of justification.

(1)   A Strategic Acquisition should emphasize the specific strategic objectives being achieved and the alternatives which have been considered. Two-Pagers for projects should show appropriate long-term returns to the Product Line (i.e., above the cost of capital), but the primary focus should be strategic, such as an important proprietary product or technology, entry into a strategic geography, product extensions, management expertise, etc.

(2)   A Financial Acquisition should be justified on the basis of extraordinary returns due to "fit" with the Product Line, such as sales growth, cost reduction, complementary products, technology or services, etc. Two-Pagers for these projects should show rapid present value paybacks (under 4 years). The Two-Pager should discuss an integration plan that will give a high degree of confidence that the financial objectives will be achieved.

Financial Policies

SUBJECT:	EFFECTIVE:	Policy No. 102
PROJECT AUTHORIZATION PROCESS	SUPERSEDES:	Page 9 OF 33

TWO-PAGERS (CONT.)

4. Format (Cont.)

(k)   Potential acquisitions (Cont.)

Two-Pagers relating to long-term strategic initiatives (such as acquisitions, joint ventures, etc.) should be submitted to the Executive Committee as early in the analysis process as possible.

5. Logistics

Two-Pagers for projects to be approved in the following quarter should be included in the Quarterly Report. Two-Pagers will be reviewed by the Executive Committee at its regular meetings. Appropriate feedback to the sponsoring Product Line will be provided by the Committee. The proposal will not be <u>approved</u> at this point, but appropriate guidance will be provided to the sponsoring Product Line. The intention of the Two-Pager process is to avoid committing (___) to any strategic expenditures or transactions before the Executive Committee has had an opportunity to review them.

Two-Pagers not part of the Quarterly Report should be submitted to (_____) (Legal Services), who is responsible for the control and distribution of all documents to the Executive Committee. All questions relating to the Executive Committee submission process should be directed to him. Refer to the Reporting Cycle Calendar for Executive Committee meeting dates.

PROJECT AUTHORIZATION DOCUMENT (PAD)

1. Introduction

A Project Authorization Document (PAD) is an authorization/approval document used for all capital expenditures, lease commitments and cash/stock acquisitions and joint ventures. Where Board approval is required, charts for Board presentation will also be prepared (see following section).

2. Scope

A PAD is required for all projects $500,000 and over and must be used by all Product Lines and Regions. Projects under $500,000 can be authorized either by shop orders or a PAD at the discretion of the Product Line. PADs are developed from Two-Pagers, therefore, a review of the scope of Two-Pagers may be appropriate. Spending overruns and changes of scope or strategy should be presented in a PAD format; authorization is always required for the total amount of the project (i.e., original authorized amount plus overrun portion or an amount relating to the change of scope of the project). The text should address these changes or new circumstances from the original approved authorization document. Overrun criteria are found in the Policy and Organization Guide (Policy 121) and are based on local currency.

Financial Policies

SUBJECT:	EFFECTIVE:	Policy No. 102
PROJECT AUTHORIZATION PROCESS	SUPERSEDES:	Page 10 OF 33

PROJECT AUTHORIZATION DOCUMENT (PAD) (CONT.)

3. **Purpose**

   The PAD serves several purposes, but it is primarily:

   (a) A management tool documenting, with sufficient specificity, what is being approved, the project's objectives and the analysis supporting the request;

   (b) A means to trigger the project's start and a reference for tracking capital spending; and

   (c) A vehicle for local legal approval (where this is necessary).

4. **Format**

   All PADs should include: (1) a standard Cover Page with signatures; (2) text describing the project, key performance indicators, operating and financial value drivers, competitive benchmarks, and key issues; and (3) standard supporting schedules showing the project's impact.

   (a) <u>Cover Page</u> - The purpose of the Cover Page is to provide standard summary key financial information as well as a common document to authorize the project (see Section on Examples). Cover pages may be modified in order to report additional summary details for acquisitions, joint ventures etc. Outside North America, the Regional President's approval is required, in addition to the Product Line President's.

   Data presented on a cover page may vary depending on the objective of the project (e.g., non-P&L projects such as office expansions or computer systems should include relevant statistics only and exclude Cash Flows, NPV, etc.). For acquisitions and JVs valued over $100 million, the impact on total (___), including EPS, must be disclosed on the cover page and discussed in the text.

   (b) <u>Financial Projections</u> - Two bases are to be used for a project's financial projections - Economic and Fiscal.

   (1) Economic analysis forms the basis for the project's analysis: Cash Flows, NPV, Value Contribution, etc. The time frame begins with the project start date and continues for 12-month periods. For example, a project starting in July should show "economic " results for the periods July-June through the forecast horizon.

   (2) Fiscal (reporting) analysis, however, forms the basis for comparing the project's results with historical and forecasted results of the Product Line it supports which are on a fiscal year basis. For comparability, the economic analysis mentioned above must be restated to a calendar year basis for the relevant periods, (i. e., from July-June to January to December).

Financial Policies

SUBJECT:	EFFECTIVE:	Policy No. 102
PROJECT AUTHORIZATION PROCESS	SUPERSEDES:	Page 11 OF 33

PROJECT AUTHORIZATION DOCUMENT (PAD) (CONT.)

4. Format (Cont.)

    (b)   Financial Projections (cont.)

        The cover page Summary and discussions in the text should be based upon the relevant product line financial reporting information (e. g., sales, pretax income, etc.) and marketing information, which should still be on a fiscal year basis.

    (c)   Text - The text should be concise (5-10 pages depending on the project's complexity). Discussions of the history of the Product Line, facility or unit proposing the project, unless relevant to the proposal, are not to be included. At a minimum the following areas should be covered.

        (1)   Project Description should describe the project, explaining what is being proposed and why and address key issues.

        (2)   Business Perspective should briefly discuss the historical and forecast financial results on the accompanying charts (see section on Examples). This discussion should include an overview and description of the business. (The historical period should be one business cycle or at least 5 years.) In addition to the operation's financial results, for P&L projects the discussion should also provide a perspective on the business environment and how it is expected to develop over the forecast period.

        (3)   Linkage to Product Line Strategy should discuss how the proposed investment supports the Product Line's strategic plan. The Product Line's Strategic Plan consists of one or more strategic initiatives and a base-line business case. each with associated capital resource requirements. The discussion should provide perspective on the specific strategy the proposal supports including the current status of implementation. If the proposal involves a shift to a new strategy, this should be clearly discussed, including the impact on the overall Product Line Strategic Plan, if relevant.

        (4)   Market Segment Assessment (where appropriate) should discuss penetration and dynamics (including life cycle) of the target market segment. In addition to discussing the data on the accompanying Marketing Segment Spreadsheet (see Examples section for formats), there should also be an analysis of the competition, their market segment share, strengths and weaknesses, strategies and alliances or affiliations. In addition to discussing existing competitors, an assessment should be made of possible new competitors entering the market and the threat of substitute products or technology on the business.

Financial Policies

SUBJECT:	EFFECTIVE:	Policy No. 102
PROJECT AUTHORIZATION PROCESS	SUPERSEDES:	Page 12 OF 33

PROJECT AUTHORIZATION DOCUMENT (PAD) (CONT.)

4. **Format (Cont.)**

  (c)   <u>Text</u> (Cont.)

     (5)   <u>Benchmarks</u> should include Key Performance Indicators or Financial Value Drivers of the business such as efficiency/productivity measurements, relative market share, sales growth, margins, cost structure, etc. which impact the NPV most significantly.   Data should be provided using internal comparisons (similar operations in similar area) and/or external comparisons (competition's results) wherever available.   If appropriate, data should be shown on an "including/ excluding/incremental i. e., this project" basis.

     (6)   <u>Financial Assumptions Driving Base Case</u> should be clearly stated and discussed. Assumptions should include market linkages, sales, margins, profitability and capital measures and other key financial value drivers.

     (7)   <u>Risks/Opportunities/Alternatives</u> should describe the risks, (market, regulatory, environmental, technological, financial, substitute products, new market entries, etc.) associated with the proposal. Response to potential risks/opportunities should be outlined. In addition, any alternatives considered should be discussed. This discussion should be concise and demonstrate that the proposed project is the best choice presently available. Alternatives should not be developed merely to satisfy this requirement; if there are no reasonable alternatives to a project, this should be clearly stated. Also include an exit contingency strategy, if required (for multiple stage projects, a "Sensitivity of Failure" analysis should show what the project would cost if the current stage was not successful and future stages were not undertaken).

     (8)   <u>Sensitivity Analysis</u> should be prepared for key value drivers showing the impact on relevant statistics - NPV, IRR, NPV Payback and Value Contribution. This analysis should be in tabular format identifying the value drivers and the impact changes in the drivers would have on the relevant statistics. A 2 to 3 line table showing a range in each statistic should be included to illustrate graphically the impact of changes in the value drivers. This analysis should address both the sensitivity of the project to changes in the drivers, as well as a textual description of the potential impact of these changes on the associated strategy.

     (9)   <u>Strategic Acquisitions</u> should emphasize the specific strategic objectives being achieved and the alternatives which have been considered. These projects should generate appropriate long-term returns to the Product Line, but their primary justification should be strategic, such as an important proprietary product or technology, entry into a strategic geography, etc.

Financial Policies

SUBJECT: **PROJECT AUTHORIZATION PROCESS**	EFFECTIVE:	Policy No. 102
	SUPERSEDES:	Page 13 OF 33

PROJECT AUTHORIZATION DOCUMENT (PAD) (CONT.)

4. **Format (Cont.)**

   (c) Text (Cont.)

   (10) Financial Acquisitions should be justified on the basis of extraordinary returns due to "fit" with the Product Line, such as sales growth, cost reduction, complimentary products, technology or services, etc. These projects should show rapid present value payback periods. These projects should show a thorough integration plan that will give a high degree of confidence that the objectives will be achieved. Business Cycle performance should be developed showing historical performance of the target through one complete cycle, if available.

   (11) Other Relevant Issues: for projects over $100 million, address the project's incremental impact on reported results (_____) (Contact Business Planning if assistance is required.) In addition, the following points should be addressed: functional impacts; business cycle positioning; JV/alliance partner involvement; buyer/supplier issues such as shortages/overages, number of buyers/suppliers and relative strength, contracts, the need to retain or obtain each type of buyer/supplier, industrial trends; and key construction or manufacturing concerns about location, shared facility, equipment or process technology.

   (d) Post-Completion Review - At the request of the Executive Committee, a post-completion review of the project may be required. The Executive Committee will determine the date. The post-completion review will consist of an assessment of strategic objectives and opportunities cited in the original PAD. This assessment should not be viewed as a number exercise.

   (e) Supporting Schedules - Standard supporting schedules for the project are to be attached to the PAD. These include a schedule of Fixed Assets, a spending schedule and calculation of deferred taxes (if appropriate), NPV schedule and standard Value Contribution analysis. (see Examples section for formats)

5. **Logistics**

   The PAD authorization process is driven by the timing of the project sponsor's capital spending programs rather than a Corporate schedule. In general, every PAD submitted should have been preceded by a Two-Pager as early in the process as possible.

   Submission/Distribution of PADs to the appropriate management approval level should be made as soon as the document is ready for approval. The approval procedure is driven by the delegation authorities of the CEO and Product Line President as set forth in the Policy and Organization Guide (Policy 121-125). All PADs which will be submitted to the Executive Committee for approval must first be reviewed by the Business Planning Department. In addition, if the PAD is for an acquisition, it must also be reviewed by the Corporate Development Department. It is the responsibility of the project sponsor to ensure that their

Financial Policies

SUBJECT: **PROJECT AUTHORIZATION PROCESS**	EFFECTIVE:	Policy No. 102
	SUPERSEDES:	Page 14 OF 33

PROJECT AUTHORIZATION DOCUMENT (PAD) (CONT.)

4. Logistics (Cont.)

PAD is submitted to both of these departments with sufficient time for review and feedback to the sponsor prior to the Executive Committee submission. Refer to the Reporting Cycle Calendar for Executive Committee meeting dates. It is the responsibility of the Product Line and Regional Management Centers to control the numbering and distribution of PADs and have approved copies on file.

(_____) (Legal Services) is responsible for control and distribution of all documents, including PADs, submitted to the Executive Committee and Board of Directors. All questions relating to the Executive Committee and Board submission process should be directed to him. Product Line and Management Center level approved PADs (e.g., Product Line President approved) over $1.0 million should be sent (_____) for distribution, for information only, to the Executive Committee; approved PADs under $1.0 million should remain within the Product Lines or sponsoring function.

Coordination and timely distribution of PADs are the responsibility of each Product Line, supported by Regional and Corporate Services.

BOARD CHARTS

Projects requiring Board of Directors' approval may be presented using charts to summarize the corresponding PAD. The PAD will be included in the Board Agenda book.

In general the following guidelines apply to Board Charts.

(a)   Bullet point format summarizing key points.

(b)   Financial and project information - summary information on the project; impact of project on total (___) results, if appropriate. For multi-phase projects, the sponsors should include a summary chat explaining each phase of project and results achieved to date.

(c)   The last chart should be the authorization (which should be reviewed by Legal Services).

(d)   Number of charts should be kept to a minimum. The number will depend on the size and complexity of the project.

Financial Policies

SUBJECT: **PROJECT AUTHORIZATION PROCESS**	EFFECTIVE: ——————— SUPERSEDES:	Policy No. 102 ——————— Page 15 OF 33

FUNCTIONAL SPECIALISTS AND GUIDELINES

The following is a summary list of functional departments and issues:

FUNCTIONAL DEPARTMENTS	ISSUES
Business Development	Mergers, Acquisitions, Divestitures, Corporate Strategy
Business Planning	Valuation Methodology, Financial Analysis
Controller's Office	Accounting/Reporting
Corporate Engineering	Technical, Engineering
Corporate EH&S	Pollution Control/Environmental Health & Safety
Corporate R&D	R&D
Corporate Risk Management	Insurance
Human Resources Division	Human Resources (include International)
Treasurer's Office	Financing
International Treasury	Foreign Exchange
Information Systems	IS
Legal Services	Legal (including approval authorities and authorization requests)
Tax	Tax
All Relevant Departments	Acquisitions/Joint Ventures/Divestments

A breakdown of issues by department and corporate personnel responsible for resolving these issues follows.

Financial Policies

SUBJECT: **PROJECT AUTHORIZATION PROCESS**	EFFECTIVE:	Policy No. 102
	SUPERSEDES:	Page 16 OF 33

FUNCTIONAL SPECIALISTS AND GUIDELINES (CONT.)

	ISSUE/PROJECT	SPECIALIST CONTACT
Business Development	Mergers, Acquisitions & Divestitures, Corporate Strategy	
Business Planning	Valuation Framework and Issues, Value Contribution, Financial and Sensitivity Analysis, Incremental Financial Impact	
Controller's Office	Mergers, Acquisitions, Divestments Reporting FASB Issues, Policies Procedures Audit Issues	
Corporate Engineering	Technical Content: Adequacy of design engineering and project management plan HAZOPS Review Adequacy of pilot testing (if relevant) Process control philosophy and vendor choice New site selection Loss prevention and fire protection	
Corporate EH&S	Should be involved at an early stage where there are significant EH&S issues irrespective of the size of the project. In particular Process Changes and Safety, Environmental Discharges. Acquisitions/Divestments Environmental Issues, New site selection/ Site shutdown, Environmental Permitting	
Corporate R&D	Licenses and Technology Acquisition (if relevant) Patent issues New Processes/Technology	

Financial Policies

SUBJECT: **PROJECT AUTHORIZATION PROCESS**	EFFECTIVE: SUPERSEDES:	Policy No. 102 Page 17 OF 33

FUNCTIONAL SPECIALISTS AND GUIDELINES (CONT.)

	ISSUE/PROJECT	SPECIALIST CONTACT
Corporate Risk Management	Insurance Due Diligence	
	Acquisition/Divestment Joint ventures/partnerships	

	Insurance Requirements
	    Leases
	    Miscellaneous contracts	

	Safety, Loss Prevention & Fire Protection	

	Insurance Coverage, including surety
	  bonding (placing or canceling)
	    New Capacity (new construction)
	    Plant closures
	    New Markets
	    Acquisitions/divestitures
	    Joint ventures/partnerships	

Corporate HR	Employee Benefits - NA	
	Pension & Savings	
	Group Benefits (Insurance)	
	Compensation	
	Relocation - Domestic	
	Outplacement, Employee Assistance Programs (EAP)	

Financial Policies

SUBJECT: **PROJECT AUTHORIZATION PROCESS**	EFFECTIVE:	Policy No. 102
	SUPERSEDES:	Page 18 OF 33

FUNCTIONAL SPECIALISTS AND GUIDELINES (CONT.)

	ISSUE/PROJECT	SPECIALIST CONTACT
International Human Resources	Pension, group insurance and other employee benefit issues outside North America and expatriate package formulation and administration. Contacts for compiling information on labor/employment environment in foreign countries, acquisition and divestiture activity as well as ongoing operations. Expatriation	
Treasurer's Office	Domestic Treasury Issues including Cost of Capital, Cash Management and Short/Long-Term Obligations. Cost of Capital Abroad	
International Treasury	Funding Overseas Acquisitions, International Economic Conditions and Prospects - By Regions/Country, Foreign Exchange Rates - Historical/Projected, Foreign Interest Rates - Historical/Projected, Cash Flow From Foreign Operations - Dividends/Service, Fees, etc.	
Information Systems	All Issues	

Financial Policies

SUBJECT:	EFFECTIVE:	Policy No. 102
PROJECT AUTHORIZATION PROCESS	SUPERSEDES:	Page 19 OF 33

FUNCTIONAL SPECIALISTS AND GUIDELINES (CONT.)

	ISSUE/PROJECT	SPECIALIST CONTACT
Legal Services (a)	Approval Authority	
	Employee Benefits	
	Environmental	
	Finance	
	International	
	Patent/Trademark	
	Real Estate	
	Securities	
	Tax	
Tax	All Tax Issues	

(a) Copies of memoranda and other material regarding submission to the Executive and Operating Committees and the Board of Directors should be sent to

Financial Policies

SUBJECT: **PROJECT AUTHORIZATION PROCESS**	EFFECTIVE:	Policy No. 102
	SUPERSEDES:	Page 20 OF 33

EXAMPLES

The examples of formats listed below are on the following pages.

1. **Two-Pager - Cover Page**

2. **Project Authorization Document (PAD)**
   (a) Cover Page
   (b) Gross Fixed Assets
   (c) Business Background - Profit & Loss Statement
   >> Including Project
   >> Excluding Project
   >> Incremental -the Project
   (d) Cash Flow & Value Contribution Schedule
   >> Including Project
   >> Excluding Project
   >> Incremental -the Project
   (e) Marketing Segment Spreadsheet
   >> Including Project
   >> Excluding Project
   >> Incremental -the Project
   (f) DCF Analysis & Value Contribution Calculations

Financial Policies

SUBJECT:	EFFECTIVE:	Policy No. 102
PROJECT AUTHORIZATION PROCESS	SUPERSEDES:	Page 21 OF 33

EXAMPLES

1. Two-Pagers

($000)

COVER PAGE

TWO PAGER

(P&L/NON-P&L) (f)

PRODUCT LINE/REGION _____

LOCATION/PROJECT TITLE _____

STRATEGIC PROGRAM LINK _____

PROJECT DESCRIPTION _____

Authorization Request			Planned Approval Date:	QTR/YR
Amount			Planned Start Date:	QTR/YR
Dollars	$ (a)		Planned Completion Date:	QTR/YR
Local Currency	_____			
(@ Avg. Exch. Rate of ____)			Capital Spending Class:	(c)

Current Phase				Total Program (e)			
	Capital Spending	Initial Working Cap.	Total Investment	Multi-Phase Programs	Capital Spending	Initial Working Cap.	Total Investment
Year 1	$	$ (b)	$	Phase 1	$	$ (b)	$
Year 2		(b)		Phase 2		(b)	
Etc.		(b)		Etc.		(b)	
Total	$ (a)	$	$	Total Program	$	$	$

Estimated Incremental Financial Impact (d) (e):

	Current Phase	Total Program		Current Phase		
NPV	$	$		Net Sales	Pretax Income	Net Income
Avg. Value Contribution						
Cost of Capital	%	%	Year 1	$	$	$
Payout	Years	Years	Year 2			
Profit Index (NPV/Cap. Inv.)	%	%	Year 3			
Present Value Payback	Years	Years	Etc.			
IRR	%	%				

Incremental Impact on	Reported Results for Projects over $100 million:					
	19XX		19XX		19XX	
EBIT	$ _____	% of Sales	$ _____	%	$ _____	%
Net Income	$ _____	% of Sales	$ _____	%	$ _____	%
Earnings Per Share	$ _____	N.A.	$ _____	N.A.	$ _____	N.A.

(a) Capital Spending Authorization Request Amount represents the Capital Spending portion of the Current Phase.
(b) Initial Working Capital represents the Working Capital incremental to the decision to start the project (i.e., start-up Working Capital only) and excludes increases/(decreases) resulting from ongoing business activities.
(c) Indicate: (1) New Product/Service, (2) Product Modification/Line Extension, (3) New Customer Sales, (4) Cost Reduction, (5) MIS, (6) Acquisitions/JVs. (7) Environmental, (8) Other (e.g., Maintenance & Replacement).
(d) When available, the incremental financial impact should be provided.
(e) For multi-phase capital programs, indicate total program capital spending by phase. Indicate which phase this White Paper represents.
(f) Some financial statistics may not be appropriate for a non-P&L project.

Financial Policies

SUBJECT: **PROJECT AUTHORIZATION PROCESS**	EFFECTIVE:	Policy No. 102
	SUPERSEDES:	Page 22 OF 33

EXAMPLES (CONT.)

2. Project Authorization Document (PAD)

COVER PAGE

($000)   (P&L/NON-P&L) (a)

PROJECT AUTHORIZATION DOCUMENT (PAD)

PRODUCT LINE/REGION _____ PAD NO. _____
LOCATION/PROJECT TITLE _____
STRATEGIC PROGRAM LINK _____
PROJECT DESCRIPTION _____

Authorization Request			Lease:	
Requested	$	(b)	Begins	
Budgeted			Ends	
Variance	$ _____		No. of Years	
			Capitalized Value	
			Rate Implicit in Lease	

	Current Phase (c)				Total Program (c)		
	Capital Spending	Initial Working Cap.	Total Investment	Multi-Phase Programs	Capital Spending	Initial Working Cap.	Total Investment
19XX	$	$ (d)	$	Phase 1	$	$ (d)	$
19XX		(d)		Phase 2		(d)	
Etc.		(d)		Etc.		(d)	
Total	$ (b)	$	$	Total Program	$	$	$

	Current Phase					Incremental Impact on Total Results for Projects over $100 million;			
Incremental Impact	Year 1 (e)	Year 2	Year 3	Year 4	Year 5		19XX		
Net Sales and Revenues									
Gross Margin - Amount						EBIT	$		% of Sales
- Percent						Net Income	$		% of Sales
Pretax Income - Amount						EPS	$		N.A.
- Percent									
NOPAT							19XX		
Depreciation/Amortization						EBIT	$		% of Sales
Other Sources						Net Income	$		% of Sales
Total Sources						EPS	$		N.A.
(Inc)/Dec in Working Capital									
Capital Spending							19XX		
Other Uses						EBIT	$		% of Sales
Total Uses						Net Income	$		% of Sales
Cash Flow						EPS	$		N.A.

Statistics (a) (c):	Current Phase		Total Program	
NPV	$ _____		$ _____	
Avg. Value Contribution				
Cost of Capital	_____	%	_____	%
Payout	_____	Years	_____	Years
Profit Index (NPV/Cap. Inv.)	_____	%	_____	%
Present Value Payback	_____	Years	_____	Years
IRR	_____	%	_____	%

APPROVALS   Date

(I) Product Line managers (for approval levels delegated by the Product Line President)
(II) Corporate Functional Specialists (list is included in this section)
     Follow-up Review Date (if suggested by the Executive Committee) _____
IF APPROPRIATE
(III) Product Line President AND
(IV) Regional President (ex. North America)

(a) Statistics may not be appropriate for a non-P&L project.
(b) Authorization Request represents the Capital Spending of the Current Phase (if multi-phase project).
(c) For multi-phase capital programs, indicate amount/results for this PAD (current phase) as well as for total program.
(d) Initial Working Capital represents the Working Capital incremental to the decision to start the project (i.e., start-up Working Capital only) and excludes increases/(decreases) resulting from ongoing business activities.
(e) Represents first full year of operations.
(f) For projects over $100 million.

Financial Policies

SUBJECT: **PROJECT AUTHORIZATION PROCESS**	EFFECTIVE:	Policy No. 102
	SUPERSEDES:	Page 23 OF 33

EXAMPLES (CONT.)

3. GROSS FIXED ASSETS

PRODUCT LINE/LOCATION
PROJECT NAME

GROSS FIXED ASSETS

		(1) Local Currency (000)	(2) S000 (a)
(1)	List assets requested		
(2)			
(3)			
(10)	Sub-Total	_____	_____
(11)	Contingency (XX.X%)	_____	_____
(12)	Total Request	_____	_____

CAPITAL SPENDING BY QUARTER (a)

		(1) QTR 1	(2) QTR 2	(3) QTR 3	(4) QTR 4	(5) CUM. TOTAL
(1)	19XX					
(2)	19XX					
(3)	19XX					
(a)	Avg. PAD Exchange Rate:					

(PRODUCT LINE)
PROJECT TITLE
BUSINESS BACKGROUND
P&L - INCLUDING THIS PROJECT

($000)	(1) 1991	(2) 1992	(3) 1993	(4) 1994	(5) 1995	(6) 1996B	(7) 1997F	(8) 1998F	(9) 1999F	(10) 2000F	(11) Avg. Ann. % Chg. Incr./(Decr.) 1991-1995	(12) Avg. Ann. % Chg. Incr./(Decr.) 1995-2000F
(1) Net Sales & Revenues												
(2) Gross Margin												
(3) Factory Admin.												
(4) Depr. Charged to Prod.												
(5) Gross Profit												
(6) Selling												
(7) G&A												
(8) R&D												
(9) Depr. Not Charged to Production												
(10) Operating Profit												
(11) Other Inc./(Exp.)												
(12) Pretax Income												
(13) Income Taxes												
(14) Net Income												

As a Percent of Net Sales

(15) Gross Margin												
(16) Factory Admin.												
(17) Depr. Charged to Prod												
(18) Gross Profit												
(19) Selling												
(20) G&A												
(21) R&D												
(22) Depr. Not Charged to Production												
(23) Operating Profit												
(24) Other Inc./(Exp.)												
(25) Pretax Income												
(26) % Effective Tax Rate												
(27) Net Income												

(PRODUCT LINE)
PROJECT TITLE
BUSINESS BACKGROUND
P&L - EXCLUDING THIS PROJECT

($000)	(1) 1991	(2) 1992	(3) 1993	(4) 1994	(5) 1995	(6) 1996B	(7) 1997F	(8) 1998F	(9) 1999F	(10) 2000F	(11) Avg. Ann. % Chg Incr./(Decr.) 1991-1995	(12) Avg. Ann. % Chg Incr./(Decr.) 1995-2000F
(1) Net Sales & Revenues												
(2) Gross Margin												
(3) Factory Admin.												
(4) Depr. Charged to Prod.												
(5) Gross Profit												
(6) Selling												
(7) G&A												
(8) R&D												
Depr. Not Charged to (9) Production												
(10) Operating Profit												
(11) Other Inc./(Exp.)												
(12) Pretax Income												
(13) Income Taxes												
(14) Net Income												

As a Percent of Net Sales

(15) Gross Margin												
(16) Factory Admin.												
(17) Depr. Charged to Prod												
(18) Gross Profit												
(19) Selling												
(20) G&A												
(21) R&D												
Depr. Not Charged to (22) Production												
(23) Operating Profit												
(24) Other Inc./(Exp.)												
(25) Pretax Income												
(26) % Effective Tax Rate												
(27) Net Income												

(PRODUCT LINE)
PROJECT TITLE
BUSINESS BACKGROUND
P&L - INCREMENTAL (THIS PROJECT)

($000)	(1) 1995	(2) 1996B	(3) 1997F	(4) 1998F	(5) 1999F	(6) 2000F	(7) Avg. Ann. % Chg. Incr./(Decr.) 1995 - 2000F
(1) Net Sales & Revenues							
(2) Gross Margin							
(3) Factory Admin.							
(4) Depr. Charged to Prod.							
(5) Gross Profit							
(6) Selling							
(7) G&A							
(8) R&D							
Depr. Not Charged to							
(9) Production							
(10) Operating Profit							
(11) Other Inc./(Exp.)							
(12) Pretax Income							
(13) Income Taxes							
(14) Net Income							

As a Percent of Net Sales

(15) Gross Margin							
(16) Factory Admin.							
(17) Depr. Charged to Prod							
(18) Gross Profit							
(19) Selling							
(20) G&A							
(21) R&D							
Depr. Not Charged to							
(22) Production							
(23) Operating Profit							
(24) Other Inc./(Exp.)							
(25) Pretax Income							
(26) % Effective Tax Rate							
(27) Net Income							

(PRODUCT LINE)
PROJECT TITLE
BUSINESS BACKGROUND
CASH FLOW AND VALUE CONTRIBUTION – INCLUDING THIS PROJECT

($000)	(1) 1991	(2) 1992	(3) 1993	(4) 1994	(5) 1995	(6) 1996B	(7) 1997F	(8) 1998F	(9) 1999F	(10) 2000F	(11) Avg. Ann. % Chg. Incr./(Decr.) 1991-1995	(12) 1995-2000F
Sources												
(1) Net Income												
(2) Depreciation/Amortization												
(3) Other Sources												
(4) Total Sources												
Uses												
Inc./(Dec.) in Working												
(5) Capital												
(6) Capital Spending												
(7) Other Uses												
(8) Total Uses												
(9) Cash Flow												
(10) Value Contribution												

322

(PRODUCT LINE)
PROJECT TITLE
BUSINESS BACKGROUND
CASH FLOW AND VALUE CONTRIBUTION - EXCLUDING THIS PROJECT

($000)	(1) 1991	(2) 1992	(3) 1993	(4) 1994	(5) 1995	(6) 1996B	(7) 1997F	(8) 1998F	(9) 1999F	(10) 2000F	(11) Avg. Ann. % Chg. Incr./(Decr.) 1991-1995	(12) 1995-2000F
Sources												
(1) Net Income												
(2) Depreciation/Amortization												
(3) Other Sources												
(4) Total Sources												
Uses												
Inc./(Dec.) in Working												
(5) Capital												
(6) Capital Spending												
(7) Other Uses												
(8) Total Uses												
(9) Cash Flow												
(10) Value Contribution												

(PRODUCT LINE)
PROJECT TITLE
BUSINESS BACKGROUND
CASH FLOW AND VALUE CONTRIBUTION - INCREMENTAL (THIS PROJECT)

($000)	(1)	(2)	(3)	(4)	(5)	(6)	(7)	(8)
	1995	1996B	1997F	1998F	1999F	2000F	1991-1995	Avg. Ann. % Chg. Incr./(Decr.) 1995 - 2000F
Sources								
(1) Net Income								
(2) Depreciation/Amortization								
(3) Other Sources								
(4) Total Sources								
Uses								
Inc./(Dec.) in Working								
(5) Capital								
(6) Capital Spending								
(7) Other Uses								
(8) Total Uses								
(9) Cash Flow								
(10) Value Contribution								

(PRODUCT LINE)
PROJECT TITLE
MARKETING SEGMENT SPREADSHEET - INCLUDING THIS PROJECT

	(1) 1991	(2) 1992	(3) 1993	(4) 1994	(5) 1995	(6) 1996B	(7) 1997F	(8) 1998F	(9) 1999F	(10) 2000F	Avg. Ann. % Chg. Incr./(Decr.)	
											(11) 1991-1995	(12) 1995-2000F
Relevant Market Information												
(1) Volume												
(2) Avg. Selling Price ($)												
(3) Amount												
Sales												
(4) Volume												
(5) Avg. Selling Price ($)												
(6) Amount												
(7) ⎓ Market Segment Share (6)/(3)												
Memo:												
(8) Leading Competitor Market Segment Share (a)												
(9) ⎓ Relative Market Segment Share (7)/(8)												

(a) Market segment share leader. If ⎓ is market segment share leader, use market segment share of next largest competitor.

(PRODUCT LINE)
PROJECT TITLE
MARKETING SEGMENT SPREADSHEET - EXCLUDING THIS PROJECT

	(1)	(2)	(3)	(4)	(5)	(6)	(7)	(8)	(9)	(10)	(11)	(12)
											Avg. Ann. % Chg. Incr./(Decr.)	
	1991	1992	1993	1994	1995	1996B	1997F	1998F	1999F	2000F	1991-1995	1995-2000F

Relevant Market Information

(1) Volume
(2) Avg. Selling Price ($)
(3) Amount

Sales

(4) Volume
(5) Avg. Selling Price ($)
(6) Amount

(7) ⏝ Market Share (6)/(3)

Memo:

(8) Leading Competitor Market Segment Share (a)
(9) ⏝ Relative Market Segment Share (7)/(8)

(a) Market segment share leader. If (⏝) is market segment share leader,
use market segment share of next largest competitor.

326

(PRODUCT LINE)
PROJECT TITLE
MARKETING SEGMENT SPREADSHEET - INCREMENTAL (THIS PROJECT)

	(1)	(2)	(3)	(4)	(5)	(6)	(7)
	1995	1996B	1997F	1998F	1999F	2000F	Avg. Ann. % Chg. Incr./(Decr.) 1995-2000F

Relevant Market Information
(1) Volume
(2) Avg. Selling Price ($)
(3) Amount

(___) Sales
(4) Volume
(5) Avg. Selling Price ($)
(6) Amount

(7) (___) Market Share (6)/(3)

Memo:
(8) Leading Competitor Market Segment Share (a)
(9) (___) Relative Market Segment Share (7)/(8)

(a) Market segment share leader. If (___) is market segment share leader, use market segment share of next largest competitor.

DISCOUNTED CASH FLOW ANALYSIS AND VALUE CONTRIBUTION - EXAMPLE

Project Name - New Mixing Machine

Assumptions
- Cost - $25,000
- Economic Life - 6 years
- Hurdle Rate (Discount Rate of 12%)

Financials	(1) Initial Investment	(2) Year 1	(3) Year 2	(4) Year 3	(5) Year 4	(6) Year 5	(7) Year 6
Net Sales		$6,795	$15,000	$20,500	$21,500	$24,000	$28,000
Cost of Goods Sold		3,500	8,250	9,225	9,675	10,800	12,600
Gross Margin		3,295	6,750	11,275	11,825	13,200	15,400
Margin %		48%	45%	55%	55%	55%	55%
Depreciation/Amortization		2,500	5,000	5,000	5,000	5,000	2,500
Other/Operating Expenses		456	502	552	607	668	734
Pretax Profit		339	1,248	5,723	6,218	7,532	12,166
Cash Operating Taxes (a)		122	449	2,060	2,238	2,712	4,380
NOPAT		$217	$799	$3,663	$3,980	$4,820	$7,786
Depreciation		2,500	5,000	5,000	5,000	5,000	2,500
Other Non-Cash Items		900	1,080	(72)	(763)	(763)	(382)
Decrease/(Increase) in W/C		(2,378)	(2,872)	(1,925)	(350)	(875)	(1,400)
Capital Expenditures	(20,000)	(5,000)	-	-	-	-	-
Proceeds From Sale/Terminal Value		-	-	-	-	-	8,500
Cash Flow	$(20,000)	$(3,761)	$4,007	$6,666	$7,867	$8,182	$17,004

Present Value (at 12%)

	(1) Initial Investment	(2) Year 1	(3) Year 2	(4) Year 3	(5) Year 4	(6) Year 5	(7) Year 6
Capital Expenditures	$(20,000)	$(4,464)					
Forecast Period Cash Flow		1,106	$3,194	$4,745	$5,000	$4,643	$4,308
Proceeds from Sale of Assets/Terminal Value							4,306

NPV

Present Value - Cash Flows From Ops.	$22,996
Present Value - Proceeds From Sale	4,306
Present Value of Investment	(24,464)
Net Present Value of Project	$2,838

Additional Information
IRR: 15.1%
Cost of Capital: 12%
Present Value Payback: 6.0 Yrs.
Profitability Index: 1.12

Value Contribution

	(2) Year 1	(3) Year 2	(4) Year 3	(5) Year 4	(6) Year 5	(7) Year 6
Pretax Operating Income	$339	$1,248	$5,723	$6,218	$7,532	$12,166
Taxes	(122)	(449)	(2,060)	(2,238)	(2,712)	(4,380)
Inc/(Dec) in Deferred Taxes						-
Depreciation/Amortization	2,500	5,000	5,000	5,000	5,000	2,500
NOPAT Cash Flow	2,717	5,799	8,663	8,980	9,820	10,286
Average Gross Assets	22,500	25,000	25,000	25,000	25,000	
Average Net Working Capital	1,189	3,814	6,213	7,350	7,963	asset
Capital Employed	23,689	28,814	31,213	32,350	32,963	sold
Minimum $ Required Return @ 12%	2,843	3,458	3,746	3,882	3,956	
Value Contribution (NOPAT CF - Min. Required Return)	$(126)	$2,341	$4,917	$5,098	$5,864	

(a) Income tax provision less increase in deferred taxes.

EXHIBIT 20-2   Sample Policy and Procedure—Capital Investment Guidelines:
New Products, Increased Capacity, Equipment Replacement,
and Cost Reduction

MAJOR INDUSTRIAL COMPANY

This major industrial company uses a policy and procedure for capital investments called
Capital Investment Guidelines. The guideline includes supplemental financial information
such as the required evaluation time period, lost revenues/profits through the introduction
of new products, and the use of spreadsheets. Specific guidelines are presented for different
categories of capital investments such as new products and increased capacity, equipment
replacement and cost reduction.

New products and capacity projects are evaluated over the product's anticipated life
cycle. Detailed instructions include required time period evaluations, computation guidelines for sales, cost of sales, selling, general and administrative expenses (S.G.&A.),
depreciation, taxes, investments, working capital, cash flows, internal rate of return (IRR),
net present values (NPV), payback period and sensitivity analysis.

These calculations can be seen in the financial summary (page 333) which is broken
down into three sections: (1) profit and loss, (2) cash flow, and (3) financial returns. Since
this project illustration has an estimated life of five years, all calculations are based on five
periods with the sixth year used for additional investment and/or working capital requirements (page 333).

Exhibit 20.2 illustrates that this project has an internal rate of return of 36.8%, and a
payback period of 2.3 years. However, using the guidelines for sensitivity analysis such as
−5% of sales prices, +10% of product cost, +10% of investment, −20% of unit volume,
+10% of DSO, and +15% of inventory turns, the section on sensitivity analysis calculates
the financial returns for the internal rate of return, net present value, payback and return on
sales. These various calculations illustrate the risk of the project based on the various
guidelines. The ideal project will have a higher upside potential than downside risk. Projects
that have the reverse should be looked at very carefully for other positive elements that the
project would offer. Reduction in sales and cost overspending creates the greatest risk to
the financial success of the project.

Equipment replacement and cost reduction projects follow a similar procedure. In this
evaluation process, two sensitivity items are used to calculate the risk of the project. They
include lower cost savings and increased investment spending. In either case, the element
of risk is shown on page 333.

CAPITAL INVESTMENT GUIDELINE

SUPPLEMENTAL FINANCIAL INFORMATION

Introduction

The last section of the main Capital Authorization Request document is the financial section. A standard financial summary has been developed and should be the first page of every financial section. The details which support this summary page will vary by type of capital investment. Included in this exhibit are two examples of financial models which can be used for various types of capital investments.

General Definitions

Currency:

  All C.A.R.'s should be prepared in U.S. dollars at the current year's pegged (budget) rates.

Time Period:

  In general, a five year financial evaluation is standard. However, if the project supports a shorter or longer life a different time period can be used. Any variance to the five year standard must be explained in the Executive Summary.

Cannibalization:

  Existing sales and cost of sales lost through introduction of new products or an increase is existing product volumes must be reflected in the Financial Summary. Any unamortized tooling on cannibalized product should also be written off.

Format:

  The financial models included in this exhibit are Lotus® worksheet.

Reproduced by permission

NEW PRODUCTS AND CAPACITY

In general, investments in new products and capacity will use a financial model driven by increased sales volumes. The assumptions used to compute the increased sales and cost of sales must be supported by Marketing, Engineering, and Manufacturing.

Time Period:

   Investments in new products and capacity should be evaluated over the product's anticipated life cycle.

   The capital investment cash outflow should be shown in Year 0.

   Sales, working capital and operating income assumptions should be reflected in the period the sales begin (usually Year 1).

   Working capital and other asset recovery assumptions should always flow the year after the final year (standard is year six).

Sales:

   New Product Investment—Gross sales should be developed from detailed assumptions for unit volumes and selling price by product and by country. Intercompany sales volumes and intercompany mark-up should be ignored.

   In general, it is usually easier to set up a separate profit & loss statement for each country or region. The Financial Summary would then be a consolidation of all countries.

   Capacity Investment—Gross sales should be developed as follows:

   If projected sales volumes have less capacity with new equipment then, projected sales volumes minus current capacity (without the new equipment) times current sales price equals gross sales.

   If projected sales volumes have more capacity with new equipment then, capacity with new equipment minus current capacity (without the new equipment) times current sales price equals gross sales.

   Intercompany sales volumes and intercompany mark-up should be ignored.

Cost of Sales:

   Cost of sales should also be developed from detailed assumptions for unit volumes and product cost. Product cost assumptions should be based on the place of manufacture. Warranty expense should also be included in cost of sales, and should be calculated based on current or projected warranty rates. Again, intercompany activity is ignored.

Gross Margin:

   Gross Margin is calculated as the difference between Sales and Cost of Sales.

Gross Margin %:

   Gross Margin % is calculated by dividing gross margin dollars by sales dollars.

S,G&A Expenses:

The Financial Summary must be fully burdened through Operating Income, including promotion and other SG&A assumptions that most directly reflect the selling country and distribution channel.

S,G&A %:

S,G&A % is calculated by dividing S,G&A dollars by sales dollars.

Operating Income:

Operating Income is calculated as the difference between Gross Margin and S,G&A Expenses.

Operating Income %:

Operating Income % is calculated by dividing Operating Income dollars by sales dollars.

Book and Tax Depreciation:

In most countries there is a difference between book depreciation and tax depreciation. The book depreciation used in the operating income assumptions must be in accordance with the depreciation lives outlined in the company's Policies and Procedures.

Tax depreciation will vary by country. If this information is not available, contact Business, Planning & Analysis or the Corporate Tax Department.

Depreciation is a non-cash item and must be added back to operating income to arrive at cash flow.

Taxable Income:

Operating Income plus book depreciation, minus tax depreciation equals taxable income.

Taxes:

Taxes should be calculated on taxable income at the management reporting income tax rate of 35%.

Taxes should be calculated regardless of the current tax position and shown as cash flow in the year accrued.

If the project is heavily biased toward a higher or lower tax entity, that different rate may be used (vs. the standard 35%).

Investment:

The cash outflow of the initial investment should be shown in year 0.

The investment, net of accumulated tax depreciation should be reported as positive cash flow in the year after the final year (standard is year six).

Working Capital:

Working capital includes Trade Accounts Receivable, Inventory, and Trade Accounts Payable. Assumptions for DSO, inventory turnover and accounts payable should be clearly identified in the detailed financials.

Initial working capital investment begins in the same year as sales (usually year 1). Any increase or decrease to working capital requirements are reflected as cash flow over the time period.

The working capital recovery assumptions should always flow the year after the final year (standard is year six).

Total Cash Flow:

Total cash flow is calculated as follows:

Operating Income
      + Book Depreciation
      − Taxes
      − Investment
      − Working Capital

Cumulative Cash Flow:

Cumulative cash flow is the current year's cash flow plus all of the prior periods cash flow.

Internal Rate of Return (IRR)

The discount rate that equates the present value of future cash flows to the cost of the investment.

In Lotus®, IRR is an @ function computed as follows: @IRR(Guess at IRR%,Cash flow stream).

Net Present Value (NPV):

The present value of future cash flows discounted at the (Firm Name) cost of capital rate minus the present value of the cost of the investment.

In Lotus®, NPV is an @ function computed as follows: @NPV(Cost of Capital,Cash flow stream).

Payback Period:

The length of time required for the net cash flows to return the cost of the investment. Usually expressed in years.

Return on Sales:

Return on sales is calculated by dividing the sum of all year's operating income by the sum of all year's sales.

Sensitivity Analysis:

IRR, NPV, Payback period, and Return on Sales should be recalculated for sensitivity to the following events:

Sales (Price)	−5%
Product Cost	+10%
Investment	+10%
Unit Volume	−20%
DSO	+10%
Inventory Turns	+15%

FINANCIAL SUMMARY
(In 000's of USD)

PROFIT & LOSS

PROFIT & LOSS	0	1	2	3	4	5	6
				YEAR			
SALES	0	38,000	49,250	60,500	76,250	87,500	0
COST OF SALES	0	22,140	28,978	35,815	45,288	52,125	0
GROSS MARGIN	0	15,860	20,273	24,685	30,963	35,375	0
GROSS MARGIN %	0.0%	41.7%	41.2%	40.8%	40.6%	40.4%	0.0%
S,G,& A EXPENSES	0	9,500	12,313	15,125	19,063	21,875	0
S,G,& A %	0.0%	25.0%	25.0%	25.0%	25.0%	25.0%	0.0%
OPERATING INCOME	0	6,360	7,960	9,560	11,900	13,500	0
OPERATING INCOME %	0.0%	16.7%	16.2%	15.8%	15.6%	15.4%	0.0%

CASH FLOW

CASH FLOW	0	1	2	3	4	5	6
				YEAR			
BOOK DEPRECIATION	0	750	750	750	750	250	
TAX DEPRECIATION	0	(500)	(857)	(612)	(437)	(313)	
TAXABLE INCOME	0	6,610	7,853	9,698	11,713	13,437	
TAXES at 35%	0	(2,313)	(2,748)	(3,394)	(4,099)	(4,703)	
INVESTMENT	(3,500)	0	0	0	0	0	781
WORKING CAPITAL	0	(7,903)	(2,420)	(2,330)	(3,313)	(2,375)	18,340
TOTAL CASH FLOW	(3,500)	(3,106)	3,542	4,586	4,738	6,672	19,121
CUMMULATIVE CASH FLOW	(3,500)	(6,606)	(3,065)	1,521	6,259	12,931	32,052

SENSITIVITY ANALYSIS

FINANCIAL RETURNS	Base Case	Sales -5%	Cost +10%	Investment +10%	Unit Volume -20%	DSO +10%	Inv Turns +15%
INTERNAL RATE OF RETURN	36.8%	15.5%	-3.5%	34.5%	33.6%	31.8%	28.1%
NET PRESENT VALUE	16,036	11,414	8,496	15,935	12,527	15,768	15,559
PAYBACK	2.3	3.5	4.7	2.7	2.7	2.2	2.0
RETURN ON SALES	15.8%	12.9%	10.2%	15.8%	16.4%	15.8%	15.8%

UNIT VOLUMES, NET SALES PRICE AND PRODUCT COST

		YEAR 1	YEAR2	YEAR3	YEAR4	YEAR5
NEW OR ADDITIONAL PRODUCT:						
Product A	Unit Volume	500	600	700	800	900
	Unit Net Sales Price	50.00	50.00	50.00	50.00	50.00
	Unit Product Cost	30.00	30.00	30.00	30.00	30.00
Product B	Unit Volume	100	100	100	100	100
	Unit Net Sales Price	25.00	25.00	25.00	25.00	25.00
	Unit Product Cost	15.00	15.00	15.00	15.00	15.00
Product C	Unit Volume	200	250	300	350	400
	Unit Net Sales Price	35.00	35.00	35.00	35.00	35.00
	Unit Product Cost	20.00	20.00	20.00	20.00	20.00
Product D	Unit Volume	400	500	600	700	800
	Unit Net Sales Price	45.00	45.00	45.00	45.00	45.00
	Unit Product Cost	25.00	25.00	25.00	25.00	25.00
CANNIBALIZED PRODUCT:						
Product E	Unit Volume	(200)	(200)	(200)	(200)	(200)
	Unit Net Sales Price	50.00	50.00	50.00	50.00	50.00
	Unit Product Cost	35.00	35.00	35.00	35.00	35.00
Product F	Unit Volume	(100)	(100)	(100)	0	0
	Unit Net Sales Price	45.00	45.00	45.00	45.00	45.00
	Unit Product Cost	25.00	25.00	25.00	25.00	25.00
TOTAL PRODUCT:						
NEW PRODUCT	Unit Volume	1,200	1,450	1,700	1,950	2,200
	Net Sales $	52,500	63,750	75,000	86,250	97,500
	Product Cost $	30,500	37,000	43,500	50,000	56,500
CANNIBALIZED PRODUCT	Unit Volume	(300)	(300)	(300)	(200)	(200)
	Net Sales $	(14,500)	(14,500)	(14,500)	(10,000)	(10,000)
	Product Cost $	(9,500)	(9,500)	(9,500)	(7,000)	(7,000)
NET	Unit Volume	900	1,150	1,400	1,750	2,000
	Net Sales $	38,000	49,250	60,500	76,250	87,500
	Product Cost $	21,000	27,500	34,000	43,000	49,500
COST OF SALES:						
	Product Cost $	21,000	27,500	34,000	43,000	49,500
	Warranty @3%	1,140	1,478	1,815	2,288	2,625
	Cost of Sales $	22,140	28,978	35,815	45,288	52,125
SENSITIVITY:						
	Unit Volume	1.00				
	Net Sales $	1.00				
	Product Cost $	1.00				

SG&A, BOOK DEPRECIATION, TAX DEPRECIATION, WORKING CAPITAL

Category	Input	YEAR 0	YEAR 1	YEAR2	YEAR3	YEAR4	YEAR5
S,G&A EXPENSES:							
Net Sales $		0	38,000	49,250	60,500	76,250	87,500
Promotion	5%	0	1,900	2,463	3,025	3,813	4,375
Salesmen's Comp	4%	0	1,520	1,970	2,420	3,050	3,500
Other Marketing	2%	0	760	985	1,210	1,525	1,750
Distribution	2%	0	760	985	1,210	1,525	1,750
Transportation	1%	0	380	493	605	763	875
G&A	6%	0	2,280	2,955	3,630	4,575	5,250
R&D	3%	0	1,140	1,478	1,815	2,288	2,625
CEA	1%	0	380	493	605	763	875
GEA	1%	0	380	493	605	763	875
Total		0	9,500	12,313	15,125	19,063	21,875
BOOK DEPRECIATION:							
Investment							
Tooling	3	(1,500)	500	500	500	0	0
Equipment	8	(2,000)	250	250	250	250	250
Total		(3,500)	750	750	750	250	250
TAX DEPRECIATION:							
Investment							
Tooling	Varies By	(1,500)	214	367	262	187	134
Equipment	Country	(2,000)	286	490	350	250	179
Total		(3,500)	500	857	612	437	313
WORKING CAPITAL:							
Product Cost $		0	21,000	27,500	34,000	43,000	49,500
DSO	50 *	0	(5,278)	(1,563)	(1,563)	(2,188)	(1,563)
Inventory Turns	4.0 *	0	(5,250)	(1,625)	(1,625)	(2,250)	(1,625)
A/P Days	45 *	0	2,625	768	858	1,125	813
Total		0	(7,903)	(2,420)	(2,330)	(3,313)	(2,375)

SENSITIVITY:		
Investment	1.00
DSO	1.00
Inv Turns	1.00

* Working Capital Ratios are based on a 360 day year.

EQUIPMENT REPLACEMENT AND COST REDUCTION

In general, investments in equipment for replacement and cost reductions will use a financial model driven by economic benefits such as reduced labor, material, inventory and overhead costs. The assumptions used to compute the economic benefits must be supported by Engineering and Manufacturing.

Time Period:

Investments in equipment for replacement or cost reduction should be evaluated over the anticipated life cycle of the product manufactured by the equipment.

The capital investment cash outflow should be shown in Year 0.

The cost reduction assumptions should be reflected in the period the benefits are generated (usually Year 1).

Working capital and other asset recovery assumptions should always flow the year after the final year (standard is year six).

Sales:

As a result of investing in equipment for replacement or cost reduction, incremental sales can be derived from lower cost, higher quality products being brought to market in less time. However, this is difficult to quantify and usually never used to financially justify these types of investments. Therefore, the incremental sales will be zero for these types of investments.

Cost of Sales:

Under most circumstances, the economic benefits will be reported as a product cost reduction in cost of sales. There should be a separate page which summarizes how the cost reductions were calculated. Each of the cost reductions (i.e., labor, material, overhead) should also be identified in the key measurement section of the Executive Summary.

Also, as a result of investing in new equipment, certain costs may increase and therefore, offset some of the identified savings. These costs will include increased depreciation on new equipment, ongoing software support, maintenance, indirect costs, etc.

Gross Margin:

Gross Margin is calculated as the difference between Sales and Cost of Sales.

Gross Margin %:

Gross Margin % is calculated by dividing gross margin dollars by sales dollars.

S,G & A Expenses:

The Financial Summary must be fully burdened through Operating Income. Most often, equipment investments such as replacements and cost reductions do not impact SG&A expenses.

S,G & A%:

S,G & A% is calculated by dividing S,G & A dollars by sales dollars.

Operating Income:

Operating Income is calculated as the difference between Gross Margin and S,G & A Expenses.

Operating Income %:

Operating Income % is calculated by dividing Operating Income dollars by sales dollars.

Book and Tax Depreciation:

In most countries there is a difference between book depreciation and tax depreciation. The book depreciation used in the operating income assumptions must be in accordance with the depreciation lives outlined in the company's Policies and Procedures.

Tax depreciation will vary by country.

Depreciation is a non-cash item and must be added back to operating income to arrive at cash flow.

Taxable Income:

Operating Income plus book depreciation, minus tax depreciation equals taxable income.

Taxes:

Taxes should be calculated on taxable income at the management reporting income tax rate of 35%.

Taxes should be calculated regardless of the current tax position and shown as cash flow in the year accrued.

If the project is heavily biased toward a higher or lower tax entity, that different rate may be used (vs. the standard 35%).

Investment:

The cash outflow of the initial investment should be shown in year 0.

Working Capital:

Working capital includes Trade Accounts Receivable, Inventory and Trade Accounts Payable. In some cases, equipment replacement and cost reduction investments will result in inventory reductions. The cash flow impact from these reductions should be reflected in the working capital calculation. Most often, with these types of Capital Authorization Request's trade accounts receivable and trade accounts payable will not be impacted.

Total Cash Flow:

   Total cash flow is calculated as follows:

   > Operating Income
   > + Book Depreciation
   > − Taxes
   > − Investment
   > − Working Capital

Cumulative Cash Flow:

   Cumulative cash flow is the current year's cash flow plus all of the prior periods cash flow.

Internal Rate of Return (IRR):

   The discount rate that equates the present value of future cash flows to the cost of the investment.

   In Lotus ®, IRR is an @ function computed as follows: @IRR(Guess IRR%,Cash flow stream).

Net Present Value (NPV):

   The present value of future cash flows discounted at the acceptable cost of capital rate minus the present value of the cost of the investment.

   In Lotus®, NPV is an @ function computed as follows: @NPV(Cost of Capital,Cash flow stream).

Payback Period:

   The length of time required for the net cash flows to return the cost of the investment. Usually expressed in years.

Return on Sales:

   Return on sales is not applicable to equipment replacement and cost reduction Capital Authorization Requests.

Sensitivity Analysis:

   IRR, NPV, and Payback period should be recalculated for sensitivity to the following events:

Cost Saving	−10%
Investment	+10%

FINANCIAL SUMMARY
(In 000's of USD)

PROFIT & LOSS				YEAR			
	0	1	2	3	4	5	6
SALES	0	0	0	0	0	0	0
COST OF SALES	0	(600)	(1,200)	(1,200)	(1,200)	(1,200)	0
GROSS MARGIN	0	600	1,200	1,200	1,200	1,200	0
GROSS MARGIN %	0.0%	0.0%	0.0%	0.0%	0.0%	0.0%	0.0%
S,G,& A EXPENSES	0	0	0	0	0	0	0
S,G,& A %	0.0%	0.0%	0.0%	0.0%	0.0%	0.0%	0.0%
OPERATING INCOME	0	600	1,200	1,200	1,200	1,200	0
OPERATING INCOME %	0.0%	0.0%	0.0%	0.0%	0.0%	0.0%	0.0%

CASH FLOW				YEAR			
	0	1	2	3	4	5	6
BOOK DEPRECIATION	0	750	750	750	250	250	0
TAX DEPRECIATION	0	500	857	612	437	313	0
TAXABLE INCOME	0	850	1,093	1,338	1,013	1,137	0
TAXES at 35%	0	(297)	(382)	(468)	(354)	(398)	0
INVESTMENT	(3,500)	0	0	0	0	0	750
WORKING CAPITAL	0	2,000	0	0	0	0	0
TOTAL CASH FLOW	(3,500)	3,053	1,568	1,482	1,096	1,052	750
CUMMULATIVE CASH FLOW	(3,500)	(447)	1,120	2,602	3,697	4,749	5,499

	SENSITIVITY ANALYSIS		
FINANCIAL RETURNS	Base Case	Cost Saving -10%	Investment +10%
INTERNAL RATE OF RETURN	42.5%	39.4%	36.1%
NET PRESENT VALUE	3,104	2,872	3,018
PAYBACK	1.3	1.3	1.4
RETURN ON SALES	n/a	n/a	n/a

SG&A, BOOK DEPRECIATION, TAX DEPRECIATION, WORKING CAPITAL

Category	Input	YEAR 0	YEAR 1	YEAR2	YEAR3	YEAR4	YEAR5
COST REDUCTIONS:							
Direct Labor		0	100	200	200	200	200
Overtime		0	200	400	400	400	400
Material		0	50	100	100	100	100
Overhead		0	150	300	300	300	300
Scrap		0	100	200	200	200	200
Total		0	600	1,200	1,200	1,200	1,200
BOOK DEPRECIATION:							
Investment							
Tooling	3	(1,500)	500	500	500	0	0
Equipment	8	(2,000)	250	250	250	250	250
Total		(3,500)	750	750	750	250	250
TAX DEPRECIATION:							
Investment							
Tooling	Varies By	(1,500)	214	367	262	187	134
Equipment	Country	(2,000)	286	490	350	250	179
Total		(3,500)	500	857	612	437	313
WORKING CAPITAL:							
DSO		0	0	0	0	0	0
Inventory	4.0	0	2,000	0	0	0	0
A/P Days		0	0	0	0	0	0
Total		0	2,000	0	0	0	0
SENSITIVITY:							
Investment		1.00					
Cost Reduction		1.00					

EXHIBIT 20-3 Sample Policy—Increase in Investments in Existing Lines of Business, Equity Investments, and Intercompany Long-term Loans

MAJOR INTERNATIONAL COMPANY

Exhibit 20-3 shows how a major international company establishes its capital investment policy. This company uses a Request for Change in Investment form that pertains to equity investments and long-term loans. The Appropriations Request form is used for the review of proposed capital expenditures. Proposals for changes in investment, capital expenditures, divestitures and disposal of assets are accompanied by memoranda with an analysis and explanation of assumptions to support the recommendation. The company uses an internal rate of return concept for determining the viability of a capital project to its determined hurdle rate.

PAGE	OF	NUMBER	SUBJECT
			INCREASE IN INVESTMENTS IN EXISTING LINES OF BUSINESS, EQUITY INVESTMENTS AND INTERCOMPANY LONG-TERM LOANS

REQUEST FORMAT

In support of the Request for Change in investment form, submit a memorandum including the following information:

1. Summary statement of reasons for recommending the additional investment.

2. The proposed source of financing for the increased investment, whether it be from cash balances, short-term or long-term external financing, guaranteed debt, or intercompany loans. The increased investment's impact on dividend policy and, when financed by debt, the projected repayment terms should be included.

3. Summary table of previous investments, loans, and guarantees.

4. Detailed statements of earnings (by product line, etc.)—five years historical and five years projected.

5. Summary balance sheets—five years historical and five years projected.

6. Summary of internal cash flows and cash returns to five years historical and five years projected.

7. In the case of intercompany loans, projected terms of repayment.

8. Advantages and disadvantages of investment by   vs. third-party borrowing by the subsidiary or affiliate.

9. Projected internal rate of return to   if requested action is approved.

10. Any other factors considered relevant by management.

Reproduced by permission.

NUMBER	SUBJECT	PAGE	OF
	APPROPRIATION REQUESTS		

APPROPRIATION REQUEST
Summary (Page 1)

1. COMPANY OR DIVISION	2. PLANT OR LOCATION	3. APPROP. NO.	4. SUPPL. NO.

5. PROJECT TITLE

7. AMOUNT

FIXED ASSETS	$_____
CAPITALIZED INTEREST	_____
WORKING CAPITAL	_____
EXPENSE	_____
TOTAL REQUEST	$_____

6. PROJECT DESCRIPTION

8. CATEGORY OF CAPITAL EXPENDITURE

1. ☐ INCREASED CAPACITY
2. ☐ COST REDUCTION
3. ☐ NEW VENTURE
4. ☐ STRAIGHT REPLACEMENT
5. ☐ PRODUCT LEADERSHIP/COMPETITIVE PRESSURES

6. ☐ COMPLIANCE WITH OUTSIDE REQUIREMENTS
7. ☐ ADMINISTRATIVE REQUIREMENTS
8. ☐ RESEARCH/DEVELOPMENT
9. ☐ STRATEGIC REQUIREMENT
10. ☐ ENGINEERING/ENGINEERING DESIGN

9. PROJECT STATUS (FIXED ASSETS ONLY)

THIS REQUEST $_____ PREVIOUS AUTHORIZATION $_____ TOTAL COST $_____

PROJECT WAS ☐ WAS NOT ☐ INCLUDED IN THE _____ CAPITAL EXPENDITURES FORECAST FOR $_____
_____ Date

PROJECT WAS ☐ WAS NOT ☐ INCLUDED IN THE _____ FIVE YEAR PLAN FOR $_____
_____ Year

10. SUMMARY OF FACILITIES TO BE RETIRED
(SEE FORM #681 P.M. INC. ATTACHED)

ORIGINAL COST $_____   LOSS OR (GAIN) ON DISPOSITION $_____

11. FORECAST OF CASH OUTLAY (FIXED ASSETS ONLY)

___ Q 19 ___	___ Q 19 ___	___ Q 19 ___	___ Q 19 ___	YEAR 0 TOTAL
$	$	$	$	$

YEAR 1 TOTAL	YEAR 2 TOTAL	YEAR 3 TOTAL	SUBSEQUENT	TOTAL CASH OUTLAY
$	$	$	$	$

ESTIMATED COMPLETION DATE _____

12. REQUIRED APPROVALS

_____ _____
Originator/Coordinator   Date

_____ _____
                            Date

_____ _____
                            Date

_____ _____
Operating Company Controller   Date

_____ _____
Operating Company Vice President   Date

_____ _____
Vice President Finance   Date

_____ _____
Vice President Operations   Date

_____ _____
Operating Company President   Date

13. INCREMENTAL PROFIT ANALYSIS AND TOTAL CASH FLOW (PAGE 3)

A. PAYBACK PERIOD _____ YEARS

B. RETURN ON INVESTMENT _____ %

C. PROJECT LIFE _____ Years

14. APPROVAL

_____ _____
VICE PRESIDENT & CONTROLLER   Date

_____ _____
VICE PRESIDENT - PLANNING   Date

_____ _____
VICE PRESIDENT - CHIEF FINANCIAL OFFICER   Date

_____ _____
EXECUTIVE VICE PRESIDENT   Date

_____ _____
CHAIRMAN, PRESIDENT, VICE CHAIRMAN   Date

PAGE OF	NUMBER	SUBJECT
		APPROPRIATION REQUESTS

"TIME SCHEDULE OF INVESTMENT"

CASH (INFLOWS)/OUTFLOWS OF THE INVESTMENT

Fixed Assets

The cash flows for each asset classification, excluding capitalized interest, will be stated on this schedule. The cash amount for each asset classification may be stated in detail for each time period or in total for each asset classification and time period.

Working Capital

Working capital required will include capital required for additional inventory levels, receivables, payables, etc. which usually result in the first year or first several years of the project. In the last year of the project's life, the working capital requirements will be recognized as an addition to cash flow.

The working capital, if any, required by the investment will also be stated in the same manner as the cash (inflows)/outflows required for the investment.

Total Project Investment

The total project investment is the net of the Total Fixed Asset (line 11) and the total Working Capital Amounts (line 16).

NUMBER	SUBJECT	PAGE	OF
	APPROPRIATION REQUESTS		

APPROPRIATION REQUEST
TIME SCHEDULE OF INVESTMENT (PAGE 2)
(Amounts in Thousands)

PLANT OR LOCATION | DATE
PROJECT TITLE

(INFLOWS)/OUTFLOWS — INVESTMENT CASH OUTLAYS

PERIOD	LINE NO	YEAR 0 19__ -Q	YEAR 0 19__ -Q	YEAR 0 19__ -Q	YEAR 0 19__ -Q	YEAR 0 TOTAL	YEARS 1	YEARS 2	YEARS 3	SUB-SEQUENT	TOTAL
FIXED ASSETS:		$	$	$	$	$	$	$	$	$	$
Land	1										
Land Improvements	2										
Buildings	3										
Building Equipment	4										
Machinery and Equipment	5										
Data Processing Equipment	6										
Furniture and Fixtures	7										
Transportation Equipment	8										
Leasehold Improvements	9										
Other (Specify)	10										
Total Fixed Assets	11										
WORKING CAPITAL:											
Increase/(Decrease) in Accounts Receivable	12										
Increase/(Decrease) in Inventories	13										
Increase/(Decrease) in Other Current Assets	14										
Increase/(Decrease) in Current Liabilities	15										
Total Working Capital	16										
Total Project Investment	17	$	$	$	$	$	$	$	$	$	$

PAGE	OF	NUMBER	SUBJECT
			APPROPRIATION REQUESTS

"INCREMENTAL PROFIT ANALYSIS AND TOTAL CASH FLOWS"

The information requested (_____) is required to arrive at the net cash flows generated during the project's economic life. These flows, excluding capitalized interest, are the basis to calculate the return on investment using the internal rate of return discounted cash flow method and to determine the payback period. The revenues and expenses stated are estimates; however, they should reflect a realistic evaluation of the project's economic worth. Inflation assumptions should be based on the latest five year plan with a continuation of the fifth year rates for subsequent years. Alternative inflation factors may be assumed if there is sufficient justification for their use in a particular project. When the Request is prepared for an asset which will replace one that is presently operational, the estimated revenues and expenses should reflect the incremental values only.

The detail required to arrive at the cash flows are outlined below for those items which required explanation:

Manufacturing Costs/(Savings)—When the nature of the investment is strictly cost reduction (no incremental sales revenue), the savings resulting from the investment will be recognized as a reduction in manufacturing costs.

Other Variable Costs will include indirect labor, fringe benefits, maintenance, power, etc. These expenses should be itemized on a separate schedule.

Depreciation will be computed on the same basis as used in the relevant income tax return. However, when use of the tax method does not materially affect an investment's R.O.I., the straight line method can be used for expediency. The capitalized amount of the asset, excluding capitalized interest, will be depreciated over its useful life. When assets having different depreciable lives are included in the same project, the respective depreciable life for each asset is used to calculate the yearly depreciation. For example, if a project with a 15–year economic life included a building with a 50–year depreciable life, depreciation for the building is based on the 50–year life. This residual or undepreciated value of any asset whose depreciable life exceeds the project's life will be included as an addition to the cash flow in the last year of the project's life.

Other Operating Costs will include shipping, marketing, research and development, and general and administrative expenses (property taxes and insurance) associated with the proposal. These expenses should be detailed on a separate schedule.

Non-Recurring Costs will be expensed in those years in which it is estimated they will be incurred. Normally, they will be incurred in the first year or first several years of the project.

PAGE OF	NUMBER	SUBJECT
		APPROPRIATION REQUESTS

Since the payback period represents the time period required to recoup the total investment, the cash inflows not the net cash flows are used to derive the time period. In the illustration, the cash flows in years 1 and 2 must be adjusted by the working capital requirements since they are already part of the total investment. These adjusted amounts will then represent the cash inflows.

The cash flows are determined for each year of the project's life and their present values are computed to arrive at the rate of return. Whenever the cash flows generated differ in any given year or years, the present value of the cash flow must be computed separately for each of those years. (Cash flows should not be averaged over the project's life except where the flow for each year is exactly the same. In the illustration the cash flows for years 3 through 14 are estimated to be exactly the same.)

Year	Cash Flows	Discount Factors	Discount Rate— 43% P.V. of Cash Flows	Discount Factors	Discount Rate— 45% P.V. of Cash Flows
0	$(600M)	1.00	$(600M)	1.00	$(600M)
1	$(153M)	0.70	$(107M)	0.69	$(106M)
2	$ 316M	0.49	$ 155M	0.48	$ 152M
3–14	$ 501M	1.12	$ 563M	1.05	$ 526M
15	$1,066M	0.005	$ 5M	0.004	$ 4M
			$ 16M		$(24M)

To determine the return on investment to the nearest whole percent, interpolate:

$$43\% + (2\% \times 16/40) = 43.8\%$$

Notes:

Year zero is the year in which the capital investment is initially made in whole or in part. The discount factor in year zero is always one.

PAGE OF	NUMBER	SUBJECT
		APPROPRIATION REQUESTS

X.   "INCREMENTAL PROFIT ANALYSIS AND TOTAL CASH FLOWS" (Cont'd.)

Income Taxes—Taxes represent the combined Federal and State tax rates used to arrive at the tax liability.

The Investment Tax Credit as treated under the Tax Act of 1982 requires that either:

(1) reduce the basis of fixed assets additions eligible for investment tax credit (ITC) by 50% of the ITC or,
(2) accept an initial ITC that is 2% less than the full ITC.

It is the Company's policy to use the latter alternative for both book and tax purposes.

The Tax Act of 1982 does not apply to property constructed or acquired under a contract entered into after August 13, 1981, which was binding on July 1, 1982.

Depreciation is the same amount included in Line No. 2 above.

Project Investment is the net of the capital required for the investment and the working capital (if any).

A. ILLUSTRATION

Assume:

1.   The amount of the investment proposal is $1,000,000 with $600,000 expended in the initial year (year zero) and $400,000 in the following year (year one).

2.   The project's economic life is 15 years.

3.   The investment will consist of a building and equipment. The former has a 50–year depreciable life and the latter a 15–year depreciable life. In this example, for expediency, depreciation for each asset is calculated on a straight line basis using the depreciable life of each asset as the base. However, the preferred method is the method used in the relevant income tax return. Since the depreciable life of the building is greater than the economic life of the project, the residual value is recognized as additional working capital in the last year of the project's life (35/50 of $700,000).

4.   Working capital in the amounts of $60,000 and $15,000 are required in the first and second years of the project's life. These amounts will be recognized as an addition to cash flow in the last year of the project's life.

DECISION-MAKING STRATEGIES

- Determine the susceptibility of changes in technology or the risk of obsolescence.
- Develop desired methods of calculating capital investment proposals.
- Choose a calculation method that reflects both the risk of the project and the time value of money.
- Develop a cash flow statement for each individual project.
- Determine the desired minimum payback period: high risk, short payback; low risk, longer payback.
- Determine the discounted cash flow rate with cost of capital, or current cost of obtaining funds.

21

LEASING—AN ALTERNATIVE FINANCING METHOD FOR INCREASING ROI RATES

In today's business environment, alternative methods of acquiring and financing assets need to be considered. For example, assets may be acquired by purchasing for cash, borrowing monies from a bank, or financing internally or from a leasing arrangement. This chapter explores how leasing can be used to increase return on investment by freeing up capital to be used for other investment opportunities.

Leasing has become a major vehicle for acquiring the use of an asset. It is a contract that involves two parties; the owner of the asset is referred to as the lessor, and the user who leases the asset is referred to as the lessee.[1] Within the leasing process, four parties participate. They are the lessor, the lessee, the equipment vendor, and a financing source such as a bank or independent leasing company. Depending on the type of lease, that is, operating lease versus capital lease, various elements of the financial statements are impacted. For example, under the operating lease, the lessor records both the value of the asset, depreciation, and incurred debt, both short- and long-term, whereas the lessee does not record the asset on the balance sheet but does record the expense of leasing on the earnings statement. Under a capital lease, the lessee records the asset, depreciation, and debt, as well as expense entries on the earnings statement, such as depreciation and interest. The lessor does not record any entries on the balance sheet, but does record revenues generated from the leasing transaction on the earnings statement. Thus, return on investment rates can vary depending on what lease is used.

ADVANTAGES OF LEASING

Leasing provides many advantages to a company. In many instances, companies may find that leasing provides a temporary solution to solving the costly acquisition of capital assets. Reviewing the advantages of leasing supports this statement.

- It provides a way of conserving cash flow initially by not requiring large initial outlays of cash.
- It creates a situation of "pay while using," since payments are made over long periods of time and usually coincide with the usage.
- It frequently circumvents constraints put on by capital budget policies and procedures and thus provides quicker approval.
- It shifts the risk of technological obsolescence back to the lessor.
- It puts the responsibility and legal ownership back to the lessor.
- It aids in forecasting cash requirements, since payments are usually fixed.
- It improves ratio performance, particularly return on investment.
- It provides the ability to test capital assets before making commitments to purchase them.
- It can provide off-balance-sheet financing.
- For tax purposes, depreciation and interest expenses can be shifted to parties that benefit the most.
- It provides a hedge against inflation by the ability to negotiate longer term and make payments with cheaper dollars.
- It can assist a company in meeting peak seasonal production requirements by permitting it to lease for short periods of time.
- Excessive usage of the asset by the lessee may make ownership not feasible.
- It allows a company to acquire assets on a piece-by-piece basis, thereby filling any voids in the capital investment program.
- It can increase discounted cash flow rates due to lower earlier cash outflows versus higher cash outflows when the asset is purchased.
- It provides greater flexibility in finding a financing source.

Based on the above advantages, it is easy to see why leasing has become so popular as a vehicle for acquiring assets. There are many disadvantages, however, any of which may discourage companies for entering into a leasing agreement.

CHAPTER 21

DISADVANTAGES OF LEASING

- It usually means a higher cost of borrowing, since the lessee will be required to pay for the lessor's built-in profit objective, as well as lost residual values, which are shifted to the lessor.
- Disclosure of leasing commitments are usually footnoted on the balance sheet, thus making analytical decisions difficult or misleading.
- Leasing arrangements are not always scrutinized from an analytical point of view, as is the case with capital investments.
- There is no availability of tax benefits, such as depreciation and interest expenses, due to lack of ownership and not creating any equity for the company.

SOURCES OF LEASES

Leasing can be acquired from many sources. As the leasing industry prospers, many players have entered this field over and above independent leasing companies. They still remain a major source of leasing.

- *Independent leasing companies.* This is the traditional type of leasing organization that leases all types of assets to almost everyone. Many independent leasing companies now specialize or concentrate on market segments such as automobiles and computers. A typical transaction between lessor, lessee, and vendor flows as follows:

1. Lessee enters into a lease commitment with any required deposits. The lessor makes the necessary arrangements to acquire the asset (see item #2) and delivers the asset to the lessee. The lessee makes periodic payments to the lessor as per the lease agreement.

2. Lessor arranges financing for the asset and pays the vendor for the asset. The asset is then delivered to the lessor or someone else whom the lessor designates. The vendor makes periodic payments to the financing source for the purchase of the asset.

Some of the above transactions happen concurrently.

- *Brokers.* These are intermediaries who bring together all the necessary parties, that is, lessor, lessee, and financial institution for the sole purpose of consummating a leasing arrangement. They are generally involved in large leasing arrangements such as aircraft and large computers.

• *Banks* provide all the necessary arrangements for consummating a lease, such as the paperwork and financing.

• *Insurance companies.* Some insurance companies form leasing subsidiaries, while others purchase individual leases or portfolios on the secondary market.

• *Finance companies* perform both consumer and operating leases.

• *Pension funds* serve as a pool of funds for lease portfolios and purchased leases from others.

LEASE TERMINOLOGY

Both operating leases and capital leases have been referred to by different names. Table 21.1 shows synonyms used to describe these types of leases.

TABLE 21-1   Operating and Capital Lease Synonyms

Operating Lease Synonyms	*Capital Lease Synonyms*
operating	capital
real	direct finance
true	finance
rental	installment sales contract
off-balance sheet	deferred sales contract
off the books	open-end lease with a bargain purchase option
closed-end	$1.00 purchase option
open-end lease with fair market value purchase option	nominal purchase option
tax	peppercorn (British)
guideline	full payout
non-guideline	full payoff
walk away	sales type
	non-tax
	secured transaction

OPERATING LEASE VERSUS CAPITAL LEASE DEFINED

The Financial and Accounting Standards Board (FASB) established guidelines for defining whether, under certain criteria, a lease can be classified as a capital lease. The four tests of substance are:

1. Will title pass from the lessor to the lessee?
2. Does the lease contain a bargain purchase option?
3. Is the lease life greater than or equal to 75% of the economic life?
4. Is the present value of the minimum lease payments greater than or equal to 90% of the fair market value of the asset?

If the answer to all these questions is yes, then the lease is considered a capital lease. If the answer to all these questions is no, then the lease is considered an operating lease.

CALCULATING THE IMPACT OF LEASING VERSUS PURCHASING

Because leasing involves the acquisition of an asset and creates certain cash flows over an extended period of time, it is possible to use capital investment techniques to evaluate which is the better decision—lease or purchase. The method that appears to be most appropriate is the net present value method (NPV). See chapter 20 for a full discussion.

We will use a simple set of facts to illustrate the different types of analyses that can be used depending upon the circumstances. Certain variables will be used to illustrate different methods of calculation. The facts are as follows:

Lease
Lease payments, $2,700 per month
Length of lease, 48 months
No residual of salvage value
Cash saving per year, $35,000

Purchase
Cost of asset, $85,000
Life of asset, 4 years
Depreciation method, sum-of-the-years digits
Tax rate, 35%
No salvage value
Cash savings per year, $35,000
Cost of capital rate, 15%

Using the above data, the cash flows and net present values for both a lease and purchase opportunity can be made, as shown in Table 21-2. The table

TABLE 21-2 Lease versus Purchase Without Any Recognition for Borrowing of Funds

Year	0	1	2	3	4
Purchase					
Initial cost of assets	($85,000)				
Cash savings		$35,000	$35,000	$35,000	$35,000
Depreciation		(42,500)	(21,250)	(10,625)	(10,625)
Cash savings before taxes		(7,500)	13,750	24,375	24,375
Taxes @ 35%		(2,625)	(4,813)	(8,531)	(8,531)
Cash savings after taxes		(4,875)	8,937	15,844	15,844
Plus depreciation		42,500	21,250	10,625	10,625
Net cash flows	(85,000)	37,625	30,187	26,469	26,469
Discount factors @ 15%	1.000	.870	.756	.658	.572
Net present values	(85,000)	32,734	22,821	17,417	15,140
Cumulative NPVs	(85,000)	($52,266)	($29,445)	($12,028)	$ 3,112
Lease					
Cash savings		$35,000	$35,000	$35,000	$35,000
Lease payments		32,400	32,400	32,400	32,400
Cash savings before taxes		2,600	2,600	2,600	2,600
Taxes @ 35%		(910)	(910)	(910)	(910)
Cash savings after taxes	1,690	1,690	1,690	1,690	1,690
Discount factors @ 15%		.870	.756	.658	.572
Net present values		1,470	1,278	1,112	967
Cumulative NPVs		$ 1,470	$ 2,748	$ 3,860	$ 4,827

illustrates which decision is preferable, using the net present value method as a criterion.

The results show that the purchasing decision generates a cumulative net present value of $3,112 versus $4,827 for leasing. Therefore, leasing will generate higher earnings throughout the life of the asset. This illustration does not assume any borrowing and repayment of funds to finance the acquisition of the asset. It also assumes an estimated 15% cost of capital rate and not the actual cost of borrowing. These decisions must be resolved before any calculations are made so as to coincide with the company's policy of calculating purchase versus lease opportunities.

Year	0	1	2	3	4
TABLE 21-3 Lease versus Purchase Decisions with Recognition of Borrowing Funds					
Purchase					
Initial cost of asset	($85,000)				
Borrowing	85,000				
Cash savings		$35,000	$35,000	$35,000	$35,000
Interest payments		(6,800)	(5,100)	(3,400)	(1,700)
Depreciation		(42,500)	(21,250)	(10,625)	(10,625)
Cash savings before taxes		(14,300)	8,650	20,975	22,675
Taxes @ 35%		(5,005)	(3,028)	(7,341)	(7,936)
Cash savings after taxes		(9,295)	5,622	13,634	14,739
Loan repayment–principal		(21,250)	(21,250)	(21,250)	(21,250)
Plus depreciation		42,500	21,250	10,625	10,625
Net cash flows		11,955	5,622	3,009	4,114
Discount factors @ 8%		.926	.857	.794	.735
Net present values		11,070	4,818	2,389	3,024
Cumulative NPVs		$11,070	$15,888	$18,277	$21,301
Lease					
Cash savings		$35,000	$35,000	$35,000	$35,000
Lease payments		32,400	32,400	32,400	32,400
Cash savings before taxes		2,600	2,600	2,600	2,600
Taxes @ 35%		(910)	(910)	(910)	(910)
Cash savings after taxes		1,690	1,690	1,690	1,690
Discount factors @ 8%		.926	.857	.794	.735
Net present values		1,565	1,448	1,342	1,242
Cumulative NPVs		$ 1,565	$ 3,013	$ 4,355	$ 5,597

The comparison can also be made using the initial data, but assuming that the asset is financed through borrowing at a rate of 8% with an annual repayment of $25,500. Table 21-3 illustrates how borrowing affects the decision to lease or purchase.

Based on Table 21-2, leasing was preferred over purchasing, since the cumulative net present values were higher by $1,715 ($4,827−$3,112). The results in Table 21-3 illustrate that purchasing is more favorable, since cumulative net present values are higher by $15,704 ($21,301 − $5,597). Since $85,000 was borrowed to finance the purchase of the asset, the outflows of cash were spread over four years through the repayment of the principal. When discounted at the 8% rate, the cash outflows are less significant in future years and have less of an impact in the current period, even though there are interest payments.

These illustrations provide some insight as to decisions regarding lease versus purchase opportunities. You can see how the method of financing changes the ultimate decision. Therefore, when making a lease versus purchase decision, it is important to determine all the facts, including how the asset is going to be financed under a purchase arrangement. Keep in mind that there are many other variations as to how assets are purchased or leased. Whatever the financing arrangements, all the facts must be reflected in determining both outflows and inflows of cash. Once this is developed, illustrations like Tables 21-2 and 21-3 can be used to make sound economic decisions.

DECISION-MAKING STRATEGIES

- Develop policies and procedures for make versus buy decisions and lease versus purchase decisions in keeping with the return on investment objectives of the company.
- Review lease agreements when leases are up for renewal.
- Always do a lease versus buy analysis on all lease agreements. Be sure to analyze the impact on return on investment.
- Make leases a part of your planning process.
- Investigate leasing as a tool for acquiring machinery and equipment to meet peak periods.
- Evaluate leasing on assets that have rapid technological changes (e.g., computers).
- Establish a company philosophy on ownership versus leasing.

NOTE

1. The ideas of leasing are based on the ideas presented in chapter 20A, *Handbook of Budgeting,* Third Edition, edited by Robert Rachlin and H.W. Allen Sweeney, *1996 Cumulative Supplement.* Copyright © 1996. Reprinted by permission of John Wiley & Sons, Inc., New York.

22

HOW TO EVALUATE ENERGY CONSERVATION USING ROI TECHNIQUES

As discussed in earlier chapters, any investment that derives greater benefits than costs should be considered a sound investment, assuming it adds incremental profit to the business. This same concept can apply to energy conservation.

As with capital investment opportunities, developing quantitative data for measuring energy opportunities with alternative investment opportunities is important. Since the true economic cost includes opportunity costs of foregone investments, energy conservation opportunities should be considered profitable only when their expected rate of return is greater than what could be realized from alternative investment opportunities.

Many energy conservation opportunities may be found during a close examination of operations, but may be rejected due to an unfavorable return on investment or a longer than expected payback period. In addition, the cost of energy in the future will play an important part in the decision. Without recapping the pros and cons of these techniques, which were discussed in an earlier chapter, I list the data necessary to calculate these concepts:

- ECO, or energy conservation opportunities
- FC, or first cost
- AOC, or annual operating cost
- AFS, or annual fuel savings
- PFP, or projected fuel price
- EL, or estimated lifetime

The FC is the estimated dollar cost of labor and materials necessary to implement the project. The AOC, AFS, PFP, and EL will determine the annual benefits, excluding any salvage value of the investment. Therefore, the net annual savings can be defined by the following equation.

Energy Equation

$$\text{Net annual savings (S)} = (\text{AFS} \times \text{PFP}) - \text{AOC}$$

Using these data as a basis, both the payback period and return on investment can be computed.

HOW THE PAYBACK PERIOD IS CALCULATED

The payback period is calculated by dividing the first cost, FC, by the net annual savings, S.

Payback Equation

$$\text{Payback period} = \frac{\text{FC}}{(\text{AFS} \times \text{PFP}) - \text{AOC}} \text{ or}$$

$$\text{Payback period} = \frac{\text{FC}}{\text{S}}$$

The payback period is then compared to the expected lifetime, EL, of the investment to determine the approximate recovery of the investment. A payback period of less than one-half the lifetime of an investment would generally be considered profitable where the lifetime is ten years or less. Keep in mind the disadvantages that exist in the payback period method, which also apply in this application.

FIGURING RETURN ON INVESTMENT USING DEPRECIATION CHARGES

Applying the ROI concept, the depletion of the investment over its economic life is accounted for through depreciation charges, DC. Using the depreciation charges, the calculation is:

ROI with Depreciation Charges Equation

$$\text{DC} = \frac{\text{FC}}{\text{EL}}$$

which relates to the return on investment as follows:

$$ROI = \frac{S - DC}{FC} \times 100\%$$

OTHER ENERGY INVESTMENT
MEASUREMENT TECHNIQUES

Other measurement techniques are available that supplement the previous two methods. They are the benefit/cost analysis, the time to recoup capital investment, and the discounted cash flow (DCF) technique.

Benefit/Cost Analysis Technique

This method requires the direct comparison of the present value benefits (savings) generated by a given investment with its costs. This comparison is referred to as the benefit/cost ratio. A ratio greater than 1 implies that the expected net benefits (after discounting) will exceed the initial costs, and therefore the investment will be considered profitable. A benefit/cost ratio less than 1 implies that an investment will not be profitable.

Time to Recoup Capital Investment Technique

This concept is similar to the payback period method except that discount rates are taken into consideration when computing the payback period.

Discounted Cash Flow (DCF) Technique

This concept uses discounting to arrive at the rate in which the discounted cash flows equal zero. Table 22-1 will be used for discounting calculations. Note that the discount factors are cumulative using a 15% discount rate.

ILLUSTRATION

The following is an example of a company considering a capital investment in the manufacturing process for energy conservation purposes. The following facts will be used:

TABLE 22-1   Cumulative Discount Table at a 15% Rate

Year (EL)	Cumulative Discount Rate (D)
1	.86957
2	1.62571
3	2.28323
4	2.85498
5	3.35216
6	3.78449
7	4.16043
8	4.48733
9	4.77159
10	5.01877

Note: This table is calculated from the equation

$$PV = \frac{1 - (1 + D) - EL}{D}$$

Assumptions
Cost of design and installation, $400,000
Average savings, 100,000 MBtu of natural gas per year
Estimated lifetime, 10 years
Average cost of fuel, $3.50 per MBtu
Objective rate, 15%

Based on those assumptions, will this be a profitable investment? Table 22-2 illustrates the calculations of the payback period and return on investment.

Based on the return-investment rate, this appears to be an attractive investment. Using the same data, let us calculate the benefit/cost analysis and the time to recoup investment.

Benefit/cost analysis. To arrive at this ratio, the present value (PV) of the future savings must be calculated for a 15% discount (D) for ten years (EL). The present value of the net annual savings (S) is:

TABLE 22-2   Calculating the Payback Period and ROI Rate

Payback Period

Net Annual Savings

$$S = (AFS \times PFP) - AOC$$
$$S = 100{,}000 \times \$3.50 - 0$$
$$S = \$350{,}000 \text{ per year}$$

Payback Period (PP)

$$= \frac{FC}{S}$$

$$PP = \frac{\$400{,}000}{\$350{,}000} = 1.14 \text{ years}$$

Return-on-Investment Rate

$$DC = \frac{FC}{EL}$$

$$DC = \frac{\$400{,}000}{10} = \$40{,}000 \text{ per year}$$

$$ROI = \frac{S - DC}{FC} \times 100\%$$

$$ROI = \frac{\$350{,}000 - \$40{,}000}{\$400{,}000} \times 100\%$$

$$ROI = 77.5\% \text{ per year}$$

$$PV = S \times PV$$
$$PV = \$350{,}000 \times 5.01877$$
$$PV = \$1{,}756{,}570$$

This results in a benefit/cost ratio (B/C) of 4.39 as follows:

$$B/C = \frac{PV}{FC}$$

$$B/C = \frac{\$1{,}756{,}570}{\$400{,}000}$$

$$B/C = 4.39$$

This investment can be considered profitable even after discounting.

Time to recoup investment. This can be approximated by referring to the discount table for comparison with the earlier calculation of the payback period, which was 1.14 years. The number coming closest to 1.14 years is 1.62571, which indicates that the investment will be entirely recouped in about two years, considering the time value of money. While this is longer than the original payback period of 1.14 years without discounting, it does provide a better indication of the profitability of this investment because it includes opportunity costs. If the correct discount rate is used, any investment recouped in a period less than its lifetime should be considered profitable.

DECISION-MAKING STRATEGIES

- Make energy conservation opportunities part of your company's investment decision analysis.
- Evaluate energy conservation projects using return on investment techniques and the policies and procedures thereof.
- Plan energy projects similar to planning capital assets.

Appendix A

PRESENT VALUE TABLES

Years	1%	2%	4%	6%	8%	10%	12%	14%
1	0.990	0.980	0.962	0.943	0.926	0.909	0.893	0.877
2	0.980	0.961	0.925	0.890	0.857	0.826	0.797	0.769
3	0.971	0.942	0.889	0.840	0.794	0.751	0.712	0.675
4	0.961	0.924	0.855	0.792	0.735	0.683	0.636	0.592
5	0.951	0.906	0.822	0.747	0.681	0.621	0.567	0.519
6	0.942	0.888	0.790	0.705	0.630	0.564	0.507	0.456
7	0.933	0.871	0.760	0.665	0.583	0.513	0.452	0.400
8	0.923	0.853	0.731	0.627	0.540	0.467	0.404	0.351
9	0.914	0.837	0.703	0.592	0.500	0.424	0.361	0.308
10	0.905	0.820	0.676	0.558	0.463	0.386	0.322	0.270
11	0.896	0.804	0.650	0.527	0.429	0.350	0.287	0.237
12	0.887	0.788	0.625	0.497	0.397	0.319	0.257	0.208
13	0.879	0.773	0.601	0.469	0.368	0.290	0.229	0.182
14	0.870	0.758	0.577	0.442	0.340	0.263	0.205	0.160
15	0.861	0.743	0.555	0.417	0.315	0.239	0.183	0.140
16	0.853	0.728	0.534	0.394	0.292	0.218	0.163	0.123
17	0.844	0.714	0.513	0.371	0.270	0.198	0.146	0.108
18	0.836	0.700	0.494	0.350	0.250	0.180	0.130	0.095
19	0.828	0.686	0.475	0.331	0.232	0.164	0.116	0.083
20	0.820	0.673	0.456	0.312	0.215	0.149	0.104	0.073
21	0.811	0.660	0.439	0.294	0.199	0.135	0.093	0.064
22	0.803	0.647	0.422	0.278	0.184	0.123	0.083	0.056
23	0.795	0.634	0.406	0.262	0.170	0.112	0.074	0.049
24	0.788	0.622	0.390	0.247	0.158	0.102	0.066	0.043
25	0.780	0.610	0.375	0.233	0.146	0.092	0.059	0.038
26	0.772	0.598	0.361	0.220	0.135	0.084	0.053	0.033
27	0.764	0.586	0.347	0.207	0.125	0.076	0.047	0.029
28	0.757	0.574	0.333	0.196	0.116	0.069	0.042	0.026
29	0.749	0.563	0.321	0.185	0.107	0.063	0.037	0.022
30	0.742	0.552	0.308	0.174	0.099	0.057	0.033	0.020

Years	15%	16%	18%	20%	22%	24%	25%	26%
1	0.870	0.862	0.847	0.833	0.820	0.806	0.800	0.794
2	0.756	0.743	0.718	0.694	0.672	0.650	0.640	0.630
3	0.658	0.641	0.609	0.579	0.551	0.524	0.512	0.500
4	0.572	0.552	0.516	0.482	0.451	0.423	0.410	0.397
5	0.497	0.476	0.437	0.402	0.370	0.341	0.328	0.315
6	0.432	0.410	0.370	0.335	0.303	0.275	0.262	0.250
7	0.376	0.354	0.314	0.279	0.249	0.222	0.210	0.198
8	0.327	0.305	0.266	0.233	0.204	0.179	0.168	0.157
9	0.284	0.263	0.225	0.194	0.167	0.144	0.134	0.125
10	0.247	0.227	0.191	0.162	0.137	0.116	0.107	0.099
11	0.215	0.195	0.162	0.135	0.112	0.094	0.086	0.079
12	0.187	0.168	0.137	0.112	0.092	0.076	0.069	0.062
13	0.163	0.145	0.116	0.093	0.075	0.061	0.055	0.050
14	0.141	0.125	0.099	0.078	0.062	0.049	0.044	0.039
15	0.123	0.108	0.084	0.065	0.051	0.040	0.035	0.031
16	0.107	0.093	0.071	0.054	0.042	0.032	0.028	0.025
17	0.093	0.080	0.060	0.045	0.034	0.026	0.023	0.020
18	0.081	0.069	0.051	0.038	0.028	0.021	0.018	0.016
19	0.070	0.060	0.043	0.031	0.023	0.017	0.014	0.012
20	0.061	0.051	0.037	0.026	0.019	0.014	0.012	0.010
21	0.053	0.044	0.031	0.022	0.015	0.011	0.009	0.008
22	0.046	0.038	0.026	0.018	0.013	0.009	0.007	0.006
23	0.040	0.033	0.022	0.015	0.010	0.007	0.006	0.005
24	0.035	0.028	0.019	0.013	0.008	0.006	0.005	0.004
25	0.030	0.024	0.016	0.010	0.007	0.005	0.004	0.003
26	0.026	0.021	0.014	0.009	0.006	0.004	0.003	0.002
27	0.023	0.018	0.011	0.007	0.005	0.003	0.002	0.002
28	0.020	0.016	0.010	0.006	0.004	0.002	0.002	0.002
29	0.017	0.014	0.008	0.005	0.003	0.002	0.002	0.001
30	0.015	0.012	0.007	0.004	0.003	0.002	0.001	0.001

Years	28%	30%	35%	40%	45%	50%
1	0.781	0.769	0.741	0.714	0.690	0.667
2	0.610	0.592	0.549	0.510	0.476	0.444
3	0.477	0.455	0.406	0.364	0.328	0.296
4	0.373	0.350	0.301	0.260	0.226	0.198
5	0.291	0.269	0.223	0.186	0.156	0.132
6	0.227	0.207	0.165	0.133	0.108	0.088
7	0.178	0.159	0.122	0.095	0.074	0.059
8	0.139	0.123	0.091	0.068	0.051	0.039
9	0.108	0.094	0.067	0.048	0.035	0.026
10	0.085	0.073	0.050	0.035	0.024	0.017
11	0.066	0.056	0.037	0.025	0.017	0.012
12	0.052	0.043	0.027	0.018	0.012	0.008
13	0.040	0.033	0.020	0.013	0.008	0.005
14	0.032	0.025	0.015	0.009	0.006	0.003
15	0.025	0.020	0.011	0.006	0.004	0.002
16	0.019	0.015	0.008	0.005	0.003	0.002
17	0.015	0.012	0.006	0.003	0.002	0.001
18	0.012	0.009	0.005	0.002	0.001	0.001
19	0.009	0.007	0.003	0.002	0.001	
20	0.007	0.005	0.002	0.001	0.001	
21	0.006	0.004	0.002	0.001		
22	0.004	0.003	0.001	0.001		
23	0.003	0.002	0.001			
24	0.003	0.002	0.001			
25	0.002	0.001	0.001			
26	0.002	0.001				
27	0.001	0.001				
28	0.001	0.001				
29	0.001	0.001				
30	0.001					

Appendix B

COMPOUND TABLES

Year	1%	2%	3%	4%	5%	6%	7%
1	1.010	1.020	1.030	1.040	1.050	1.060	1.070
2	1.020	1.040	1.061	1.082	1.102	1.124	1.145
3	1.030	1.061	1.093	1.125	1.156	1.191	1.225
4	1.041	1.082	1.126	1.170	1.216	1.262	1.311
5	1.051	1.104	1.159	1.217	1.276	1.338	1.404
6	1.062	1.120	1.194	1.265	1.340	1.419	1.501
7	1.072	1.149	1.230	1.316	1.407	1.504	1.606
8	1.083	1.172	1.267	1.369	1.477	1.594	1.718
9	1.094	1.195	1.305	1.423	1.551	1.689	1.838
10	1.105	1.219	1.344	1.480	1.629	1.791	1.967
11	1.116	1.243	1.384	1.539	1.710	1.898	2.105
12	1.127	1.268	1.426	1.601	1.796	2.012	2.252
13	1.138	1.294	1.469	1.665	1.886	2.133	2.410
14	1.149	1.319	1.513	1.732	1.980	2.261	2.579
15	1.161	1.346	1.558	1.801	2.079	2.397	2.759
16	1.173	1.373	1.605	1.873	2.183	2.540	2.952
17	1.184	1.400	1.653	1.948	2.292	2.693	3.159
18	1.196	1.428	1.702	2.026	2.407	2.854	3.380
19	1.208	1.457	1.754	2.107	2.527	3.026	3.617
20	1.220	1.486	1.806	2.191	2.653	3.207	3.870
25	1.282	1.641	2.094	2.666	3.386	4.292	5.427
30	1.348	1.811	2.427	3.243	4.322	5.743	7.612

Year	8%	9%	10%	12%	14%	15%	16%
1	1.080	1.090	1.100	1.120	1.140	1.150	1.160
2	1.166	1.188	1.210	1.254	1.300	1.322	1.346
3	1.260	1.295	1.331	1.405	1.482	1.521	1.561
4	1.360	1.412	1.464	1.574	1.689	1.749	1.811
5	1.469	1.539	1.611	1.762	1.925	2.011	2.100
6	1.587	1.677	1.772	1.974	2.195	2.313	2.436
7	1.714	1.828	1.949	2.211	2.502	2.660	2.826
8	1.851	1.993	2.144	2.476	2.853	3.059	3.278
9	1.999	2.172	2.358	2.773	3.252	3.518	3.803
10	2.159	2.367	2.594	3.106	3.707	4.046	4.411
11	2.332	2.580	2.853	3.479	4.226	4.652	5.117
12	2.518	2.813	3.138	3.896	4.818	5.350	5.936
13	2.720	3.066	3.452	4.363	5.492	6.153	6.886
14	2.937	3.342	3.797	4.887	6.261	7.076	7.988
15	3.172	3.642	4.177	5.474	7.138	8.137	9.266
16	3.426	3.970	4.595	6.130	8.137	9.358	10.748
17	3.700	4.328	5.054	6.866	9.276	10.761	12.468
18	3.996	4.717	5.560	7.690	10.575	12.375	14.463
19	4.316	5.142	6.116	8.613	12.056	14.232	16.777
20	4.661	5.604	6.728	9.646	13.743	16.367	19.461
25	6.848	8.632	10.835	17.000	26.462	32.919	40.874
30	10.063	13.268	17.449	29.960	50.950	66.212	85.850

Year	18%	20%	24%	28%	32%	40%	50%
1	1.180	1.200	1.240	1.280	1.320	1.400	1.500
2	1.392	1.440	1.538	1.638	1.742	1.960	2.250
3	1.643	1.728	1.907	2.067	2.300	2.744	3.375
4	1.939	2.074	2.364	2.684	3.036	3.842	5.062
5	2.288	2.488	2.932	3.436	4.007	5.378	7.594
6	2.700	2.986	3.635	4.398	5.290	7.530	11.391
7	3.185	3.583	4.508	5.629	6.983	10.541	17.086
8	3.759	4.300	5.590	7.206	9.217	14.758	25.629
9	4.435	5.160	6.931	9.223	12.166	20.661	38.443
10	5.234	6.192	8.594	11.806	16.060	28.925	57.665
11	6.176	7.430	10.657	15.112	21.199	40.496	86.498
12	7.288	8.916	13.215	19.343	27.983	56.694	129.746
13	8.599	10.699	16.386	24.759	36.937	79.372	194.619
14	10.147	12.839	20.319	31.691	48.757	111.120	291.929
15	11.074	15.407	25.196	40.565	64.350	155.568	437.894
16	14.129	18.488	31.243	51.923	84.954	217.795	656.84
17	16.672	22.186	38.741	66.461	112.14	304.914	985.26
18	19.673	26.623	48.039	85.071	148.02	426.879	1477.9
19	23.214	31.948	59.568	108.89	195.39	597.630	2216.8
20	27.393	38.338	73.864	139.38	257.92	836.683	3325.3
25	62.669	95.396	216.542	478.90	1033.6	4499.880	25251.
30	143.371	237.376	634.820	1645.5	4142.1	24201.432	191750.

GLOSSARY

ABC analysis. Provides management with a set of three inventory on-hand classifications based on annual volume.

accountability centers, or accountability segments, or responsibility centers. Segments of a business for which managers have responsibility and authority to manage an operation.

accountability segments. See *accountability centers.*

accounts receivable—net to working capital. Measures the impact of accounts receivables on the liquidity of the company.

acid test ratio. Supplements the current ratio by measuring liquidity and the ability of the company to meet its current obligations.

activity-based costing. A costing concept that associates costs with specific activities that are used to create these costs.

adjusted net income method. A technique that adjusts net earnings to a cash basis by adding or subtracting all transactions that affect or do not affect actual cash.

asset utilization. Utilizing a company's assets to maximize profits.

assignable costs. Costs that are incurred by a specific project.

average collection period. Indicates how long it takes a company to collect its receivables from customers.

Baumol Model. Concept that treats cash as an inventory item with the expectation that settling cash transactions can be predicted with certainty.

bond discount. Bonds sold at less than par, or face, value.

bond premium. Bonds sold at greater than par, or face, value.

bonds. Instruments issued by companies agreeing to pay bondholders a specific amount of interest over a specified period of time.

book costs. Costs in which accounting allocations of prior expenditures are made to the current period.

break-even point. The point at which net sales equal variable costs plus fixed costs.

business plan. Documents developed annually by each business segment that outline the tactics and strategies necessary to achieve future earnings and growth objectives.

373

business segments. Major divisions of a company defined by functional responsibilities.

business segment implications. Short-range consequences associated with a capital project decision; concerned with how the business segment will be affected operationally by the capital project.

Capital Asset Pricing Model. Method of calculating the cost of equity capital through the use of generally accepted financial theories that equate the cost of equity capital to the sum of a risk-free cost of money and risk premium to account for the company's systematic risk.

capital assets. Assets capable of being sold or transferred to other owners.

capital budgeting process. Procedure that reviews capital requests and allocates capital resources.

capital employed. Total assets less current liabilities.

capital expenditure evaluation. Concepts such as payback and discounted cash flow used to measure expected future returns on a proposed capital investment.

capital investment. Any investment in an asset or activity that impacts the corporate cash flow for a period of more than one year.

capital structure. The permanent long-term financing of the company represented by debt and equity components.

cash cycle. The time period beginning when cash is disbursed to purchase raw materials and ending when cash is collected from the sales of finished goods inventory or services.

cash disbursements. Payments to creditors and employees for goods and/or services received.

cash flow. Accounting net income plus depreciation charges as applied in capital expenditure evaluation.

cash receipts and disbursements method. A method that forecasts cash by tracing through all the items of income and expense.

cash turnover. Indicates the rapidity with which cash moves within the company.

common equity. Sum of common stock, capital in excess of par value, and earnings retained in the business.

compounding. A method used to compute the future value of money using compound interest rates.

contribution margin. A concept of break-even that determines how many units are necessary to recover both fixed and variable costs and yet generate a desired profit.

contribution pricing. A pricing approach where the best price is the one that generates the highest contribution.

controllable costs. Costs that are influenced by management during a specific period of time.

conversion cost method. A pricing method that emphasizes the conversion costs and shifts the emphasis on products that have high material costs.

corporate discount rate. The discount rate to be utilized in the calculation of present value measures for all projects, which is based on cost of corporate capital plus a rationing premium.

cost centers, or cost segments. Segments of a business that incur costs but do not generate revenues.

cost of capital. The average rate of earnings that investors require to induce them to provide all forms of long-term capital to the company.

cost of debt. Interest rate after corporate income taxes that would prevail on newly issued long-term debt.

cost of equity. Rate of return required by those who invest in stock of the company, and determined by the use of the Capital Asset Pricing Model.

cost of sales to inventories. Measures the turnover of inventory.

cost-plus pricing. Developing a price from the bottom up.

cost savings projects. Projects that anticipate sufficient economic value over and above existing costs.

cost segments. See *cost centers.*

current assets. Assets used in the normal course of business that can be converted into cash more quickly than other assets.

current assets to current liabilities. Referred to as the current ratio.

current dollar basis. A recommended method of analysis that bases all cash flows on actual amounts expected to be expended or received during each year, that is, includes escalation for both inflation and real price increases or decreases as opposed to constant dollar basis, which considers cash flows in terms of a based year value of the dollar by excluding the effects of inflation.

current liabilities. Debts of a company that fall due within the current calendar or fiscal year.

current liabilities to shareholders' equity. Measures the share creditors have against the company as compared to the shareholders.

current ratio. Measures the ability of the company to meet its current obligations.

day's sales on hand. Indicates the average length in days that inventory is held before it is sold.

day's sales outstanding. A ratio referred to as the collection period, which indicates the average age of net customer's accounts receivable.

DCF. See *discounted cash flow.*

debt financing. A form of financing in which the borrower agrees to repay the borrowed principal plus interest in specified amounts on specified dates.

debt to equity. Measures the extent to which a company is financed by long-term debt or borrowed capital, and permanent contributed capital.

depository transfer checks. Checks without signatures drawn against the bank of deposit.

direct costing, or variable costing. A costing approach that allocates only variable costs to the product.

direct labor. The amount of labor needed to convert manufacturing materials into a finished product.

direct materials. Materials used to manufacture a product that ultimately become a part of the product.

discounted cash flow, or DCF. A basic theory holding that a dollar today is worth more than a dollar in the future.

discounted cash flow return on investment (DCFROI). A rate of return on an investment that is calculated by determining the discount rate that equates the present value of future cash inflows to the present value of the investment cash flows; the maximum cost of capital to finance the project and break even.

discounting. A method that shifts the value of money to be received in the future back to the present.

discount rate. Based on the interest charged on risk-free securities and adjusted for risk elements for both internal and external factors.

dividend payout. A ratio that indicates how a company divides its earnings between common shareholders and reinvesting them within the company.

dividend yield. Measures the expected return to investors. Calculated by dividing the market price per share into the dividends per share.

drafts. Negotiable instruments used like checks that are drawn against a company rather than a bank.

earnings before interest and taxes (EBIT) to interest. Measures a company's ability to meet its interest payments on both short- and long-term debt. Calculated by dividing EBIT by interest.

economic life. Period of time whereby economic conditions might shorten or limit the continuation of operating a specific asset.

Economic Order Quantity (EOQ) Model. An inventory management technique that determines a product's optimal order quantity, or a level of inventory that minimizes both the order and carrying costs.

economic value added (EVA). Measures short-term shareholder values.

elasticity pricing. A strategy whereby a decrease in price causes a sharp increase in demand.

end of period discrete discounting. Method of discounting based on discrete cash flows received at the end of each period.

entry pricing. A strategy of pricing below the existing competitive level to establish a position in a specific market.

equity financing. Capital permanently invested by investors.

expansion projects. Projects aimed at expanding production, increasing sales in existing markets, and achieving sales in new markets.

expense segments. Functions measured along organizational structures.

financial leases. Leases usually in effect for longer periods of time than operating leases. See *operating leases.*

fixed assets (net) to shareholders' equity. Measures the amount of capital invested in nonliquid assets.

fixed costs. Costs that do not fluctuate with levels of activity.

floatation costs. Costs of issuing and selling a bond.

full absorption costing. A costing approach where both variable and fixed manufacturing costs are charged to all units produced and become an expense in the period when inventory is sold.

gross margin percentage. Indicates the margin of sales over the cost of sales.

high-price strategy. A pricing technique whereby higher than usual prices are established on selected products.

human assets. Assets in people; incapable of being sold.

human resource accounting. The concept of capitalizing costs incurred in the training and future development of employee rather than expensing.

human resource behavioral/variables method. The use of statistical analyses of variations in leadership ability correlated with increases in earnings, productivity, and other income factors.

human resource cost approach. Measures an investment in human resources similar to the capital expenditures investment concept.

human resource economic approach. Suggests that the value of an employee is based on the marketplace.

human resource goodwill method. Calculates earnings in excess of an industry average and attributes a proportion of this to human factors.

human resource value approach. Relates the value of human resources as a function of the wages or earnings of the company.

in and out pricing. A pricing strategy that prices products high and reduces them when the sought-after segment of the market becomes saturated.

incremental analysis. Method of analysis that compares the results of an investment to projections of what would occur without the investment, that is, the change in expected cash flows as a result of the investment.

incremental cost method. A markup method of pricing that emphasizes the conversion costs and shifts the emphasis on products that have high material costs.

indirect costs. Costs not directly traceable to a specific unit of production.

insurance value. The amount at which a company is willing to insure an employee.

internal rate of return, or IRR, method. Solves for the discount or interest rate that discounts cash flow to equal the investment.

inventory. An asset representing merchandise in the form of either raw materials, in-process merchandise, or finished goods.

inventory to current assets. Measures how much of the current assets are tied up by inventory.

inventory to total assets. Measures the percentage of inventory in relation to the total assets of the company.

inventory to working capital. Measures the impact of inventories on the liquidity of the company.

inventory turnover. Measures the efficiency of a company to move inventory.

investment segment. A unit of an organization whereby investment dollars are controlled and that is measured by the amount of earnings generated from a specific amount of investment.

job earnings. Calculation of MBO job value less the discounted cash flow of salary, training, and related employee benefits.

job order costing. A cost system method that accumulates costs of an identifiable product known as a job, and follows the product through the production stages.

just-in-time (JIT) inventory. A management system used in manufacturing that estimates how much inventory is necessary to keep the production line running efficiency.

leverage. A ratio that answers the fundamental question on how a company finances its assets. Calculated by dividing total assets by the stockholders' equity.

liquidity. The ability to convert current assets into cash in short periods of time.

loss leader pricing. Selling certain items at near or below cost to attract buyers for other products.

maintenance and replacement projects. Projects needed for the continuance of existing machinery and equipment.

managing ratios. Ratios that assist in evaluating the various components of the balance sheet.

manufacturing overhead. The manufacturing costs of producing a product over and above direct materials and direct labor.

margin of safety. Calculation of break-even that indicates how much sales can decrease before losses can be expected.

margin pricing approach. Establishes an acceptable margin rate based on sales dollars.

marketable securities. An asset representing temporary investments of excess cash in securities and held for short periods of time.

marketing assets. Accounts receivable and inventories that are generally controllable by the sales territory.

marketing contribution. The sum of net sales by marketing territory, less cost of sales and selling expenses; used by the marketing territory to sell the product.

markup pricing. Pricing that uses a percentage above the total cost of a product to arrive at a specific profit.

MBO job value. The value of a job measured through a management by objectives (MBO) process.

net cash flows. Total cash flows for each period including inflows (e.g. from operations, tax benefits) and outflows (e.g., investments, tax costs).

net income to net sales. Measures the profitability of every dollar of sales; also referred to as the profitability rate.

net income to shareholders' equity. Measures the return generated from the owners' equity in the business when considering all risks.

net income to total assets. Represents the return on funds invested in the company by both owners and creditors.

net income to working capital. Measures the ability of a company to use working capital to generate net income.

net present value. Economic advantage or disadvantage of an investment expressed in terms of a value at any point in time by discounting all future net cash flows at a particular cost of capital and adding the discounted values.

net present value, or NPV, method. Calculates the net present value of cash flows using a given discount rate.

net sales. Revenues received from customers for the exchange of goods sold or services rendered; they are the prime source of revenues for a company.

net sales to accounts receivable--net. Measures the turnover of receivables.

net sales to fixed assets-net. Measures how efficiently a business is able to use its investments in fixed assets.

net sales to working capital. Measures the ability of working capital to support levels of sales revenue.

new product introduction projects. Projects whose primary objective is providing facilities for the introduction of new products.

NPV method. See *net present value method.*

obsolescence. An asset or product having no value due to conditions that make it obsolete.

operating leases. Leases not classified under accounting regulations as capital leases, and usually in effect for shorter periods of time.

opportunity costs. Represent a benefit that is foregone as a result of not using another alternative.

out-of-pocket costs. Costs that require cash outlays either currently or in the future.

PACs. See *preauthorized checks.*

Pareto's law. A rule of thumb that says 80% of any output usually comes from 20% of the input.

payback period method. Calculated by dividing total investment dollars of a capital investment proposal by the annual cash flows.

performance ratios. Ratios that follow the trend of the overall performance of the company.

period costs. Costs incurred as a function of time as opposed to levels of activity.

physical assets, or fixed assets. Investments fixed in nature, including land, factories, machinery, equipment.

physical life. The time when an asset will be worn out and cease to function without any form of replacement.

preauthorized checks (PACs). Checks without a signature issued by a payee with a prearranged agreement with a payor.

preauthorized debits. A system similar to PACs, but without the need to issue checks.

present worth index. Measure used for ranking the present value of a project's net cash flows calculated as a ratio of the present value of net cash inflows to the present value of net cash outflows.

present worth payout. Measure used to evaluate the risk of a project by determining the length of time the company's investment funds remain unrecovered; determined by calculating the time it takes for the cumulative present value of the cash flows to become positive.

present worth profile. Graph or chart that indicates the net present value of a project at any discount rate within a predetermined range.

price-earnings ratio. The current price of a stock divided by current or projected earnings; measures investor confidence.

process costing. A cost system method that accumulates costs by a process or operation as it flows through production.

product costs. Production costs that relate to the product's unit output and are charged to the product's cost when it is sold.

Production Order Quantity Method. Similar to the EOQ model, but assumes that inventory flows in a continuous manner, or when inventory accumulates over a period of time.

profit centers, or profit segments. Segments of a business with both revenue and expense responsibility.

profit contribution ratio. Computed by dividing the contribution margin by net sales.

profit improvement projects. Projects anticipated to add additional profit to existing earnings.

profit segments. See *profit centers*.

profitability rate. Measures how much earnings are generated from each dollar of sales.

profitability ratios. Ratios that evaluate components of the statement of income and effectively show how well a manager is performing at the given level of responsibility.

programmed costs. Costs that result from specific decisions without any consideration of volume activity or passage of time.

psychological pricing. A pricing strategy that prices a product just below the round-dollar amount.

quality-improvement projects. Projects that bring about a general improvement of the quality in keeping with a company's quality standards.

quick assets. Includes cash in banks, marketable securities, and accounts receivable—net.

quick ratio. A ratio that is similar to the current ratio but that places more emphasis on those liquid assets that can easily be converted into cash.

remote disbursements. A method of creating float by lengthening the time it takes a check to clear through the banking system and be presented for payment.

responsibility center. See *accountability centers.*

return on assets (ROA). An internal ratio measurement that indicates the dollar return per dollar of invested assets. Calculated by multiplying the profit margin percentage times the turnover rate.

return on capital employed. Earnings divided by capital employed (total assets less current liabilities).

return on investment (ROI). A management tool that measures both past performance and future investment decisions in a reasonably systematic manner.

return on investment equation. A pricing approach that determines the price needed to achieve a desired return on investment.

return on marketing assets. Marketing contribution as a percentage of net sales multiplied by net sales divided by marketing assets.

return on net assets (RONA). A ratio that relates profitability to asset management. Calculated by dividing net sales by net assets. Net assets defined as all assets except cash equivalents and marketable securities, less all liabilities except notes payable, current portion of long-term debt, long-term debt, and all shareholders equity accounts.

return on shareholders' equity. Earnings divided by shareholders' equity. Measures the profit return that stockholders receive on their investment.

return on total assets. Earnings divided by total assets.

risk-free securities. Associated with U.S. Treasury bills.

rule of three. Evaluates an organization by dividing it into three components.

selling expenses to net sales. Measures the cost of selling a product.

sensitivity analysis. Process by which the critical assumptions and uncertainties in forecasting the results of an investment are identified and quantified.

shareholder value. Represents the economic value of a company and is defined as the sum of the cash flows in the future in today's current value of the dollar.

source and application of funds. Indicates how money flows through a business by highlighting where the cash was used and where it was spent.

standard costs. Anticipated or predetermined costs of producing a unit of output under given conditions.

statement of cash flows. Provides the necessary information relating to the cash receipts and cash payments of a company during a specific period of time.

statement of income. A financial statement that reflects how much net income was made during a given period by recording all transactions of income and expenses.

strategic implication. The long-range consequences associated with the specific capital project decision; concerned with how the segment of a company is positioned competitively, legally, and financially for the future.

sunk costs. Costs incurred in prior periods.

technological life. The life of a asset as limited by advancing technology.

total debt to total assets. A ratio that measures how much of the total funds are being supplied by its creditors. Calculated by dividing total assets into total debt.

transfer pricing. The price charged to another internal part of the company.

turnover rate. Indicator of how capital-intensive a business is, or how many dollars in investment are needed to support dollars in revenues.

typical pricing strategy. A pricing strategy generally established by the marketplace in that it uses what is accepted by the customers as being a fair price.

unassignable costs. Costs that cannot be directly traced to a specific product and/or segment of the business without arbitrarily allocating them.

uncommitted funds. Cash available for capital budgeting that has not been appropriated to a specific project.

uniform discrete discounting. Method of discounting based on the receipt of expenditure of cash more or less evenly throughout a period.

variable costing. See *direct costing.*

variable costs. Costs that change in direct proportion to levels of activity.

volume strategy. A pricing strategy in which low margins are accepted and profits are generated from high volume.

weighted average cost of capital. Weighs all components of capital, assigns given values for each capital component in accordance with contractual and calculated rates, which results in a weighted average cost figure.

wire transfers. Movement of funds from one location to another by electronic means to avoid the loss of time inherent in the mail system.

working capital. Computed by subtracting current liabilities from current assets.

zero balance accounts. Checks drawn against an account with no required balance.

Z-Score Model. A model that uses five key ratios that objectively weighs and develops a total score that is used to predict a company's ability to survive.

INDEX